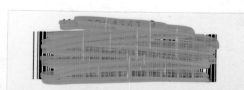

The Restored Monarchy
1660 – 1688

Each volume in the 'Problems in Focus' series is designed to make available to students important new work on key historical problems and periods that they encounter in their courses. Each volume is devoted to a central topic or theme, and the most important aspects of this are dealt with by specially commissioned studies from scholars in the relevant field. The editorial Introduction reviews the problem or period as a whole, and each chapter provides an assessment of the particular aspect, pointing out the areas of development and controversy, and indicating where conclusions can be drawn or where further work is necessary. An annotated bibliography serves as a guide to further reading.

PROBLEMS IN FOCUS SERIES

The Restored Monarchy 1660 – 1688

EDITED BY

J. R. JONES

First published 1979 by
THE MACMILLAN PRESS LTD
London and Basingstoke
Associated companies in Delhi Dublin
Hong Kong Johannesburg Lagos
Melbourne New York Singapore and Tokyo

Photoset, printed and bound
in Great Britain by
REDWOOD BURN LIMITED
Trowbridge & Esher

British Library Cataloguing in Publication Data

The restored monarchy, 1660–1688.
   – (Problems in focus series).
   1.   Great Britain – History – Restoration, 1660–1688
   I. Jones, James Rees   II. Series
   942.06'6   DA445

   ISBN 0–333–21431–5
   ISBN 0–333–21432–3   Pbk

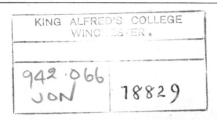

Contents

Preface

HISTORIANS are pattern-makers. What they call historical periods
are in reality arbitrarily divided segments of time, centering on some
particular characteristics that attract attention and act as foci. Often
this is because these particular characteristics have relevance to the
concerns, problems and issues of our own time, and consequently we
tend to read into the study of the past our own values, assumptions
and prejudices. So some writers dismiss the Restoration as a period of
harsh reaction, others as a time of triviality and empty frivolity, after
the allegedly crucial English Revolution of the 1640s and 1650s.
Others over-simplify by uncritical use of such sweeping concepts as
the Commercial Revolution or the Scientific Revolution.

As the essays in this collection show, the Restoration as a period
forms a far less arbitrary unit than do most of those used by historians.
Political developments of an unusual kind provided a general framework for most aspects of life. The period began when the first Convention Parliament re-established the monarchy, evidently (but
temporarily) to the satisfaction of most of the people. It ended with an
explicit revocation of that earlier decision, when the nation deserted
James in the face of William's intervention, and the second Convention Parliament declared the throne vacant.

Of course there is no necessary reason why a period primarily determined by domestic political developments should be equally applicable and useful for the study of developments and events in other
fields. For example in foreign affairs the Restoration period itself
divides into two distinct phases; initially the Dutch wars of 1665–7 and
1672–4; but later a time of virtual isolation from Europe. In the administration of government and the law generally, and of finances
particularly, a start was made to resolve some formidable problems,
but their solution was to prove to be a long-term process. In the case of
religious life a solution was quickly achieved, even though its long-
term implications were only gradually to make themselves felt. The
decisive victory of the Anglicans described by Dr Beddard determined
the shape of the next two centuries; the nation was irrevocably divided

into separate Anglican and Dissenter communities, their enmity miti-
gated after 1687 by a toleration based on expediency, not principle.
Another enduring impression on national life was made by the emergence of political parties, the first Whigs and the original Tories. There
was spectacular progress (to use a term that few of Charles II's subjects would have understood) in other areas of life. Overseas trade
expanded, especially with the colonies. London grew steadily in size
and wealth, despite the Plague and the Great Fire. For the first time it
became an intellectual centre of excellence, with an international influence and reputation.

A realisation of the variety and complexity of life and developments
in Restoration England emerges from the essays in this volume. They
are all enriched by the original research that each of the contributors
has undertaken and published. This not only gives them fresh insights
but also enables them to offer individual interpretations in fields in
which they are experts. But they do not lose sight of the need to outline
principal developments, and of the value to the reader and student of
surveys of the various interpretations that have been put forward on
major issues by other scholars.

J. R. JONES

Introduction:
Main Trends in Restoration England

J. R. JONES

I

THE Restoration period has tended to be neglected by both professional historians and students. Until quite recently it has been generally accepted that the dramatic events and changes of the 1640s and 1650s, described by Victorian historians as the Puritan Revolution but now generally called the English Revolution, were more important in their effects, and therefore more deserving of study and research. The England of Charles II and James II has often been dismissed as a chronicle of wasted time, an inconclusive period whose main characteristics were negative or trivial and ephemeral – public and private immorality and self-indulgence, political factionalism, religious persecution, a dishonourable and unsuccessful foreign policy. Now, however, as the essays in this volume and the associated bibliographical lists indicate, an increasing amount of research and attention is being devoted to the study of Restoration England, and particularly of those areas of life in which we can see the early but crucial stages of long-term developments. Politically the main development was the emergence of parties that divided the nation into opposing camps; at the time this was seen as a symptom of failure, or even of impending disaster, but England avoided another civil war and became the first state to incorporate in its political system rival political parties. Away from politics, and very largely independent from them, important changes were beginning to operate that were over the next century to transform most aspects of life and produce in England the first 'modern' society and the pioneer industrialised economy.

Historians of the Restoration period have too often allowed their interpretation and judgements to be unduly influenced by their attitude to controversial issues of their own day. Nineteenth-century liberals, taking their cue from Hallam, Mackintosh and above all Macaulay,

For Notes to the Introduction, see pp. 205–7.

were prejudiced against the Stuart sovereigns and their ministers as enemies of constitutional liberty.[1] Similarly evangelical and non-conformist writers deplored their influence – as irreligious profligates they were charged with cynically corrupting the morals of a whole generation. On the other side apologists for the later Stuarts, mostly writing in the Edwardian and inter-war years in a time of reaction against Victorian dogmatism, were sympathetic to France and to Catholicism.[2] Not surprisingly their conclusions were biased. Charles and James, like their father, were presented as champions of the ordinary people against a predatory aristocracy who were merging with a new capitalist class of merchants, bankers and entrepreneurs. The pro-Catholic and pro-French policies of the Court were presented as a defensive campaign, a last stand, against the materialism and philistinism of the bourgeoisie who, with industrialisation, were to impoverish and degrade the lives of most of the nation.

The controversies and debates which now interest historians of the Restoration period are no longer so directly related to our contemporary political concerns, but derive far more from differences and variations in interpretation and evaluation of the evidence. There is no longer any pressing need to act in a partisan manner as a prosecutor or defence advocate of policies or individuals. But no one can claim that we know everything about developments during the period; there are still important unanswered questions as well as issues on which the student will find conflicting judgements and divergent interpretations. For example, were Charles II's foreign policies essentially dynastic, and against the national interest? Is it helpful to talk of English mercantilism during the Restoration period? Did the undoubted expansion of overseas trade have any significant connection with official policies and the statutes passed for its encouragement? Did the wars against the Dutch help or hinder? Was there any connection between periods of depression or recession and those in which political tensions and instability were most marked? Can it be argued that the 'new' science was reconciled without difficulty with traditional beliefs, and that the former's importance and value were easily and generally accepted? Was this a period of administrative regression, in which the quality of government declined as a result of the abandonment of new methods introduced during the Interregnum?

These are some of the basic questions which are discussed in the individual essays of which this volume is composed. In this introduction an attempt is made to provide an overall impression, to form a context into which the chapters covering separate topics can be fitted.

II ENGLAND AS SEEN FROM EUROPE

England during the Restoration period was of little account in European affairs. Its politics, culture, literature and religious life were completely different in essential respects from those which were accepted as normal or regular by contemporary European observers. England was notorious for its instability and turbulence, symbolised above all by the most shocking event of the century, the trial and execution of Charles I. This reputation was perpetuated after 1660 by recurrent crises that threatened to plunge the country into another disastrous series of civil wars. England's idiosyncratic constitution and anachronistic system of law provided mysteries that few foreigners could, or tried to, understand. Few Europeans (except Dutchmen) could understand spoken or written English; consequently the nation's history and literature were little known. The xenophobia of ordinary people, even in London with its relatively cosmopolitan population, was a real deterrent to visits by foreigners. Half Europe hated England as the country in which their Catholic coreligionists were savagely if intermittently persecuted; the judicial murders of priests and recusants alleged to be involved in the Popish Plot of 1678–81 were well publicised in France, Spain and Italy.[3] The other, Protestant, half of Europe had little contact with the established Church of England (which with a very few exceptions was entirely insular in its outlook), and was baffled by the multiplicity of sects and heresies which had proliferated during the Interregnum and mostly survived after 1660.

England made a positive impression in very few ways. Under Cromwell the Commonwealth had suddenly emerged as a formidable power, but this proved to be only a temporary phenomenon – like the brief life of a comet – not the addition of a new power to the European system. Only the Dutch, and to a lesser extent the Spaniards and Danes, were directly affected by the strength of the virtually new English fleet that had hammered the Dutch in the war of 1652–4. London, however, fascinated travellers. Its prodigious size and its continued expansion, despite the catastrophes of the Plague and the Fire of 1666, were a source of wonder. That a relatively small and peripheral country should support a metropolis of over 500,000 inhabitants (more than 10 per cent of the population of England and Wales) was not necessarily seen as a sign of strength. London drained the provinces of people and wealth, and foreign visitors were contemptuous of the squalor and meanness of provincial towns. There were few of any size – Bristol, Norwich, Newcastle – and these compared unfavourably with the corresponding secondary urban centres in France and the Netherlands.

In most ways England occupied an intermediate position between what would be regarded as the normal institutions, social forms and conventions of European monarchies and those that existed in the United Provinces. The King had far more limited powers than his fellow-monarchs (with the exception of Poland), but even these were constantly threatened. There were the paradoxes of a socially dominant aristocracy and landowning gentry, who had been forcibly displaced from power, offices and influence under the Commonwealth but still continued to neglect the profession of arms; of a Protestant and married but hierarchically organised clergy; of a culture that still persisted in looking back to the barbaric glories of the Elizabethan and Jacobean ages, but which in polite circles was increasingly imitative of the prevailing French modes.[4] In the eighteenth century, in the age which invented John Bull and 'Rule Britannia', Englishmen were to glory in the differences that distinguished them from Johnny Frenchman and other comic or sad stereotypes of foreigners. But in Restoration England the basic causes of that later boundless and arrogant self-confidence did not yet exist.

A critical and questioning spirit was active at all levels of society. Foreigners were astonished by the interest shown in state affairs by ordinary people, including many who had no votes in parliamentary elections. Men and women of superior means and social standing were not invariably treated with respect, especially in London. It is now fashionable to talk of a 'deferential' society, but in detailed accounts of everyday life deference is often noticeable by its absence. In travelling, at markets or elections, in business transactions, men recognised those whom they accepted as worthy of respect, but those outside the limits of such recognition could often have their pretensions rudely or even savagely rejected or challenged. The Anglican clergy, in particular, were acutely conscious of hostility or (even more wounding) contempt. Clarendon, speaking for most of an older and more formal generation, regarded the prevalent critical spirit as an unfortunate legacy of the Interregnum. He believed that paternal authority had crumbled, and that consequently subjects in general were failing to display a 'firm and constant obedience and resignation' to the King. He thought that society was being poisoned by the continuation of habits acquired during the Interregnum, when it had been legitimate to disobey, slander and cheat a usurped government, but which were now undermining all authority: selfishness, distrust of others, 'murmuring' (constant expressions of grievances), a readiness to give credit to libels and gossip, an appetite for luxury and wealth.[5] Foreign diplomats echoed his judgements. They reported that everyone and everything was up for sale, that most office-holders were concerned to make hay while the sun shone. Certainly French, Dutch, Spanish and other diplomats never had any difficulty in finding ministers, courtiers, peers and M.P.s ready to accept money in return for serving the interests of a foreign power.

III PEPYS AS AN OBSERVER

Englishmen of the Restoration period, anxious at the possibility of another civil war, buffeted by the natural disasters of the plague and fire, humiliated by the failures of the second and third Dutch wars, alarmed at the growth of French military and naval power, and impressed against their will by the arrogance and confidence of Louis XIV, had little reason to feel secure. But despondency and pessimism were far from being all-pervasive, and the picture painted by sober Victorian historians of an age of failure and degeneracy is far too black. All students of Restoration England have one almost unique and certainly priceless advantage over those of other periods: they can step at will into the bustling, exciting but strange life of everyday London through the magic doorway of Pepys's *Diary*, now accessible to everyone (and not just specialists and scholars) in a superb new edition.[6] Although Pepys was at times anxious and afraid (for the future of the nation as well as of his own career) the underlying resilience and vitality that is apparent throughout, his energy and drive to advance himself and carry out his duties to his superiors' satisfaction, an unfailing curiosity about everything human and natural, a shrewd judgement based on acute powers of observation and an unfailing fund of commonsense were characteristics that he shared with many of his generation, although few men combined them so effectively. In his *Diary* Pepys describes customs and attitudes that seem primitive or savage to us, and conditions in which we can hardly understand how life was mentally or physically supportable. But by giving an account of his own many-sided activities he helps us to understand the emergence of new ways of thought that we can recognise as 'modern', that is of our own time.

Pepys is the best known, but by no means the only, creative administrator of the period. He was one of the first generation of long-service professionals on whose efficiency and relative honesty (that is, by the standards of the time) effective government depended. He, Downing, Blathwayt, Bridgeman and Lowndes provided continuity and dependability in a time when their ministerial superiors were constantly changing and, partly because of their insecurity, gave first priority to faction-fighting at Court and in Parliament.[7] As Dr Tomlinson demonstrates (see pp. 115–16) the professional administrators developed business-like administrative methods that were to be improved and generally adopted during the ordeals of the French wars that followed 1688.

One of the most striking differences between the pattern of everyday life described in the *Diary* and that of our own times is the ease and frequency with which Pepys moved from one social or occupational group to another. Appallingly bad communications kept him confined for most of the year to London and its riverside dependencies, but he was not like us barred by the need for specialised skills from participating in a wide range of activities. In his daily routine Pepys moved between his office and the company of naval officers and administrators, the Court where he was in frequent contact with Charles, James and the chief ministers, and the commercial and mercantile communities of the City, Wapping and Deptford. His entries testify to the raw energy, keen competitive spirit and coarse lack of scruple of those with whom he had business dealings. It is easy for historians, with a lofty over-view, to write off as unsuccessful competitors of the Dutch these merchants, ship-owners, contractors, captains and bankers. But as Dr Jackson argues (see pp. 153–4) they were in fact establishing the bases for Britain's spectacular commercial expansion over the next century.

Pepys was a member of the Royal Society, and particularly interested in the application of new scientific methods and mathematical techniques to solve navigational problems. He helped to launch an investigation into accurate means of determining a ship's longitude, and he was also concerned with the improvement of charts. The former line of research eventually succeeded, with the development of the chronometer, but, as Dr Hunter demonstrates (see pp. 181–3), the applied results of the so-called Scientific Revolution were relatively disappointing. Nevertheless the achievements of gifted individuals, notably Newton, Hooke, Boyle and Ray, made a major impact on contemporary European scientists, and the still small but growing band of intellectuals and popularisers of scientific discoveries and philosophical innovations.[8] The role of the Royal Society, and the reception of Sprat's propagandist *History*, are discussed below (pp. 180–7), but one aspect has wider relevance. Intellectual and scientific questions were not debated in such an envenomed atmosphere of bitter controversy as had been the case commonly in the years before the civil wars, when theological differences had affected all intellectual discussion. Indeed the Royal Society explicitly barred theology as the one subject which should not be included in its terms of reference, because of the controversy which it could be expected to provoke. This provision, and the opening of membership to men of all religions, are significant steps in the secularisation of thought and it is not surprising that high churchmen were sceptical of the claims made for science by Sprat, and by the polymath who also became a bishop himself, John Wilkins.

IV RELIGION AND TOLERATION

The gradual, grudging and partial acceptance of religious toleration (finally put into statutory form in 1689) is another example of the demotion of religion from its previously dominant position. The cause of toleration, and the work of those who like Locke justified it for altruistic and idealist reasons with philosophical arguments, has always attracted favourable attention from the liberal majority of historians.[9] Most students have to make a real effort of imagination to understand the reasons that were used against toleration, and to credit its enemies with sincerity. But although for us the intellectual arguments for toleration seem to be indisputably superior, its ultimate establishment was due primarily to political calculation and to a spread of religious indifferentism. In the 1660s and 1670s the Country opposition, and then the first Whigs, hoped to derive electoral advantage from taking up toleration, although they did little in practice to relieve Dissenters' grievances. Similarly Charles and James thought that they could obtain political gains, when they issued their Declarations of Indulgence (1662, 1672, 1687, 1688), although there was also an ulterior motive in that they wished to extend effective religious liberty to Catholics as well as Protestant Dissenters. This was as a first step to giving the former equality in status and privileges to members of the established Anglican Church. James also officially commended toleration on economic grounds, emphasising the commercial advantages that would result from the ending of all attempts to enforce religious uniformity.[10] This was an argument that had previously been associated with supporters of the Country opposition who admired the Dutch Republic, and argued that its tolerance had been a major contributory cause of its unique prosperity and wealth.

When toleration was passed in a statutory and permanent form in the Indulgence Act of 1689, it was a grudgingly conceded and limited measure that merely exempted Protestant Dissenters from legal penalties. Nevertheless although rather shoddy arguments and considerations of political expediency were in practice more persuasive than those based on principle, love and charity, toleration was irreversibly established. Charles's and James's Declarations were legally disputable. Had they achieved their ulterior objective of rendering the King independent from both Parliament and the Anglican allies of the Crown, then it would have been possible for toleration to be amended or even withdrawn at the King's will – in the same way that Louis XIV by his Edict of Fontainebleau (1685) revoked Henri IV's Edict of Nantes. But by the time of the Revolution of 1688 the climate of English opinion had changed, and although the high-flying Tories and their clerical allies might later try to reduce the concessions granted to Dissenters, there was never again a danger that they might be totally withdrawn, as had happened in 1674.

V   THE CONCEPT OF RESTORATION

The instability and confusion that followed Oliver Cromwell's death, and were intensified after the fall of Richard Cromwell in April 1659, had enhanced the appeal of the exiled and dispossessed monarchy. Apparent political disintegration led most men to believe that only if the King came into his own again could the nation hope to enjoy its constitutional and legal rights, and properties, without fear of further arbitrary interference from self-constituted and oppressive military governments. At the level of everyday life even the poorest felt the army as a burden on their narrow backs, resenting the excises and requisitioning that were needed to support an arrogant, self-interested and politicised army of mercenary soldiers and ambitious officers. Naturally those with a more substantial stake in society resented their exclusion from their accustomed positions of influence – J.P.s, militia officers, on corporations and in the parishes – and hated their supplanters, who in 1659–60 were mostly the dependants of the Rump or the leading military politicians. However the euphoria of April and May 1660 did not last for long. Divisions quickly reappeared in society, and the early revival of the old pre-war split between Court and Country was exacerbated by the religious differences caused by the reimposition of religious uniformity in 1661–2. Cynicism was bred by the short-sighted and irresponsible behaviour of Charles, his courtiers and most of his ministers; their greed for money and places, their reckless extravagance and exhibitionist behaviour, could be maintained only at the expense of the public. Commonwealth hypocrites had apparently been succeeded by frivolous rakes. Much more fundamentally the King, who in 1660 had been careful to establish his credentials as a constitutional ruler, gave serious cause as early as 1662 for fears and suspicions that he intended to follow absolutist policies, and that he favoured Catholicism. These suspicions were never entirely to disappear during the period.

It is a cliché to conclude that the Restoration failed to restore national unity, social and religious harmony and political stability. But it is less often appreciated that this failure did not in itself entirely discredit the concept of Restoration. Indeed this concept provided the main principle that underlay the ultimately successful political settlement, that which followed the Revolution of 1688.

Today our residual belief in progress, and our awareness of the importance or irresistibility of change in human affairs, lead us to dismiss the expectations that men held in 1660 as unrealisable. We see that the old pre-1642 world could not be brought back from a dead past. Interregnum changes and developments could not really be ignored as if they had never happened. Almost everyone in 1660 thought otherwise. There was a general belief that historical events operated on a cyclical pattern, with situations repeating themselves. At the time of the Restoration it was almost universally thought that now the wheel had turned full circle, bringing back the situation that had existed before the crisis of 1641–2 that had precipitated the civil war. Men now had the opportunity to learn from the mistakes committed at that time, and to achieve the lasting settlement that all but fanatics and republicans wanted. Clarendon and nearly all the first set of Charles II's ministers and advisers had been constitutionalist moderates in 1640–2, and were sincerely intent on ensuring that the restored monarchical government would use only strictly legal methods.[11]

If government and administration could be kept strictly within the framework of the law and precedent, then subjects of every class and status group would in a spirit of trust and certainty obey royal authority without question. But in practice such harmony and trust never developed – partly because the frantic scramble for offices and places in the summer of 1660 left large numbers of disappointed claimants resentful and all too ready to attribute their failure to corruption on the part of those who controlled patronage. As shown below (see pp. 105–110), Clarendon's initial attempt to institute an administration controlled by the Privy Council proved to be ineffective. But we should not underestimate the strength of the continuing, if unsatisfied and repeatedly disappointed, desire for a successful restoration of unity, stability and domestic peace. The post-Restoration generation did not all consciously want to participate in politics, in the sense of introducing new policies and changes. After each adventurous ministerial policy collapsed, or opposition projects failed, in a welter of dismissals, faction-fighting and general recriminations, there were renewed calls for a new act of restoration. This happened in 1669–70, after Clarendon had been destroyed but his successors and supplanters found themselves powerless to control or manage Parliament. After the collapse of the Cabal, Danby consciously appealed to this conservative sentiment, promising a return to the good old laws and ways.[12] Similarly the notion of a return of the old world and its values forms the theme of John Dryden's *Absalom and Achitophel*, which promised a new age of peace once Shaftesbury and the first Whigs had been defeated. The poem concludes:

> Henceforth a Series of new time began,
> The Mighty Years in long Procession ran:
> Once more the Godlike David was Restored,
> And willing Nations knew their lawful Lord.[13]

VI CHARLES II'S ART OF KINGSHIP

The Restoration came unexpectedly to Charles, but we tend to forget that many contemporaries believed that his hold on his three kingdoms would always be precarious. Over the long term, indeed, it can be argued that ultimately Charles realised that the survival of the monarchy and the preservation of the legitimate succession were about all that he could hope to achieve. When he recovered his right Charles was already a realist; the bitter years in exile and the humiliations he had suffered left him a young man without illusions. He had nothing further to learn about what may be called the black political arts of machiavellian statecraft. No scheming courtier or designing politician surpassed or even equalled him in the techniques of dissimulation (the artful concealment of his true intentions or feelings). Charles had the ability to penetrate other men's motives and intentions; he was quick to identify, and quite callous in exploiting, their weaknesses, and he was always on his guard against being deceived or outwitted by any servant or opponent. When he wished to do so Charles could behave in a cold or even cruel manner, and his habitual amiability was often assumed in order to put men and women off their guard. As the portraits of his last years show, he developed into a formidable, even intimidating, monarch.

The reality was far removed from the foolish myth of the 'Merry Monarch'. Yet Charles apparently let himself be used for long periods by men and women whose ulterior purposes he detected, and whom he certainly despised. His major failings as a sovereign were indolence and inconsistency. As two of the essays show (Chapters 1 and 3) these defects created serious political and governmental confusion and weakness. Charles was probably a more intelligent man than his cousin Louis XIV, but he failed to devote himself to business in anything resembling a systematic fashion, so that he could not avoid relying on servants and ministers whom he knew to be untrustworthy. Since he was not prepared to undertake such time-consuming work as the reading and appreciation of reports, despatches and accounts he was dependent on others for information. There was never any possibility that he would take important business into his own hands and away from his ministers for any length of time; the only exception to this was his correspondence with his sister in the preliminary negotiations that led to the secret treaty of Dover (1670).[14]

As Dr Miller explains, inconsistency is the key-note of the reign of Charles II. Royal policy did not proceed for any length of time in a constant direction. There were no fixed, or indeed ascertainable, principles. Moreover it was not just in short-term politics, or tactics, that Charles switched from one line to another. Overall there were, at

most times during his reign, two major alternative political strategies
that Charles could follow. By repeatedly turning from one to the other
he imparted an element of confusion and deceit to all politics; even his
closest advisers could never be certain which of the two was really
being favoured. There was always the possibility that policies would
be suddenly abandoned, and with them those ministers who were
committed to a definite line.

The first alternative line of policy had been formulated in its main
principles during the years of exile by Clarendon (although even then
Charles had often deviated from it), and its promulgation in private
correspondence with supporters or possible adherents in England,
and in 1660 in the Declaration of Breda, had reassured opinion and
significantly aided the Restoration. Its basis was acceptance of the
necessity for the King to rule within the law; although sovereign, that
is possessed of supreme authority and an obligation to act at his discretion in any emergency situations (such as, for example, the Fire of
London when Charles ordered the destruction of private property so
as to form fire-breaks, in an attempt to stop the conflagration spreading),[15] the King and ministers acting under him would respect the
law. They were also expected to work in partnership and mutual trust
with those individuals and groups who by tradition accepted the
honour and duties of offices at all levels, both at Court and in the localities. Although never explicitly stated, this meant an obligation on
Charles's part to appoint to these offices only those men whose social
status, reputation for honesty, religious faith and adherence to fixed
principles of loyalty and service would in themselves command general respect. Such men would be fit representatives of the Crown.
They would not require visible backing from royal authority, but
would obtain willing obedience from respectful subjects.

At the top, in Clarendon's conception, came the Privy Council of
the great men of the kingdom – including both those who held the
great offices of state, and those who were great men of influence in
their own right because of the standing of their family or the extent of
their territorial possessions. In practice the Council was too large and
unwieldy, and many of its nominal members attended too irregularly,
for it to control administration, so that smaller committees emerged
to make major policy decisions. Secondly, co-ordination and communication between the central government and its servants in the
counties (J.P.s, office-holders in corporations and parochial church-
wardens and overseers) were to be maintained by the bench of judges.

Before 1640 this had been done by the prerogative courts (the Star
Chamber, Council of the North and Council of Wales and the
Marches). Not only was there no suggestion from laymen of reviving
these courts after 1660, but the judges were at first far more independent than in the past. For the first decade of the reign their commissions were 'during their good behaviour', which meant that a
reason would have to be produced for their dismissal (although not for
their suspension). This would also mean that if they were consulted
about a principle of law or the constitution they would be independent in their judgement, but for this very reason they were not regularly consulted until the terms of their commissions had been altered.
The change to the formula 'during pleasure' put them entirely at the
King's disposal, and by James's reign the bench of judges was being
constantly changed, or purged, for what were really political purposes, so that they could be employed as auxiliaries in the enforcement of policy, as well as of the law.[16]

The third branch of government in the traditional concept consisted of the militia.[17] This was as much for the purpose of internal
security, or policing duties during critical periods, as for defence
against invasion by a foreign power. Although never entirely convincing in either role, the merit from the constitutional point of view of the
militia was that it was a substitute for the kind of professional, standing armies that most European sovereigns were striving to establish or
expand at this time. Standing armies were synonymous in the minds
of Englishmen with tyranny, and specifically with royal absolutism.[18]
They preferred an amateur force, largely untrained and badly armed,
because it was organised on a county and not a national basis, and for
the reason that a force officered by the gentry was unlikely to be a
threat to the rule of law. After Venner's abortive terrorist rising in
London at the end of 1660 opinion tolerated a small professional army,
but any move to expand its strength aroused alarm, and in 1679 (at a
time of acute crisis when the King's life was alleged to be in danger
from papist assassins) it was proposed to disband it.

The most contentious part of the traditional policy to which
Charles was committed by Clarendon was the re-establishment with
coercive powers of an established Church of England governed by
bishops.[19] This was the most unpopular part of the Restoration settlement, but also the one with the most important long-term effects.
England was to remain divided along confessional lines between Anglican and Dissenter until the late nineteenth century, but of course the

original purpose of the religious legislation passed by the Cavalier Parliament was not to divide the nation or to persecute Dissenters but to eliminate them, and restore religious unity. This concept of unity within one church was a central and essential part of the Clarendonian scheme of government; he regarded it as necessary if the King's authority was to become impregnable. As the tactical offer of bishoprics to the presbyterians Calamy and Baxter showed, there was no question in official minds of *jure divino* episcopacy in and after 1660; bishops were to act as royal servants in Parliament (they were reinstated in the Lords by a statute of 1661), and they provided a direct chain of command into their dioceses, extending to the parochial clergy, which was far more extensive than anything possessed by the lay authorities (which is why James tried to make use of it by commanding the reading of his Declaration of Indulgence from every pulpit in 1688).

More generally the function of the church was to consecrate the state and its agencies; there was to be no attempt to revive Laud's provocative attempts to make the Anglican Church independent of the temporal authorities. The clergy took a vehement stand on the divine character of monarchy. Preachers regularly stressed the duty of unconditional obedience by all subjects to the King, and the absolute inadmissibility of any resistance, even to a tyrant. James was to be dismayed in 1688 when he discovered that this doctrine could not be taken at its face value, but from the Restoration there was an implicit qualification to Anglican divine right theory. The monarchy that the church upheld was what George Morley in his Coronation sermon of 1661 termed 'Political (not Despotical) Monarchy' which governed the people 'by equal and just laws made with their own consent to them'.[20] This ideal was never within sight of being achieved. Ostentatious and shameless royal immorality (especially by a young King) was nothing unusual, but as early as 1662 Charles gave proof of his essential unreliability.

It was the first, almost totally abortive, Declaration of Indulgence that revealed the existence of an alternative line of political strategy, and of a group of advisers who favoured a break with the constitutional royalism and steadfast Anglicanism advocated and practised by Clarendon. The basis of this alternative policy was to extend toleration to Catholics and most Protestant Dissenters, in return for which they would be expected to assist the Court, and acquiesce in the permanent strengthening of the powers of the royal prerogative. Two

questionable assumptions underlay this alternative policy. The
Church of England as restored and reconstituted in 1660–2 under
episcopal government was not universally popular, and a few years'
experience showed that coercive legislation was not going to achieve
religious uniformity. But Charles, James and some of their advisers
were guilty of miscalculation in jumping to the conclusion that the established church was more of a liability than an asset, and they
greatly exaggerated the actual or potential influence of Dissenters and
Catholics. Even when James achieved independence from Parliament, in 1686–8, these alternative auxiliaries were to prove less adequate and serviceable than the traditional allies of the Crown, the
Anglican nobility, gentry and clergy. The second assumption was disproved much earlier, although James ignored this warning, to his
great cost. The doctrines of passive obedience to royal authority and
non-resistance in all circumstances never prevented the Anglican
clergy from defending their corporate interests and privileges whenever these were threatened, and they could count on an immediate
response from a large bloc of peers and M.P.s. They forced the withdrawal of the first Declaration of Indulgence of December 1662, and
the fall of Clarendon in 1667 did not lead to the elimination of the Clarendonian interest.

VII THE POLICIES OF ABSOLUTISM

There were two main phases of absolutist policies, and one episode
may possibly fit into the same category. The first sustained attempt to
make the King independent of the co-operation of his subjects, and
especially of Parliament, was made by the Cabal ministry in 1668–73,
and is associated with the secret treaty of Dover with Louis XIV, the
third Dutch war and the Declaration of Indulgence of 1672. The
second by James in 1687–8 involved the establishment of toleration by
prerogative means (Declarations of Indulgence in 1687 and 1688), and
a campaign to obtain a collaborationist Parliament by wholesale
modelling of the corporations and repeated purges of local office-
holders. There was also one other political experiment during the
period about whose real character and aims it is still impossible to be
categorical. In 1678 Lord Treasurer Danby raised an army for the os-
tensible purpose of making war on France. No such war resulted and
it is possible that none was ever intended, but that the army was
raised in order to establish arbitrary government in England. This

would have involved (as had been planned in 1672) the dissolution of the existing Parliament, with no intention of calling another in the foreseeable future, and the use of the army to overawe or, if necessary, to crush opposition.[21]

Louis XIV's absolutist style of government provided the obvious and, up to the 1690s, generally successful model for other rulers. Many former exiles had first-hand experience of it. Many army officers from the British Isles served Louis. Ministers envied the freedom from constitutional restrictions of their French opposite numbers. Unlike his cousin, Louis could promulgate laws, and impose taxes in most provinces, by royal edict. The aristocracy that had earlier dominated the French Court and the provinces, and claimed as of right to share in the administration of government, had been reduced to submissive obedience. Even in the greatly expanded professional army, in which the nobles held most of the commissions, royal authority was directly established through the new military bureaucracy of *intendants* directed by Louvois, and these officials were also extensively used to supervise civil administration. Towns were closely controlled and policed. The *Parlements* were reduced to obedience. Provinces which retained their representative assemblies, their *états*, were brought under effective control by royal governors.

A second model of absolutism existed, cruder and less systematic, but far nearer to home, in Scotland. During the 1670s the northern kingdom was controlled by Lauderdale and then, from 1679, by James himself. A formidable army formed the basis of a rough and repressive regime. Parliament was managed and subordinated. The powers of the Crown were substantially increased, and an unpopular episcopal church imposed on a largely antagonistic people. Of course conditions were far more favourable for the establishment of absolutism in a poorer country, where many of the nobility were dependent on royal patronage, and the tribal Highlanders could be easily mobilised. The single-chamber Scottish Parliament had no tradition of independence, and never gained the initiative in legislation, and the Scottish episcopal church was always completely dependent on royal support.[22]

Consequently although some of Charles's ministers hoped ultimately to achieve the same kind of absolute power that Louis or Lauderdale possessed, and this was certainly James's objective in 1687–8, a rapid and total transformation of the system of English government was not a practical possibility. Absolutism could be established only after the achievement of royal independence from Parliament, such as the Tudors had enjoyed. But although Charles was not constitutionally obliged to call a parliamentary session every year, his financial needs made him choose to do so; there was a session every year up to 1681, with the exceptions of 1672 and 1676. The frequency of these sessions affected ministerial behaviour. Ministers learnt from the fall of Clarendon in 1667 and of Clifford in 1673 how vulnerable they were to attacks in Parliament. Unless they acquired immunity from the threat of an impeachment, ministers would never act as the whole-hearted servants of their royal master – as was the case in France.

In terms of power seventeenth-century absolute rulers based their authority on professional standing armies. Contemporary Englishmen were well aware of the use made of military force to break or overawe opposition in Europe as well as in Scotland, and no one could forget how the New Model army had enabled first the Rump and then Oliver Cromwell to rule the nation against its will for a decade.[23] Although the regiments of the Commonwealth army were paid off as quickly as possible in 1660–1, since neither Charles nor Parliament felt safe so long as it was in being, the first serious suggestion of expanding the relatively small forces that Charles retained came as early as 1662. On the grounds that the enforcement of the Uniformity Act and collection of the new Hearth tax might cause disturbances, proposals were made by some of the junior ministers (notably Bennet) to raise new forces. This was not done, but in 1666 the money levied to finance the militia was (illegally) diverted for the maintenance of newly raised independent companies, whose officers were given the same kind of commissions as those in the small regular army.[24]

In 1672–3 what critics thought was a suspiciously large army was retained in England (in addition to the forces sent abroad to fight alongside their French allies) for a planned invasion of the Dutch coast that never took place. Some M.P.s openly said that the intention had been to use the army for a coup.[25] In 1678 a much larger army was levied for exactly the opposite purpose, to support the Dutch in their defensive struggle in Flanders against a French invasion. Suspicions were intensified by two factors. Charles showed no intention of actually declaring war, even though troops were sent to protect Ostend; talk of war was construed as a cover for preparations to dissolve the Cavalier Parliament and suppress any opposition by force. Secondly the army was raised without any assurance of financial supply from

Parliament, and if this was not forthcoming (and it would not be unless war was declared) the soldiers would have to live at free quarter – requisitioning supplies and billets. Although it is impossible to be categorical about the matter, it is clear that in the autumn of 1678 Charles and Danby had at the least created an option to attempt the introduction of absolutist methods.[26]

Expansion of the army formed the first stage of James's policy of strengthening his authority, regardless of the reactions of his Tory allies who had preserved his right to the succession. After the suppression of Monmouth's rebellion in the summer of 1685, James outraged Tory principles by declaring his determination to retain a considerably enlarged army (at the expense of the militia), and even more by announcing that he would continue the commissions of Catholic officers who had been appointed in breach of the Test Act of 1673. James unlike his brother could disregard parliamentary protests; he had the financial resources to maintain a larger army without extraordinary taxation. In the medium and long term this enlarged army was to serve as the basis of a greatly strengthened monarchy, but although James had insufficient time to construct an elaborate military administration on the French model, his army does not seem to have suffered from serious organisational weaknesses. Detachments were stationed in most regions of England, whereas the bulk of Charles's forces had always been quartered around London, so that by 1688 the whole kingdom was taking on the appearance of a country under military occupation.[27]

There were, even by 1688, some important areas in which there were no real signs of developments that would have been necessary if absolutism *à la française* was to be established. The most fundamental deficiency was administrative. There were no *intendants* and no means of producing them. Before 1640 the prerogative courts had provided a training for officials (who were mostly men educated in the civil, not common, law) whose routine habituated them to looking at all problems from the point of view of advancing or protecting the King's interests. The failure to revive the prerogative courts after 1660, combined with the chronic lack of money, kept down the size of the central bureaucracy and rendered systematic and positive supervision of local government virtually impossible. The King could dismiss J.P.s at will, and did so frequently for political or factional reasons, but he had no means of ensuring that replacements would obey orders or undertake duties more efficiently, and as

James discovered in 1687–8 there was a limited pool of men available with the time, inclination and local standing on whom to draw.
There was neither the money nor the means to train and support professional administrators in the localities. When James began to model
the municipal corporations in 1687–8 he had to set up a special organisation for the purpose, and its activities provoked intense and widespread resentment.[28] The same reaction occurred when in 1686 he
revived a prerogative court, the Ecclesiastical Commission, primarily
to supervise and discipline the clergy. Each of the major cases in
which it was involved, the prosecution of Bishop Compton and that of
the fellows of Magdalen College, Oxford, turned into a set-piece political battle and test of strength and determination.[29] Centralisation
and policies pointing in that direction ran counter to the basic principles of English government and were seen at the time as attempts to
undermine the constitution.

Another notable weakness of the royal position, by comparison
with that of Louis XIV, was the lack of an ability to control, channel
and exploit economic and especially commercial activity. Charles and
James had far more limited powers in this area than their father who
had frequently, if ineffectively and often counter-productively, inter-
fered in economic life by issuing patents, licences and monopolies.
Although the Council of Trade and Plantations could have been developed for the purpose, neither Charles, James nor their ministers
applied themselves to asserting royal control as Colbert did in France.
Consequently the economic and commercial expansion that took
place owed little to assistance from the Crown, and the Court itself
was no longer (as it had been in the first half of the century) the arena
in which mercantile and industrial interests jockeyed and fought for
privileges and rights. Merchants, ship-owners, manufacturers and
middlemen, mine-owners and most frequently landowners and
farmers who wanted official action taken to rectify unfavourable conditions or to facilitate expansion and new enterprises, normally
turned to Parliament. The three most important mercantilist policies
were all embodied in parliamentary forms – the enlarged and more
easily enforced Navigation Act of 1660, the resolutions of 1664 calling
for coercive action that led to the second Dutch war, and the agitation
based on the Scheme of Trade (a claim that England was being impoverished by an unfavourable balance of trade) that produced in 1678
a ban on imports of most French manufactures and luxury commodities.[30]

However the most important barrier to absolutism remained the King's chronic lack of money (above all, ready money), and his poor credit. Even those administrators who attempted constructive changes, notably the reforming Treasury commissioners of 1667, were under too much pressure from current demands for money to be able to eliminate recognised causes of inefficiency and corrupt practices. As Dr Tomlinson shows (see pp. 98–105) a start was made and new methods were introduced that were to serve the Crown and nation well after 1688, but under Charles and James there was insufficient trust in either the solvency or the good faith of the King for a national bank to be established. Had one been attempted it would probably have been interpreted, and resisted, as a device to make him independent of Parliament.

Finally on the subject of absolutist experiments and policies, it must be emphasised that up to 1685 its advocates and champions suffered even more than their ministerial and political rivals, the defenders of constitutionalism, from Charles's inconsistency. Defenders of the *status quo* were alarmed by revelations of his preference for absolutist policies and Catholicism, but they could always rally support against them. Those who advocated such drastic changes and bold innovations ran great personal risks. When Clifford, alone of the Cabal ministers, refused to disclaim responsibility for policies that were coming under furious attack, and urged that they should be continued at all costs, he was abandoned without compunction; he had to resign in June 1673 and was dead within four months. As Danby was to discover in 1679, no minister who ran into serious difficulties could expect Charles to try to protect him.

Paradoxically when Charles did at last succeed in freeing himself from dependence on Parliament, in the last phase of his reign (1681–5), neither he nor Rochester made any attempt to institute absolutist policies. Triumphant over his Whig enemies but content to maintain his royal prerogatives intact, and having committed himself to an inactive foreign policy, Charles ruled in a loose combination with the Tory landowners and clergy who had rallied to him during the Exclusion crisis. His attitude during this last phase strengthens the view that, although he had permitted some of his ministers to embark earlier on adventurous and absolutist policies, Charles had never committed himself irrevocably.

For Rochester, the least known of his chief ministers, this last period of the reign vindicated the principles that had been embodied by his father, Clarendon. The latter's conception of government and politics was largely static. Parliament should lay the grievances of the nation (if there were any!) before the King who, out of his goodness and after consultation with the Privy Council, would initiate remedies – either by Proclamation or by introducing legislation into one of the Houses. On the other hand the Commons could not be expected to vote additional taxation to the King for life, or temporary extraordinary taxes, if the King, the Court and the government were guilty of extravagance. Clarendon did not want regular, still less annual, parliamentary sessions, fearing that these would invite Parliament to meddle with matters outside its proper sphere. The representation of grievances would be encouraged. M.P.s would be able to pose as vigilant defenders of popular interests, and to claim that it was the Court that was to blame for whatever went wrong. Regular exposure to such attacks would inevitably provoke ministerial counter-measures, and so give rise to a permanent set of political tensions. Consequently in 1663 Clarendon unsuccessfully opposed a group of younger and more dynamic ministers who persuaded the King to authorise them to initiate a systematic policy of parliamentary management that would produce a working majority (and also incidentally increase their own personal influence). Clarendon rightly foresaw not only that the use of such political inducements on a large scale would corrupt both the Court and Parliament, but that it would also make it impossible for the King to practise 'good housekeeping', that is to live within his income. For this reason he also opposed an adventurous foreign policy that ran the risk of involving the country in an expensive war.[31]

In the last phase of Charles's reign Rochester helped to create the favourable circumstances in which his father's policies could be made to work. He was the only minister to be involved in the secret agreement of April 1681 with Louis XIV by which, in return for subsidies, Charles agreed not to call another Parliament and not to intervene in Europe if called on to do so by Spain or the Dutch Republic, to whom he had treaty obligations.[32] Freed from the prospect of having to manage Parliament, Rochester carried through a drastic programme of retrenchment, and he was the only one of Charles's ministers ever to succeed in limiting royal expenditure.[33] Although he did not try to prevent the Catholics from enjoying private relief from the penal laws, Rochester's ministry gave the Church of England complete security. The press, which had become a powerful influence during the Exclusion crisis, was brought under effective censorship. A combination of

Tory political activity and a legal prosecution reduced London, the Whig citadel, to submission. Although it involved a breach of the provisions of the Triennial Act no Parliament was called, but there was no demand for one, and when Charles died his brother inherited an unprecedentedly strong position.

James retained Rochester as his chief minister for eighteen months, but he had a totally different conception of the role of ministers. He demanded obedience and loyalty, but what was in even sharper contrast with the attitude of Charles was that James did not allow ministers to formulate policy or make major decisions. James was determined to rule as well as reign, leaving his ministers no freedom of action. By the end of 1686 Rochester's position had become untenable, as he found that he was powerless to dissuade the King from following lines of policy that were almost universally distrusted as absolutist; after considerable hesitation he gave up his offices at the end of the year. James was nothing if not consistent, and pressed on with the policies that led to disaster, regardless of the advice of his ministers. It is not surprising that at the end they left the country before he did, or joined in the general defection to William.

VIII   LIFE IN RESTORATION ENGLAND

In political terms the Restoration period can only be seen as a failure. Harmony was not established; instead the nation was divided into hostile camps, Court against Country, then Whig against Tory, and Anglican against Dissenter. Several over-ambitious 'projects' or adventures – the second and third Dutch wars, the Cabal's policies, Danby's parliamentary management systems, the organisation of opposition by Shaftesbury, Monmouth's rebellion, James's attempt to pack Parliament – all ended in total failure. The fact that such a number of gambles should be attempted was in itself a symptom of the underlying instability, but the absence of widespread or large-scale violence during crises meant that politics did not actually disrupt the ordinary life of the people. Indeed the weakness of the Crown and its impotence in foreign affairs after 1674 actually proved to be economically valuable. Tax levels after 1662 were lower than they had been under the Commonwealth (or were to be after 1689), and for four years (1674–8) England was the only major European power not involved in war.

The absence of a trained and salaried bureaucracy left the

governing processes that most closely touched the lives of ordinary people in the hands of the locally-based leaders of provincial society. Obviously they interpreted their role, and undertook their duties, in ways favourable to themselves and those whom they accepted as their associates, particularly in the administration of the poor law, but most J.P.s and parochial officers tried to govern in the interests of the communities to which they belonged, as they saw them. J.P.s and militia officers, even though they were often linked by associates with a group at Court or with clients of a minister, were not prepared to accept dictation or centralisation. However the long-term trends were moving in the direction of oligarchy. An economic and social gap was beginning to open up between the more substantial landowners and the mere gentry whose horizons were confined to a part of a county and were under-capitalised. Similarly the newly established and most rapidly expanding trades (especially those with the American and West Indian plantations) required more working capital or better credit than most merchants possessed. Artisans, small producers, yeoman farmers and local retailers were finding it increasingly difficult to combine independence with a reasonable living, and in many trades those who had completed their apprenticeship found it difficult to set up on their own account. But the decline in status and living standards that affected certain sections cannot be directly attributed to political changes or developments; ironically the one group who benefited most from the Restoration, the lower clergy, were the most articulate in expressing their dissatisfaction at their poverty, which they blamed for the lack of respect which they received from most of the laity.[34]

It is a matter of historical controversy how far the new subjects of Charles II thought of themselves as oppressed by the Restoration. Certainly John Milton, in passages of eloquent entreaty that had absolutely no effect at the time, thought of it as a return to bondage.[35] Most uneducated people had been only briefly influenced by the revolutionary ideas of 1647–9. They had never had a chance to participate in political or electoral processes under any of the Interregnum regimes, so that apart from those purged in the corporations or disabled from acting as office-holders there, few men lost any political rights by the Restoration. For most humble people all governments were a burden on their backs; the less they weighed the better. After 1660 there was far less actual government – no large army that required heavy direct and indirect taxation and yet continued to

engage in requisitioning and free quarter. There were no special or
extraordinary courts, no major-generals. People seldom thought that
government intervention in their daily lives was intended for their
benefit, or to increase the prosperity of the nation. Experience taught
them that under each successive regime the purpose was to confer
special advantages on the favoured associates of those who controlled
political power. In 1667 Charles II endowed his illegitimate son, the
Duke of Richmond, with a perpetual duty of a shilling on every chal-
dron of coal shipped from the Tyne (giving him over £10,000 p.a.),[36]
but the Commonwealth had given its senior military officers similarly
generous grants, and the Long Parliament had enriched land specu-
lators and financiers.

The Restoration meant a return of decentralisation. England again
became, governmentally, a confederation of counties, and each sizeable county a confederation of hundreds, each with its own petty sessions. Without prerogative courts supervision was necessarily
intermittent and lax, and the quality and character of government at
the local level depended largely on the personal inclinations and prejudices of the men serving on the commissions of the peace or in corporations. This can be seen very clearly in the case of the two sections
who really did suffer repression during the Restoration period: the
Catholic recusants and the Protestant Dissenters. There were wide
variations in the way in which the laws were enforced; an enthusiastic
magistrate like John Arnold in Monmouthshire could initiate a sustained local persecution at a time when recusants in other counties
such as Northumberland were living undisturbed.[37]

Although repression of Protestant Dissenters was intermittent,
they did suffer severely at times of crisis – especially after 1681 when
they paid heavily for their association with the first Whigs.[38] Many
ministers and magistrates genuinely thought that they posed a threat
to internal peace and order, just as unofficial opinion identified the
Catholics with conspiracies aimed at establishing absolutism. Dissenters and recusants alternately filled the role of scapegoats. Obviously
this need for scapegoats was an admission of insecurity, but this feeling of insecurity had political rather than social or economic causes.
There is little evidence that political disaffection, for instance in the
Exclusion crisis of 1679, was directly caused by economic distress.
Socially as well as politically the first Whigs were a heterogeneous
combination of interests: aristocrats, lesser gentry, urban tradesmen,
some of the leading London merchant oligarchs, lawyers, small-

holders and tenant farmers. However it is clear that in the period immediately after the Restoration a succession of bad or indifferent harvests and the dislocation of trade (caused, at home, by the plague and, abroad, by the second Dutch war) resulted in a severe depression. This intensified fears of a renewed rebellion, but the economy recovered and trade was to expand during the rest of the period. There were no acute shortages of food. England (though not Scotland or Ireland) finally passed out of the era of what are known as crises of subsistence, that is times of near-famine with exceptionally heavy mortality and low conception rates, such as were to afflict France for another three generations.

The pace of social change was slow. Oligarchical elements – great landowners, entrepreneurs and merchants with capital – were constantly improving their position, at the expense of the lesser gentry, yeomen farmers and small masters, but undramatically and gradually. Parliament passed very few enclosure acts during this period. There were no large-scale displacements of population, but a steady drift of surplus labour to the towns and especially to London. The drastic Act of Settlement that restricted poor relief to the parish where a pauper had been born was passed, but not uniformly or harshly enforced. A more severe attitude towards the poor and criminals was being urged, but had not yet become generally accepted.

The advance of a wealthy oligarchy can be traced in two areas: building and the flowering of a metropolitan culture. Not surprisingly large-scale building came to an almost complete halt during the Interregnum, but for the half-century after 1660 architects and builders enjoyed a period of great activity and prosperity. The boom in building had a stimulating effect on many related trades: brick and tile yards, quarries, glass manufactures, internal transport, ships for importing soft-timber from the Baltic, lead mining. Calamitous fires made rebuilding necessary in London and Northampton, and large-scale development of cheap houses occurred on the eastern fringes of London and south of the Thames. But a very high proportion of the new building catered for the wealthy and very wealthy. West End streets and squares were laid out with expensive town houses for purchase on leases or letting for the London season.[39] After the fire the wealthier merchants moved out of the congested City, and residential villages to the west and on the higher ground to the north were expanded. Similarly in regional capitals, county towns and spas the greatest expansion was in town houses, assembly rooms and civic buildings. The building, rebuilding and extension of country houses were resumed. Ecclesiastical building provided another area of high demand. Cathedrals had been commonly neglected, and often vandalised, during the Interregnum, and many urban and rural church buildings were in a dilapidated condition. An immense amount of money and care had to be devoted to repair work, refurnishing and decoration, and it was not always easy to get money for the purpose; in the most extreme case Bishop Hacket had to use great pressure to raise money for the reconstruction of Lichfield cathedral which had been destroyed during the civil war.[40] Oxford and Cambridge colleges resumed building. But it is significant that the Crown was relatively inactive; parts of Whitehall and Windsor were patched up, but plans for a new palace in London and for a new country palace at Winchester came to nothing for lack of money. The only large-scale official construction project ended in total failure; engineers undertook the largest civil engineering task of the age, the construction of an immense mole to protect Tangier harbour, but it was constantly damaged by Atlantic gales and had finally to be demolished when the town was abandoned in 1683.[41]

The dominant cultural characteristics of the Restoration period were aristocratic, metropolitan and cosmopolitan.[42] Naturally during the Interregnum fashionable cultural activity had atrophied, and popular culture had largely assumed religious forms that were already partly discredited by 1660. Butler's wildly popular *Hudibras* caricatured puritans as philistines and hypocrites, and Milton's last great masterpieces were read and appreciated only by an unfashionable minority. One by-product of the Restoration, following the re-installation of the upper class in governmental offices and Parliament, and the return of a royal Court, was the re-emergence of the London season. A hectic and expensive metropolitan cultural life developed very rapidly after 1660, on a luxurious scale that could not be imitated in any provincial capital. In London alone there were theatres (with companies that included actresses for the first time), eating-places, coffee houses, clubs and societies, pleasure gardens, portrait painters, bookshops and printers, importers of luxury commodities, all catering for the fashionable or those who wished to pass as such. By comparison life in winter-time in isolated country houses or market towns seemed dull and restricting, especially to women, who could not hunt and were far less mobile than their menfolk. But participation in the London season was expensive, beyond the means of all but fairly substantial landowners and established office-holders. Few of those whose living came from the professions, trade or business had the means, the time or the temperament to engage in what was often an idle, and frequently a dissipating, way of life; as a consequence such people were frequently derided and depicted in unflattering ways in Restoration comedies – few would be in the theatre audience to express resentment.

The élite culture of the Restoration period was open to foreign, and particularly French, influences. The theatre closely followed French models. Dress, etiquette and manners aped French modes. Socially as well as politically Whitehall could almost be described as an out-station of Versailles. The impressionability of the upper classes of fashion was dangerous; their imitation of French ways aroused resentment. The frenchified fop might be derided as a figure of fun, but the culture for which many returned exiles had developed a sympathy was thoroughly impregnated with the principles and values of the Counter-Reformation, and was associated with the Court and official culture of Louis XIV. Charles and his courtiers undoubtedly set their social inferiors a disreputable example. Their exhibitionist lack of moral restraint, hectic pursuit of selfish pleasure and arrogant lack of consideration for others were morally and socially corrosive. Lives of self-assertion and self-indulgence could end, as with the sensitive poet and wit Rochester, in an abyss of moral nihilism and despair.[43] In his case this was relieved by a death-chamber conversion to (Anglican) religious faith, but generally the high culture of Restoration London was heartless, frivolous and superficial. Only in one respect did it have really valuable, if indirect, results.

Science and philosophy became fashionable. Most of the courtiers who attended the meetings of the Royal Society contributed little or nothing personally, but collectively they and Charles as patron conferred on the scientists effective protection and a certain prestige. As Dr Hunter shows (see pp. 190–4) not everyone accepted the claim that scientific investigations would necessarily act as a reinforcement for revealed religion. But in practice scientists and philosophers encountered little obstruction; it was because of his close association with Shaftesbury that Locke had to leave Oxford and take refuge in the Dutch Republic.[44]

The publications of the first generation of the members of the Royal Society were to earn for English scientists and philosophers a dazzling reputation in most of Europe. But within England the contemporary influence of more traditional and conservative thinkers and scholars was equally great. Oxford and Cambridge suffered a slow but persistent decline in the numbers of students. They failed to incorporate in their curricula the new science and philosophy, but they did provide an intellectual training and livelihood for many of the innovative geniuses, notably Barrow and Newton. However the universities gave more recognition to scholarship of a more orthodox although not necessarily traditional kind, in which achievements were far from negligible: for example George Bull earned an international reputation for his work in patristic studies.[45] The revival of anglo-saxon and medieval studies, and the working out of a genuinely critical approach to historical sources by Robert Brady, disprove the notion that universal torpor reigned in Restoration Oxford and Cambridge.[46] The universities continued to play an important role as seminaries for the education of the Anglican clergy and, despite the spread of literacy and a consistently high output of publications of all kinds, preaching remained the most important single form of intellectual influence in the lives of ordinary people.

IX   CONCLUSION

The expectations of 1660 that the restoration of the monarchy would bring about unity and harmony could not have been more emphatically disproved by political developments. Fears of royal absolutism and Catholicism, mistrust of the King and his ministers, were matched by suspicions of the sincerity of the self-appointed leaders and organisers of opposition, and alarm at the apparent danger of renewed civil conflicts. The partisan religious settlement and the failure of coercive legislation to eliminate dissent created the rift in English society between conformist and separatist that was to endure for over two centuries. When the first parties were organised during the Exclusion crisis the titles which were given to them, Whig and Tory, were originally terms of abuse denoting violence and rebellion, of either the Scottish or the Irish variety.

In Scotland and Ireland repression and rebellion were characteristics of the Restoration period, but in England civil war was avoided, if only by a narrow margin in 1685 and 1688. When revolution came in the latter year, it was virtually bloodless, and confined to the purely political sphere. It did not gather the kind of momentum that would lead (as in the 1640s) to social and political upheaval. The prime movers, William and his extensive network of English associates, retained effective control at all stages. For once the centre held. Men of zealous ill-will either shared in James's defeat, as his heterogeneous Court of opportunists, adventurers and time-servers disintegrated or, in the case of such trouble-makers in William's entourage as Mordaunt, Peyton and Montgomery, had no real opportunity to emerge as a major force, acting on their own.

Briefly, but for long enough to accomplish the durable settlement that had evaded the politicians and statesmen in 1640–2 and 1660, the nation became united (as perhaps never again until 1940). The same theme of restoration is to be found in 1688–9 as in 1660, but there was one significant difference. In the latter year the restoration of the monarchy had been seen as the key-stone of the settlement, the guarantor of constitutional liberties, the prerequisite to unity, harmony and stability. But in 1688 the universal demand was for a free Parliament; only after one had been elected was the fate of the monarchy discussed. Although its reputation had been tarnished during the Restoration period by factionalism, obstructionism, corrupt practices and abuses of privilege, Parliament stood out in 1688 as the institution that embodied the interest of the nation. Symbolically as well as in practical terms the Restoration period ends with the offer of the Crown to William and Mary by the Convention Parliament in 1689.

1. The Later Stuart Monarchy

JOHN MILLER

MOST historians, in writing about the restored monarchy, stress its weaknesses rather than its strengths, with some plausibility. The Crown's coercive powers had been reduced by the abolition in 1641 of Star Chamber, the Council of the North and High Commission. These were not revived at the Restoration. Similarly, the legislation of 1641 which declared illegal many of Charles I's unpopular fiscal devices was preserved intact and was supplemented by an Act abolishing feudal tenures and the Court of Wards. As a result, with a few minor exceptions, the King could now raise money only by means explicitly approved by Parliament. Moreover, although Parliament reverted to the traditional doctrine that the King should 'live of his own', it showed itself reluctant to enlarge his ordinary revenue too far, preferring to vote temporary extraordinary grants to meet his immediate needs. There were several possible reasons for this reluctance to grant Charles II too large a permanent revenue. As representatives of the taxpayer, MPs were never eager to vote money without a very good reason. They realised, too, that Charles was much more likely to meet Parliament regularly if he were kept short of money. There were, in fact, only two years between 1660 and 1681 when Parliament did not meet. Finally, an impoverished monarch would be unable to afford a substantial army and Englishmen had had enough of military rule. This last anxiety also underlay Parliament's refusal in the early 1660s to reform the militia and thus make of it a more effective military force.[1]

These restrictions on the monarchy, important as they were, were perhaps less significant than the restrictions which were *not* imposed. Had they wished, the Convention of 1660 and the Cavalier Parliament elected in 1661 could have refrained from giving Charles II an adequate permanent revenue and then used their financial power to reduce Charles to a figurehead. Instead they seemed to go out of their way to build up the power of the Crown. Not only did they vote an ordinary revenue which was intended to be sufficient to cover the normal costs of administration but they abandoned Parliament's two main constitutional demands of 1641–8: a share in the King's choice of ministers and in the control of the armed forces. The Commons had made these demands late in 1641 because MPs had thought the reforming legislation of that year insufficient to stop Charles I from abusing his powers. At the Restoration the King's exclusive right to control the militia was explicitly reaffirmed while his right to choose his advisers was tacitly acknowledged. Thus all the basic royal prerogatives remained intact. Apart from controlling appointments and the armed forces the King was responsible for the conduct of foreign policy and the provision of justice and, in general, he was expected to see to the day-to-day administration of the country. Thus in 1685, when Sir William Petty considered the extent of the King's powers, he concluded in some alarm that 'the King . . . can do what harm he pleases to his subjects'.[2]

This restoration of monarchical authority was quite deliberate. In the words of Roger North:

> The gentlemen of this early Parliament [1661] came up full of horror at the very thoughts of the past miseries of the civil war and firmly resolved . . . to prevent the like for the future. . . . All that was done for church and crown [was] true English policy for the preservation of law and property and not . . . the result of a chimeric loyalty.[3]

Not only Royalists but moderate Parliamentarians had abhorred Charles I's execution, and Presbyterians like Prynne were as vindictive as anyone in hounding the regicides in 1660. The radicalism of Cromwell's army had had little counterpart among civilians. England's economy was dominated by agriculture, in which custom and tradition were far more apparent than a willingness to experiment and the social and constitutional attitudes of most Englishmen were similarly conservative. The restoration of the monarchy on essentially traditional lines followed logically from men's attachment to the 'Ancient Constitution'. Moreover a strong ruler seemed necessary to guard against any resurgence of the radical 'Good Old Cause' of the 1650s, whose strength was habitually overestimated by Restoration Englishmen.[4] However archaic and impractical the monarchy may seem in the twentieth century, in the seventeenth it seemed the most effective and rational form of government. Some functions, like diplomacy or leadership in war, could be performed better by one man than by many. Experience showed, too, that only a king, elevated above even the greatest of his subjects, could exercise reasonably impartial justice among them. Because the monarchy's powers were gradually whittled away from the seventeenth century, historians have been over-eager to ascribe this to a conscious quest for power on the part of the Commons and to seek the beginnings of this process in the conflicts of Crown and Parliament under Charles II, Charles I and even Elizabeth. In fact Parliament curbed the royal prerogative only in exasperated self-defence, in reaction to the Stuarts' persistent refusal to use their acknowledged powers within the limits which their subjects regarded as proper. Parliament's quarrel in the 1640s had been with Charles I's abuse of his authority, not with the royal authority as such.[5]

The monarchy's effective powers were restored, then, because the Convention and Cavalier Parliament wanted Charles II to be an effective ruler. His subjects, like those of Elizabeth or Charles I, accepted that the Crown's powers were necessary but expected him to use those powers in the 'national interest'. Quite how this 'national interest' was interpreted is debatable. The Commons consisted mostly of landowners who were always ready to complain that land was too heavily taxed and to shift much of the burden of taxation on to trade and consumption. But MPs were also willing, on occasion, to vote heavy taxes on land if they believed this to be really necessary and they sometimes sought to protect the interests of the poorer taxpayer, as in the frequent attempts after 1664 to have the Hearth tax modified or abolished.[6] More generally, MPs expected the King to govern in a manner acceptable to the provincial gentry and not to follow his personal whims or those of a court clique. After 1660, as before 1640, one of the King's greatest assets (if properly used) was his leading subjects' acceptance that effective royal powers were necessary and their willingness to co-operate in his government: most MPs, indeed, served him as JPs or in some other capacity. If he failed to maintain their co-operation he was unlikely to provoke a rebellion – there had been no hint of a rising in England in the 1630s – but the effectiveness of his government would be seriously impaired, especially if he sought to persuade his subjects to fight for him, as Charles I did in 1639–40 and James II did in 1688. As Lord Treasurer Danby remarked in 1677: 'Till the King can fall into the humour of his people, he can never be great.' Similarly, Sir William Temple explained to William of Orange

> that the crown of England stood upon surer foundations than ever it had done in former times and the more for what had passed in the last reign, and that I believed the people would be found better subjects than perhaps the King himself believed them. That it was, however, in his power to be as well with them as he pleased. . . ; if not, yet with the help of a little good husbandry he might pass his reign in peace, though not perhaps with so much ease at home or glory abroad as if he fell into the vein of his people.[7]

Successful kingship thus required skills which were as much political as administrative. A king had to frame his policies so as to maintain the goodwill of his subjects in Parliament, the administration and the provinces. Until the early 1680s Charles II failed to do so, while James II's conduct undermined his subjects' loyalty to a point where they made little or no effort to oppose William's invasion in 1688.

II

When considering the objectives of Charles II and James II, it is well worth bearing in mind the remarks of Michael Hawkins on Charles I's regime:

> To have aims implies a degree of freedom of manoeuvre. Given the financial problems of the early Stuart government, the realisation of ambitious aims was unlikely; 'aims' were often confined to seeking a degree of financial independence which would provide manoeuvrability in other fields.[8]

Much the same could be said of the reign of Charles II. There were differences: in particular, the King's financial problems now centred on managing Parliament rather than on maximising the yield from the Crown's powers of economic regulation and its multifarious feudal and property rights. But survival was still the main priority and in some areas (notably foreign policy) financial stringency ensured that

Charles II's room for manoeuvre was as limited as his father's.

Charles's obsession with survival was partly a product of his indolent temperament: as Sir John Reresby remarked, he 'was not stirring nor ambitious, but easy, loved pleasures and seemed chiefly to desire quiet and security for his own time'. It also reflected a profound distrust of his subjects. As Burnet remarked, 'he thinks the world is governed wholly by interests and indeed he has known so much of the baseness of mankind that no wonder if he has hard thoughts of them'.[9] Historians may now stress the conservative, defensive motivation of the Parliamentarians in the civil war but that was not the way they appeared to the men of the Restoration. The simple fact remained that a large number of Englishmen had fought against their King and that he had subsequently been executed. It hardly seemed credible that the forces which had brought about such momentous events should simply disappear now that the King had been restored. Long before the Tories coined the slogan 'Forty-one is here again' in the Exclusion crisis, anxious gentlemen saw echoes of 1641 in every small disturbance or quarrel between King and Commons.[10] Charles and his advisers, too, remained fearful of rebellion. The early 1660s saw Venner's rising, the Derwentdale plot and many rumours of 'fanatic' plots and plans for republican risings. Acutely aware that it lacked the military force to put down a major rising, Charles's government sometimes over-reacted to disorders, especially in London, even when those disorders were not overtly political. After a crowd had pulled down brothels near Moorfields in 1668, some of the rioters were indicted for treason on the grounds that they had taken upon themselves a task that was properly the King's. (The decision to proceed on this charge perhaps owed something to rumours that the rioters had been egged on by Cromwellian officers.)[11] As tension rose in the 1670s Charles told successive French ambassadors that he feared a rebellion. His anxiety may have been feigned for diplomatic reasons. Louis XIV resented Charles's deserting him to make peace with the Dutch in 1674 and his preparing to make war on France in 1678, so it suited Charles to argue that he had no choice, that his subjects would rebel if he did nothing to save the Spanish Netherlands from Louis's armies. Nevertheless, it seems likely that Charles genuinely feared a rebellion in the mid 1670s and that his fears became stronger in the Exclusion crisis.[12]

This preoccupation with survival underlay much of Charles's government. It can be seen in his sporadic attempts to reform the militia and enlarge the army, which foundered because of lack of money and Parliament's hostility. It offers a possible explanation for his consistently pro-French foreign policy. Lacking an adequate army, Charles felt the need for a powerful ally who could come to his aid if his subjects rebelled. The secret treaty of Dover included a promise that Louis would come to Charles's aid if need arose. However, when Louis offered to send troops, in March 1673, Charles replied that he would accept his offer only in the direst necessity, for he realised that the coming of French troops would be more likely to provoke than to prevent disorder.[13] There were, however, other possible advantages of an alliance with France, for example to prevent the French and Dutch combining against England as they had in 1666–7.

The concern for security also helps to explain Charles's policy towards Protestant Dissent. In 1660–2 and 1668–9 Charles supported schemes to make the established church more comprehensive by removing certain features of which Presbyterians disapproved. He also tried in 1662–3 and in 1672–3 to grant a measure of toleration to all dissenters from the restored Anglican Church. Such measures probably owed something to Charles's own tolerance and to his promise of liberty to tender consciences in the Declaration of Breda. They may also have reflected Charles's desire to secure a measure of toleration for Catholics. Although he remained outwardly a member of the Church of England, Charles had considerable sympathy for Catholicism (indeed, he died a Catholic) and he was conscious of the loyalty to the Crown shown by many Catholics during the civil wars. I am not convinced, however, by arguments that this was the main reason for his attempts to secure toleration for Dissenters,[14] for such a toleration could also serve a political purpose. Remembering the 1640s and 1650s, Charles naturally exaggerated the numbers and political weight of the Dissenters. He was encouraged in this by courtiers eager to undermine the political dominance of Anglicans like Clarendon and Danby. The declaration in favour of toleration of December 1662 followed months of rumours that the implementation of the Act of Uniformity would provoke widespread disorder. Similarly the Declaration of Indulgence of 1672 was seen by Arlington (though not by some of his colleagues) as a way of keeping the Dissenters quiet during the forthcoming war with the Dutch. The relief granted to Catholics in these declarations proved politically counter-productive.[15]

Closely connected to the problem of survival against armed attack, at home and from abroad, was that of financial survival. Charles had few sources of income other than those approved by Parliament. His main concerns were thus, first, to persuade Parliament to grant further supplies and, second, to extract the maximum yield from the revenues already granted. These two problems were closely inter-related. The better the King's revenues were managed, the less he needed to depend on further grants from Parliament and the less likely it became that Parliament would become bogged down in ster-ile recriminations about waste and mismanagement. Moreover, financial problems were closely linked with other questions of men and measures. A minister like Danby, who could increase the King's revenue and secure supplies from Parliament, could make himself well-nigh indispensable and persuade the King to adopt policies which seemed necessary to propitiate the Commons. Thus financial considerations could permeate almost every aspect of Charles's government. His concern to promote trade and shipping had an obvious fiscal element, but other types of policy could also be affected. The need for money from Parliament to continue the war against the Dutch in 1673 forced Charles to cancel his Declaration of Indulgence, while the impossibility of obtaining money from Parliament after 1681 (plus his need for French subsidies) left Charles unable to hinder further French gains in the Spanish Netherlands.

If Charles II's main concerns were physical and financial survival, this was less true of James II. Taking advantage of a major upsurge in overseas trade and a much improved financial administration, the Crown's ordinary revenue climbed to an average of £1,600,000 a year in 1685–8. This was some £400,000 a year more than the notional yield of the revenues granted in 1660–3 and represented an increase of well over fifty per cent on the actual yield of those revenues for most of the 1660s. Moreover, this was a real increase, for prices had remained quite stable during Charles's reign. James's first Parliament granted him all the revenues enjoyed by his brother, plus various temporary, extraordinary revenues, designed to enable him to pay the Crown's debts, refurbish the fleet and put down Monmouth's rising. Although Professor Chandaman has shown that these grants were not reck-lessly generous, they removed any financial need to call Parliament so long as the new duties lasted and enabled James to double the size of his army, to nearly 20,000.[16] Thus James could formulate policy largely free of the financial constraints under which his brother had worked, while his larger army and the failure of Monmouth's rising reduced the danger of rebellion. He could therefore, if he chose, pursue policies far more ambitious than those of his predecessors.

The policies which James chose to pursue proved to be ambitious to the point of folly. A zealous Catholic, he sought to remove the laws forbidding Catholic worship and excluding Catholics from office, under the mistaken belief that so many people would then declare themselves Catholics that Catholicism would become the dominant religion. As these laws, the penal laws and Test Acts could legally be removed only by a Parliament, James (despite his financial independence) needed Parliament's co-operation as much as Charles had done. When the strongly Anglican Parliament of 1685 refused to do as he wished, James began to extend his powers in a dubiously legal manner. He dispensed many Catholics (and later Dissenters) from taking the test which the laws imposed on those holding public office and suspended altogether the laws against religious nonconformity. He also used the powers which the Crown had recently acquired over municipal corporations to fill their offices with Dissenters in order to secure the election of a Dissenting Parliament. His promotion of Catholicism, using methods which were seen as illegal and quasi-absolutist, eroded his subjects' loyalty. Few made any effort to save him in 1688.

III

Having examined briefly the objectives of the later Stuarts – physical and financial survival in Charles's case, the promotion of Catholicism in James's – let us now consider the means they used in their efforts to achieve those ends. I shall be concerned here not with the particular policies they adopted but with the way those policies were formulated. Later Stuart monarchy was intensely personal. The King was responsible for all major decisions and many minor ones. He picked his ministers and chose whether to accept their advice. Much thus depended on the King's character, skill and diligence. He was influenced by those around him, at Court, but he in turn did much to shape the character of the Court and thus of the advice which he received.

Charles II's conduct of government was characterised by indolence and cynicism. He was not prepared to apply himself systematically to the drudgery of administration, although he was intelligent enough to grasp the rudiments of a problem if he chose to do so. He preferred pleasure to business and preferred the company of witty men like

Buckingham or 'Bab' May to that of conscientious administrators like
Clarendon or Sir William Coventry. In the early years of his reign
especially, his kingship displayed strong signs of frivolity, which
diminished but did not disappear in the more difficult 1670s and 1680s.
But if Charles was not prepared to work hard, he was determined not
to be a mere figurehead. He trusted nobody and was convinced that
his ministers pursued their own interests more than his. As he could
not or would not check in detail on their recommendations, he sought
to play one off against another and so keep them all in awe and make
them serve him. This did not work very well. To pursue a policy of
'divide and rule' required more diligence and better information than
Charles possessed. Although he appointed some talented and conscientious ministers, he too often ignored them and paid more heed to
personal favourites who told him what he wished to hear. 'His great
dexterity', recalled the earl of Mulgrave, 'lay in cozening himself, by
gaining a little one way while it cost him ten times as much in another
and by caressing those persons most who had deluded him the often-
est.' He was always too ready to believe those who assured him that all
was well. If he sometimes accepted the need for severe economies or
other unpleasant measures, his resolve often crumbled in the face of
the importunities of his mistresses and his less responsible courtiers.[17]

Charles's lack of diligence and his openness to suggestion ensured
that he pursued his objectives with little consistency of either men or
measures. As Temple remarked

> This softness of temper made him apt to fall into the persuasion of
> whoever had his kindness and confidence for the time, how different
> soever from the opinions he was of before, and he was very easy to
> change hands when those he employed seemed to have engaged
> him in any difficulties, so as nothing looked steady in the conduct of
> his affairs, nor aimed at any certain end.[18]

This inconsistency naturally made ministers feel insecure, especially
as they could not rely on the King to defend them. Although only
Danby was dismissed as a direct result of pressure from Parliament,
no minister could feel secure after Charles had dismissed Clarendon
and pressed the Lords to condemn him on trumped-up charges.
(Charles did this because some of his courtiers argued that the Chancellor must be disgraced in order to propitiate the Commons, not because the Commons had actually demanded it.)[19] Given this

insecurity, ministers naturally concentrated on short term expedients, however little those might do to improve Charles's position in the long term. Moreover, they tried to make as much money as they could out of what might be only a short period in office and devoted as much time to attacking their rivals as to doing the King's business. As Charles did not restrain their feuds, they spilled over into Parliament; ministers and their followers attacked their colleagues for reasons of personalities as much as policy. This was seen clearly in the case of Clarendon's impeachment.

Despite such deficiencies of kingship, Charles did appoint some men of real talent, like Danby and Rochester, and defended them against their rivals, although he was most likely to do this if driven by obvious financial necessity. In the early 1680s Charles supported Rochester's campaign of retrenchment, despite the squeals of his courtiers, because he dared not risk calling Parliament. He also learned from the Exclusion crisis that there was no point in trying to propitiate the Whigs (who, he thought, wished to strip him of all effective power), so he had to rely on the Tories. Earlier the divisions within the political nation and the options open to the King had been much less clear cut. Charles had made his relationship with Parliament unnecessarily difficult by his attempts to appeal to the Dissenters (who were few, divided and of little social weight) rather than to the more numerous and powerful Anglicans. He did this on the advice of Arlington and Buckingham who were trying to drive Clarendon and his Anglican followers out of office. If Charles ended his reign in a strong position, this owed less to skilful kingship than to the fact that changing circumstances had drastically reduced the options open to him. The Tories' belief in strong monarchy had been intensified by the Exclusion crisis, so the obvious thing for Charles to do was to exploit it.

Despite his indolence and inconsistency, Charles survived because his objectives of physical and financial survival were essentially conservative and thus acceptable to most of his subjects. He was also prepared to yield to political necessity. James's aim of promoting Catholicism was far less acceptable and his relative financial independence allowed him to indulge his obsession with an unusual freedom from practical constraints. Whereas Charles's Court had contained a wide variety of competing politicians offering more or less practical solutions to the perennial problems of the monarchy, James's Court was dominated by the few (some cynical careerists,

some totally inexperienced) who were prepared to encourage his fan-
tasies and to try to put them into effect. The range of opinions represented at Court became narrower. Some Tory magnates ceased to
attend the Court or the Privy Council, while those who remained
exercised little influence. After the flexibility of Charles's reign,
decision-making under James showed a rigidity which was to prove
brittle.

Unlike his brother, James worked hard and believed that kings
should be firm and consistent. Unfortunately, he lacked Charles's intelligence. Despite his efforts, he seldom rose above the details of a
problem to see it in its entirety. Thus, like Charles, he failed to keep a
firm grasp on government, but through lack of ability rather than lack
of application. Unable to control everything himself, James (like
Charles) relied on the judgement of others, but in choosing whom to
trust he was 'more subject to persons than to arguments'.[20] Like
Charles he too often took the advice of those who told him what he
wished to hear. James was eager to believe that his plans to promote
Catholicism would succeed, despite all the indications that they
would not. The Court became increasingly introverted, impervious to
the hostile reaction to James's measures. A French ambassador com-
mented in 1688: 'The English court is very badly informed of what is
happening abroad and is even ignorant of what happens in London
and the provinces.'[21] But even when James received adequate information he was reluctant to believe anything which contradicted his
preconceptions. Having convinced himself that Dissenters would welcome the toleration which he granted, and would make it permanent
by helping to repeal the penal laws and Test Acts, James ignored any
information which did not confirm this conviction. He placed exaggerated reliance on the Dissenters' addresses of thanks, even though
many were carefully qualified and some were far from spontaneous.[22]
James's position in 1685 was extremely strong. Only political inepti-
tude and insensitivity on a heroic scale brought about his expulsion in
1688.

IV

The strongest influences on the policies of the restored monarchy
were, first, the personalities and aspirations of Charles II and James
II and, second, the advice which they received from their servants and
courtiers. There were, however, other influences and constraints on

the formulation and execution of policy. As far as its formulation was concerned, the most important constraints were those imposed by Parliament and the law courts. As for its execution, the main problem was to ensure that the King's commands were obeyed in the localities.

Charles II called Parliament mainly to vote money. After the first years of the reign, there was seldom any legislation which he really needed to pass, although James had to use Parliament if he was to repeal the penal laws and Test Acts. The need to ask Parliament for money did not necessarily restrict the King's freedom of action. It depended, first, on whether the Commons chose to use their financial power to force the King to make concessions and, second, on whether he was so desperately short of money that he had to succumb to their pressure. In other words, it was a question of the Commons' *desire* to coerce the King and of their *power* to do so.

On the first point, MPs accepted in principle that the King should govern and that they should provide the money he needed to govern properly. This did not mean that they always voted money when asked or that they always approved of his measures. They took pains to discover if the money they had voted had been misappropriated or mismanaged, notably after the humiliations of the Dutch War of 1665–7. They often complained in addresses of the misdeeds of royal officials or advised the King on the sort of objectives which he should pursue. In particular they expected him to uphold the landed interest, the Protestant interest (at home and abroad) and the Ancient Constitution. But it was one thing to criticise the King's conduct (or rather that of his ministers), and to make clear to him the ends which the Commons thought he should pursue. It was quite another thing for the Commons to try to *force* him to act on their advice. During the Exclusion crisis, it is true, some Whigs argued that the King should do whatever the Commons thought best, but more typical was the argument used in a debate on foreign policy in 1677: 'The prerogative is not at all encroached on, nor do we pretend to treat or make alliances. We only offer our advice about them and leave it with the King to do as he pleases, either make them or not make them.'[23] After 1673 the Commons became reluctant to vote taxation, fearing that Charles might use the money to raise an army to impose 'Popery and arbitrary government'. They also continued the earlier practice of appropriating supply to particular needs, but there was little sign, even in the Exclusion crisis, of any systematic attempt to withhold supply in order to extort concessions, even though both sides assumed that the

Commons would vote money if the King gave them satisfaction.

If the Commons were uncertain about the propriety of putting crude financial pressure on the King, their *power* to do so was limited, for two reasons. First, the House was far from united. MPs were mostly independent country gentlemen, preoccupied with local and private interests and by no means amenable to discipline. The proceedings of the House were often highly confused and there were sometimes long periods when nothing was said at all. MPs could be moved to great extremes of emotion – fear, anger, even joy – but such surges of feeling seldom lasted long. Thus in 1667 the Commons, furious at the mismanagement of the Dutch War, set up a committee to scrutinise the King's accounts, but this fury had long subsided by the time the committee reported in 1670 and the report aroused little interest.[24] Secondly, Charles's need for money was seldom so overwhelming that he could be forced to do as the Commons wished. His ordinary revenue was thoroughly inadequate for most of the 1660s, but by the mid-1670s it should have yielded enough to make Charles solvent, but for the burden of interest on past debts and his reluctance to economise. Thus in the 1660s when Charles needed additional supplies on a large scale the Commons were comparatively willing to grant them, while in the 1670s, when the Commons became more reluctant, Charles's need for money was not so great – provided he avoided extravagant or extraordinary expenditure.

If the Commons were unable or unwilling to put effective financial pressure on the King, their attempts to influence his choice of advisers proved still less effectual. Addresses to remove ministers were ignored, impeachments were thwarted in the Lords or by Charles's dismissing Parliament. Only Danby was dismissed as a direct result of an impeachment and even then Charles ensured that the former Lord Treasurer was not brought to trial.

Thus the Commons' power to coerce the King was limited, partly because their financial power was not all that great, partly because on some crucial occasions Charles could rely on the support of a majority in the Lords, but also because many MPs thought such coercion unconstitutional. The ideal relationship of Crown and Parliament remained one of partnership, in which King and subjects worked together for the common good. If the King failed to rule as the Commons expected, they blamed his evil advisers, although sometimes MPs came close to attacking Charles directly.[25] Usually they relied on persuasion and argument rather than coercion. MPs might often be suspicious, obtuse or cantankerous but they would co-operate in the King's government, if their loyalty and energies could be harnessed. To do this required skilled management. Ministers had to ensure that their supporters turned up and voted the right way and that those who consistently supported the official line were rewarded. They had to ensure, too, that there were competent, properly briefed spokesmen to convince suspicious squires of the integrity of the King's government and of the reasonableness of his financial demands. As most back-benchers were independent-minded, argument was more important than manipulation in pushing measures through the Commons, which meant that a wise ruler avoided outraging MPs' prejudices. Even if a king pursued unpopular policies, however, the Commons rarely succeeded in making him change them. Charles perhaps made more concessions than his predecessors, thanks mainly to his tendency to take the easy way out, but usually he was influenced more by the pressure of his courtiers (who wanted money from Parliament, regardless of the political cost) than to the arguments of the Commons.[26] One should remember, too, that Elizabeth and even Henry VIII had suffered defeats at the hands of the Commons.[27] But even if the Commons' coercive power remained limited after 1660, the fact remained that the government worked more smoothly if the King avoided measures likely to antagonise the Commons. Charles II, however, insisted on pursuing foreign and religious policies which most MPs disliked. His difficulties with Parliament thus owed more to his political insensitivity and poor management than to any new power or assertiveness on the part of the Commons.

Unlike Parliament the judges exercised only an occasional influence on royal policy-making. As they depended on the King for their appointment and promotion, they were amenable to royal pressure and saw it as their duty to uphold his authority, especially when the security of the state was involved. They were also as susceptible as others to the political passions of the early 1680s, when much of the 'justice' they dispensed was blatantly partisan. Yet even James II's judges showed that there were limits to what they would approve. They told him that he could not dispense with the 1678 Test Act (excluding Catholics from Parliament) and two of them criticised the dispensing power vigorously in the celebrated trial of the Seven Bishops in 1688. Even so, James's judges stretched the law even further than those of Charles I. Even if James did not use it very widely, a dispensing power so extensive that it allowed the King to suspend statutes altogether threatened to reduce the laws to a nullity. A king who could get the common law courts to endorse such an extension of his powers scarcely needed prerogative courts.[28]

Turning from the constraints on the formulation of policy to the constraints on its execution, Charles's regime left those in control of local administration largely to their own devices. He showed little interest in a number of areas which his predecessors had tried to regulate. He abandoned any attempt to enforce most of the great mass of social and economic legislation enacted by Tudor and early Stuart Parliaments. These laws mostly remained on the statute book, but it was left to JPs to decide whether they should be enforced. On the other hand, Charles's government took pains to exact obedience on matters affecting the revenue. By relentless vigilance and pressure it obtained a financial administration in the provinces which, by the standards of the day, was obedient, efficient and adequately paid. On other matters, the central government was moved to bursts of activity only when the security of the state was threatened. It tried persistently, if not always successfully, to control the press, even after the Licensing Act lapsed in 1679. When insurrection or invasion threatened, orders were sent to search for arms, arrest suspicious persons, call out the militia, keep watch and drive horses and cattle away from the coasts. Similarly, the government ordered the enforcement of the laws against Catholics or Dissenters only when this seemed necessary to propitiate Parliament or to reduce the danger of sedition. The government's orders were not always obeyed. JPs enforced the laws against Catholics or Dissenters only when they thought it really necessary, while James's orders to prepare to resist William's invasion aroused little response.[29]

It would be misleading, however, to concentrate too much on cases of disobedience and obstruction. On most of the basic ends of local government – above all, the maintenance of order – King and JPs were in agreement. If JPs no longer tried to regulate the marketing of grain or to enforce the apprenticeship laws, this did not greatly concern Charles II, provided the provinces remained quiet and he received his revenue. When he wished to enforce his will, he could dismiss particularly recalcitrant JPs, while he still possessed extensive local patronage (not least in the militia and commissions of the peace) which was swollen by the growth of the revenue administration in the 1680s. It is worth noting, too, that Charles II's revenue was less contentious than his father's had been. MPs might criticise the excise and Hearth

money, JPs might make difficulties about assessments, enraged pea-
sants might beat up Hearth money collectors (who received little protection or co-operation from the JPs), but even so the fiscal burden in
Restoration England was light and equitably distributed compared
with that of Charles I's reign or that of contemporary France. There
was nothing as random as Charles I's fines for encroaching on the
royal forest, nor did Charles II use for fiscal purposes monopolies and
other patents which, in effect, allowed favoured individuals to profi-
teer at the expense of the community. It is worth noting too that after
1689 the nation showed that it could bear a much heavier fiscal
burden, provided its local leaders approved the purposes for which
taxes were used and participated in their assessment and collection.[30]

Thus in local as well as central government, one of the monarchy's
greatest, if least obvious, strengths was the landed élite's responsibility and willingness to co-operate in measures which it thought
necessary. This was seen most strikingly in the early 1680s. The
Exclusion crisis had divided the political nation deeply and bitterly.
In many parliamentary boroughs the Tory minority (often closely
linked with local landed families) had been vilified by the Whigs, defeated at the polls and driven out of office. They could regain power
and wreak revenge only with the King's help, so they begged him to
use his authority and his law courts to confiscate the boroughs' charters and issue new ones which gave him greater control over appointments to municipal office. He could then use this to give his 'old
friends', the Tories, a monopoly of local power. Thanks to the polarisation of the political nation, the Tories were quite content that the
King should bend the law, provided he did so in their interests. They
participated eagerly in the purge of borough corporations which was
to help James to secure the election of an overwhelmingly Tory House
of Commons in 1685. For the first time in early modern England, a
monarch was able to manage a general election and to 'pack' Parliament, something which Elizabeth and the early Stuarts had never
dared to attempt.[31] But the Tories' co-operation was given on the tacit
understanding that James would continue to uphold their interests
and those of the Church of England. James refused to recognise this
condition and so squandered a massive accession of political strength
in his pursuit of the chimera of a Catholic England. The history of the
1680s illustrates a fundamental truth about early modern monarchy,
that a king was strongest when he ruled with his subjects' co-
operation and consent.

V

The Revolution of 1688–9 ushered in a new era in the history of the monarchy. The constitutional settlement imposed few new statutory limitations on the King's powers, mainly because William III insisted that it should not do so. The real change was that Parliament refused to grant William an adequate ordinary revenue. Experience had shown that the Stuarts could not be trusted to exercise their powers responsibly and William, besides being half a Stuart, was a foreigner with a nasty reputation for authoritarianism. Parliament therefore insisted on maintaining the financial power to impose its will on the monarch, should he abuse his powers.[32] However the Commons did not use this financial power in a systematic bid to deprive the King of effective control over the government. Most MPs still accepted in principle the King's right to rule as well as reign, even though they often criticised his conduct in particular cases. But if the Commons became sufficiently angry or fearful, they could now use their financial power to coerce the King. Thus William was forced to disband his army after the Peace of Ryswick and to revoke his grants to Dutchmen of Irish lands. Moreover, as William was very conscious of the Commons' financial power, he often refrained from using his acknowledged powers in ways that might prove contentious. Thus he chose not to use his power to dismiss judges from the bench.

After 1689 Parliament met more often and for longer than ever before. It insisted on scrutinising in detail the spending of the unprecedented sums voted for the great war of 1689–97. This scrutiny, however, did not work entirely to the King's disadvantage. For the first time ordinary MPs came to appreciate the true cost of government and especially of war. As a result, they showed an increasingly constructive and sophisticated attitude to the raising of money.[33] While the absolute monarchy of France slid towards bankruptcy in the eighteenth century, the limited monarchy of Britain raised vast sums with apparent ease. Thus after 1689, as under the early and later Stuarts, a King who co-operated with his subjects could prove stronger in many ways than one who ignored their wishes. This situation changed only when the subjects' attitude to the monarchy changed, when MPs began to use systematically the financial power which the Commons had assumed, for pragmatic and defensive reasons, in 1689.[34] This change came only with the development of mass politics, dominated by divisive ideologies. Apart from the emergence of a precocious and short-lived two-party system under Anne, it was to take more than a century for the political and constitutional implications of the Revolution of 1689 to work themselves out.

2. Parties and Parliament

J. R. JONES

I

THE appearance of two rival organised parties was, in the view of contemporaries as it has been in that of most historians, the most striking and important development in the politics of the Restoration period. There has been one recent dissentient, Robert Walcott, who suggested that the original Whig and Tory parties would be found on analysis to consist of coalitions or combinations of family connections, and interest groups based on territorial influence, but his hypothesis has been disproved by the research completed during the last two decades.[1] His approach was concerned excessively with the politics of an upper-class élite, the great aristocracy and substantial landowners, lawyers and merchants. In early modern England such persons were normally those to whom men in humbler and poorer circumstances paid either willing or reluctant deference, but however else one may describe Restoration politics the word 'normal' is hardly applicable. In times of frequent and acute crises, such as those of 1678–81 and 1687–8, men did not behave normally. Walcott, like others who have tried to apply the historical approach developed by Sir Lewis Namier to other periods, does not seem to have appreciated the importance of political issues, and ignores the passions and excitement that they aroused.

In trying to analyse the character of Restoration politics it is impossible to avoid considering a popular dimension, and in a time of rapid and unpredictable changes it is otiose to try to find a settled structure of politics such as existed at the accession of George III.[2] The emphasis in this essay will be on the fluidity of Restoration politics, and the constant adaptation to changes that was required of politicians. However, although parties came into existence a two-party system did not. Neither the first Whigs nor the first Tories regarded

For Notes to Chapter 2, see pp. 209–11; for Bibliographical Notes, see p. 198.

themselves as a party, because the term still had an obnoxious meaning. Both claimed to represent the best interests of the nation, which
were threatened by the other's activities. Party had a meaning which
was still almost indistinguishable from that of conspiracy or faction.

The second major political innovation of the period was also universally and harshly condemned, yet was to remain in constant use for
nearly two centuries; this was the systematic use of patronage to
manage Parliament, and particularly the Commons. Managerial
techniques became necessary when it had to be recognised that parliamentary sessions at fairly frequent intervals could not be avoided,
but they attracted strenuous condemnation on both political and
moral grounds. Critics feared that their sustained use could undermine the independence of Parliament, and denounced the acceptance
of favours by peers and MPs as a betrayal of trust and as evidence of
the degeneracy of the age.

Managerial techniques were first used with effect by Danby (Lord
Treasurer, 1673–9), who took full advantage of having a 'standing'
body of men on whom to work in the Cavalier Parliament that lasted
from May 1661 to January 1679.[3] This long period without a general
election also meant that there were very limited opportunities for
political opinion to form outside Westminster and the Court at
Whitehall, or for any section of the public to exert direct influence on
policy or parliamentary proceedings. The dissolution of the Cavalier
Parliament threw everything into the melting pot. Electoral techniques, almost unused since 1661, became the key factor during the
years of the Exclusion crisis. Three general elections occurred – two in
1679, and one early in 1681 – which returned Whig majorities that
overwhelmed ministerial influence in the Commons. However politics
were to be completely transformed twice again in the years before
1688. Charles deprived the Whig electoral and propaganda techniques of all their value during his last years, by his settled determination not to call another Parliament. Conditions were so different by
1685 that the elections that followed James's accession produced a
Tory majority even larger than those of the Whigs in the Exclusion
Parliaments. However, a new revolution (in the seventeenth-century
sense, of a complete turn of events) awaited the victorious Tories.
When they refused to collaborate with James, he used against them
the full armoury of political techniques that had been developed since
1661. They were pressurised by royal managers and ejected wholesale
from central and local offices. Then the King, using former Whig

techniques and itinerant agents, invaded their localities, remodelling the constituencies as preparation for a rigged general election planned for October 1688.

It can be seen, then, that there was no settled structure of politics, and that attitudes and techniques appropriate at one time were useless at another. Consequently cynicism and opportunism were common. Levels of political morality were often as debased as personal standards in Charles II's Court. Many of the ministers and politicians of the Restoration period can best be compared with a type of lizard, the chameleon, that changes its colour to match that of its background.

II

It has long been recognised that the composition of the Cavalier Parliament was constantly changing; for instance there were twenty-four new MPs in the second session (1663), while by the last session in 1678 no less than 343 seats had changed hands.[4] But such gradual and random changes do not explain the early reappearance of the old division within Parliament between Court and Country. Opposition to ministerial proposals was never negligible; there were over 100 votes in the first session against such a fundamental measure as the Corporation Bill, but on contentious religious legislation there were always sufficient Anglican zealots to swamp those who wanted a broader church settlement.[5] Generally, on less controversial matters, and on the difficult and unpalatable business of making the King financially solvent, there was a lack of effective direction and systematic attention to expediting business. Charles remonstrated with the Commons for its neglect of public matters, but by the second session his abortive Declaration of Indulgence (December 1662) had reawakened old suspicions that were never entirely to subside during the rest of the reign. Although phrased in respectful language the Commons' address was in effect a rebuke; MPs warily thanked the King for his doubtfully sincere profession 'against introducing a Government by a Military Power'; the very fact that he was suspected of doing so was ominous. They also noted his invitation to prepare fresh laws against the growth of popery, the second great issue that was to recur over the next three decades, and they made it clear that they could not accept as constitutional the prerogative powers which had been claimed to validate the Declaration.[6]

Rather than persist in the face of mounting opposition Charles quickly abandoned the Declaration, and also found it expedient to assure the members that he did not intend to dissolve Parliament. Instead Charles took the first decisive step to initiate a new type of political management that was to change the character of parliamentary politics. Clarendon relied on frequent private consultations of ministers with senior MPs of proven loyalty, who together worked out the way in which proceedings should go, but this group did not openly canvass support, or make offers and promises to win individuals.[7] The experience of the first and second sessions exposed the inadequacy of such gentlemanly methods. Those being consulted had the disadvantage of being mostly old and also inexperienced in parliamentary matters, since few old Cavaliers had sat at Westminster since early 1642. Moreover they had few contacts with the ambitious younger careerists who were pushing themselves forward, and no sympathy for their extravagant, hedonistic ways of life. It was three of these thrusting politicians (Henry Bennet, Thomas Clifford and William Coventry) whom Charles ordered Clarendon to admit to his consultative meetings, which they quickly took over and transformed. They engaged in more dynamic and undisguised forms of management, soliciting support, making promises in the King's name and approaching men whose services would be particularly valuable. They encouraged and assisted the introduction of legislation that would favour sectional interests; a bill prohibiting imports of Irish lean cattle was a massive inducement to the generally over-represented counties of the pastoral west and north countries, and also of Wales.[8]

The new managers, instead of appealing to sentiments of loyalty and relying on the willing co-operation of the faithful, engaged in techniques that involved trafficking in votes. Without realising what they were doing, they were establishing new political patterns of tensions and stresses. Those who enlisted peers and MPs by promises of appointments and gratifications required the King's constant support to implement them, but often this was not forthcoming, or they found that Charles had already made incompatible half-promises to others. Since all managers and ministers were engaged in cut-throat competition against each other, a humiliatingly visible failure to redeem promises could result in a politician being instantly deserted by his clients. On the other hand constant importuning of Charles on their behalf could alienate the latter. In these circumstances of uncertainty the power of the purse eventually proved to be decisive, and control over patronage after 1667 was held by whoever controlled the treasury.

Clarendon condemned those who undermined him, and then began to organise Parliament, as politicians without principles who were actuated solely by the pursuit of personal advancement and profit. For more than a decade, until his death in 1678, Andrew Marvell portrayed the Court as a totally corrupt body, denouncing with particular bitterness the earl of Danby (Lord Treasurer from 1673 to 1679) as a corrupter on a massive scale, and savagely condemning his dependants as betrayers of their country.[9] His venomous propaganda attacks have often been too readily accepted by historians, because they were taken at their face value by many of Marvell's contemporaries, but it would be wrong to regard management as exclusively a matter of corrupt practices. Ministers and managers had to attach themselves to distinctive policies that made a genuine appeal to peers and MPs, and provided a subject for proceedings in Parliament. Clarendon's enemies associated themselves with religious toleration and the aggressive mercantilism that led to the second and third Dutch wars, but Danby in 1673–8 made a more conservative and less adventurous appeal to traditional Cavalier principles. The efficiently organised managerial devices for which he became infamous at the time were secondary to his policy, and some of them had more limited objectives than might seem at first sight. Many of those condemned as 'pensioners' were fully employed functionaries – Pepys and Secretary of State Williamson for example – and some cash payments were a form of compensation for past losses. Many sinecure appointments were given primarily in order to ensure that MPs were in attendance during sessions.

Nevertheless Danby's followers were intensely vulnerable to political satirists who mercilessly pilloried them, exposing their weaknesses and vices. Some were derided for their poverty – '£50 a session, meat and drink, and now and then a suit' was one comment – but such paupers were shown to be dangerous because they had only their votes on which to subsist. On the other hand wealthy Court MPs were charged with having acquired their riches at the expense of the public, particularly those connected with tax administration and collection. Those who had risen from humble origins ('once a poor serving man'; 'a tailor's son') were shown to be equally dangerous, since their past record of time-serving and sycophancy made them ready and willing tools for absolutist-minded ministers. Marvell himself took great pains to keep in close and continuous contact with his own constituency, and worked to further its interests, so he had justification for emphasising and exploiting the aloofness, neglect and self-interest of many Court MPs, who had ceased to be representatives in any real sense.[10]

The organisation of an effective Court bloc of over 100 MPs resulted in the formation of an interest group that was obviously averse to a dissolution which must cost many of them their seats. During the 1660s a dissolution was seriously considered on several occasions when difficulties arose – in 1663, 1666, 1667 and 1669 – but Charles came nearest to ordering one in the spring of 1673 when the first Court bloc, organised by Clifford, was disintegrating as the Cabal's policies faltered. Danby's reconstruction of a Court interest, on a wider basis and by far more systematic methods, virtually eliminated the possibility. A dissolution would dissipate his investment in canvassing, persuasion and patronage. Many of his dependants had neglected or lost their local connections, or quarrelled with patrons, associates or the leading men in their constituencies, and the Court lacked both the financial resources and the electoral machinery to assist with their re-election. Danby knew that he could not afford to cope with a general election; on the other side of politics Shaftesbury and the Country opposition tried by all means to force Charles to dissolve, in the confident expectation that elections would at last give them the opportunity to swamp the Court.

III ELECTIONS

It would be entirely fallacious to suppose that the return in 1661 to the traditional system of parliamentary representation, with the abandonment of all the experimental innovations of the Interregnum, meant that the Commons were the nominees of a small upper-class élite of great landowners. Examination of elections and by-elections during the Restoration period reveals a picture broadly similar to that established by Derek Hirst for the first part of the century.[11] The keynote was uncertainty, particularly in the boroughs. There were no definitive, binding decisions on the subject of the borough franchises, or on other forms of procedure concerned with elections. The right to vote was established by custom, but often decades had passed since a poll had occurred. If a group of men came forward, claiming to vote, and were refused by the returning officer – for example, as the most common case, the inhabitants or householders in a borough where the freemen or the corporation claimed exclusive rights – the Commons could uphold their right to the franchise, and over-rule the returning officer. In doing so it could also reverse or ignore its own past decisions, even though these were quite explicit. Alternatively a candidate defeated in a poll of inhabitants or householders could claim that he should have been returned as he had a majority of 'real' or valid votes, and by declaring him elected the Commons could establish a more limited franchise. It would be a simplification to say that the opposition or the Whigs tried consistently to enlarge the franchise, and the Court to restrict it; instead most decisions were made on a personal and partisan basis. During the Exclusion crisis elections of 1679 and 1681 there were, however, a number of cases where a Whig candidate encouraged the commonalty to assert, for the first time, a claim to vote so as to dislodge a well entrenched corporation or gentry interest, and the Whig-dominated Commons and its committee of Privileges and Elections upheld the claim.[12]

Uncertainty about the franchise was compounded by uncertainty about the length of tenure of a newly won seat; in 1661 it proved to be nearly eighteen years, in the spring of 1679 just under three months, a little longer in the second elections of that year, but in 1681 a bare week, and in 1685 a split session of under two months. Consequently although there was more competition to be returned to Parliament than there had been before the civil war, elections were seldom very expensive by eighteenth-century standards. Electoral techniques were not yet commercialised and standardised as in the period of regular and frequent elections that followed the Triennial Act of 1694.

The general elections of the period fall into two categories. Those of 1661 and 1685 were broadly similar in that each provided an opportunity for an unorganised demonstration of loyalty, first to the newly restored Charles, and then to uphold James who had just succeeded without any of the turmoil or dire consequences that had been predicted.[13] Both sovereigns made an appeal most suited to a period of recovery and hopes of peace and stability, after a time of conflict. The dangers of continued unrest and rebellion were emphasised in 1661 by Venner's rising (an example of primitive urban terrorism), and more seriously in 1685 by the prospect of invasion by Argyll and Monmouth. A conservative reaction was already effective in both years. In 1661 fanatics, although not as yet moderate dissenters, were being repressed, but in 1685 dissenters of all kinds were under the harrow of systematic and sustained enforcement of the penal laws. On both occasions the press was closely controlled. Open opposition to the monarch ran the risk of being treated as disloyal, but organised and coherent opposition hardly existed. The 'Presbyterians' (that is, those who wanted a broad Church settlement) were totally demoralised in 1661 by the failure of their members, who had been in a majority in the Convention Commons of 1660, to make effective use of their temporary influence, and they had also been deserted by most of their leaders.[14] In 1685 the once triumphant Whigs were virtually shattered. The revelations of the Rye House Plot (1683), in which Whig stalwarts were involved in plans to stage a rising, or to murder Charles and James, had led to the executions of Russell and Sydney, and the exile of Monmouth, Grey and Wildman. Most former Whigs had disassociated themselves from the cause and their guilty colleagues, and few stood for election in 1685.

Direct royal influence was limited in both 1661 and 1685. Men of proven loyalty had already been installed in all nominated posts in local government, as justices, sheriffs and in the lieutenancy. In the corporations there was a significant difference. A purge of disaffected or unreliable office-holders followed the 1661 elections, being executed through enforcement of the Corporation Act that the new Parliament passed in its first session. But a policy of questioning the municipal charters had been under way for three years before the 1685 elections. Although the original purpose had been to strengthen royal control over the administration of justice in the towns, where the Dissenters were strongest, electoral advantages were also considerable.[15] Charters had been surrendered or declared forfeit, and then reissued with powers reserved to the King to name the principal officers. During both elections the lords lieutenant were actively engaged, but as leaders of their local communities rather than as agents of the King. They worked with some success to arrange a consensus within counties, so as to avoid contested elections. They persuaded individuals to abandon candidatures that might necessitate polls, which could cause divisions, disorders and expense. Although Sunderland, as secretary of state, suggested the names of worthy men (and these were also put to patrons) they were not obliged to accept them; there were only about twenty places in the King's own gift. Similarly although some bishops wrote to their clergy asking them to ensure the return of loyal men, this did not mean (as it did in the Exclusion elections) that they were expected to canvass voters or attend the election in droves.

The parochial clergy, like members of the lieutenancy, used their influence to foster unity among the gentry, to dissuade splinter candidatures, and to fortify the resolution of the returning officers. The latter also knew what was expected of them; they denied polls to dissidents or, if forced to have one, prematurely closed it, or changed the place and time of election without notice so as to snuff out potential challenges.[16]

Consequently the fact that the elections of 1661 and 1685 each returned an overwhelming majority of loyal members was not the result of victories at the polls, it was due primarily to the success of tactics designed to avoid polls. In contrast Whig victories in 1679 and 1681 were the direct consequence of their success in mobilising mass support.[17] Often they overwhelmed their rivals in a poll, but particularly in 1681 their pledged supporters were present in such numbers that the Tories abandoned their challenge for fear of having their own insignificant numbers revealed.

Each of the three Exclusion elections had its own distinctive character. In the spring of 1679 a long political log-jam was suddenly broken. Nearly half the seats had been held continuously by a single person since 1661; now they were thrown open to competition with very little notice and time for campaigning. They took place in a time of excitement, or near-hysteria, caused by the sensational revelations of the Popish Plot. The Court was in disarray, with Danby having to neglect electioneering in order to prepare his own defence against an impending threat of impeachment. He left his former supporters leaderless, since he had taken care not to encourage anyone to aspire to become his deputy. Courtiers and dependants received no guidance or direction, and found that their association with the fallen minister was often as much a liability with a patron as with independent voters. Danby's pensioners were collectively and individually vilified by pamphlets; it was in this election that the press first became a major electoral factor.

However the first elections of 1679 were not in any sense organised by the opposition, or by Shaftesbury who was becoming identified as its chief. The sweeping changes in membership of the Commons were in part an inevitable consequence of an excessively long-lived Parliament, and the abuse of their tenure by many of the older members. But it was also a delayed-action result of the arguments which the Country opposition had put forward about the existence of a conspiracy to introduce absolutism and popery. Those who had used these arguments with little effect within a standing Parliament now claimed credit for their far-sightedness. The issues, then, were largely negative, and there are few signs that candidates in any numbers explicitly raised the issues of how the crisis was to be resolved. There were many generalised calls for Protestant unity to be established to confront the papist menace, but the idea of excluding James from the succession, which had been raised in the last weeks of the Cavalier Parliament, did not appear as an electoral issue.

In the autumn elections of 1679 the Exclusion Bill was *the* issue, and this contributed to the polarisation of the nation into opposing party camps, Whig and Tory.[18] These elections were fought far more frequently than had ever been the case before on national rather than local issues, with the press again playing a major role. Whig writers addressed themselves to the task of persuading voters to put political considerations first, before local and personal obligations of neighbourhood and good relations, of kinship and long-standing friendship. This may seem obvious to us in times of national politics and parties, but in 1679 it meant going against the whole pattern of provincial social life and its conventions. Voters were asked to support only those pledged to Exclusion, and to reject friends and neighbours who would not give such undertakings. The Whig weekly press also publicised as examples to be followed some county elections (Essex and Buckinghamshire provided the clearest cases) in which the mass of the ordinary freeholders successfully resisted intense pressure at the polls by their social superiors, the entire body of Anglican clergy and a majority of the landed gentry, and with enthusiasm and at little or no expense returned conspicuously Whig candidates.

The Whig strategy to obtain Exclusion accepted the fact that the result would be a deeply divided nation, although since they claimed to represent the sound part of the nation the Whigs had no inhibitions about arousing passionate hostility against their opponents. Even the rejection of the Exclusion Bill by the Lords in November 1680, and the unmistakable signs that Charles was implacably opposed to it, did not cause the Whigs to modify their intransigent insistence that only Exclusion could provide national security. In the 1681 elections Whig propaganda was distinctly more vituperative about the Tories, but the main concern was to preserve and demonstrate the unity of the party. A new device was employed. Members were presented with 'instructions' which accompanied their election; these in modern parlance 'mandated' them. They were instructed to insist on Exclusion and nothing else, and until it passed they were to refuse Charles any financial supply. There was an implication that if they did not observe these conditions, there could be no possibility of their being elected to a future Parliament, but although ordinarily this would have been instantly resented as a breach of privilege, Whig members found it diplomatic to acquiesce, and many thanked their constituents for the instructions.[19]

Another feature of the 1681 elections was a determined but generally unproductive Tory attempt to organise on the same lines as the Whigs, often imitating their newly developed techniques. Suspecting that they had a minority of voters in many counties, the Tories often put forward only one candidate, particularly when one of the Whigs was less popular or wellknown, or an outsider to the locality. Tories even arranged counter instructions to newly elected members, to offset the propaganda effect of the Whig instructions. The Tory version asked members to oppose Exclusion, and to ask the King to order the enforcement of the penal laws against the Dissenters and all those engaged in political sedition.[20] By this was meant what the Tories denounced as the licentious Whig press, which had had great influence in moulding opinion but which was now in early 1681 no longer having matters its own way. The Tory challenge in the field of journalism was to be more effective than in any other, but it does not seem to have made much impact in the 1681 elections.

IV PARTIES

In order to substantiate the claim that the first Whigs, and to a lesser extent the original Tories, can accurately be described as political parties, it is first essential to offer a definition of what constituted a party in the seventeenth century, as distinct from other contemporary political entities; a faction, an interest or a connection. The Whigs and Tories pass the test of being organised bodies of men, who were not associated by personal, family or local ties alone, but were united in the pursuit of common and publicly stated objectives. Of course they were concerned with achieving power for themselves, but they were openly committed to the task of furthering or defeating certain specific policies. These policies, and the struggles that centred on them, imposed a degree of discipline and cohesion on adherents of both parties, but it was only when elections were being fought (or at least preparations for elections were being made) that mass support was sought on a nation-wide scale.

This means that parties really existed only during the years of the Exclusion crisis, when politics were no longer largely confined to sessions at Westminster of uncertain length, and held at irregular intervals. As a party in 1679–81 the Whigs energetically canvassed for popular support, particularly by organising mass petitions throughout the country. Their pamphlets and papers catered for every level of education and political awareness, and were distributed widely, being disseminated and discussed in informal political clubs that usually met in coffee houses and taverns. A more formal club, the Green Ribbon, played an important role in London, encouraging and subsidising journalists, and staging spectacular political shows – bonfires on 5 November, and monster Pope-burnings on the 17th, the two days of Protestant celebration.[21]

The Whigs were the more active of the two parties because they had to pressurise Charles and the ministers into conceding Exclusion, whereas the Tories had more limited aims and therefore a more limited range of activities. But although their role was to act as royal auxiliaries, it is important to realise that they were not the creation of the Court, or royal dependants.[22] Their independent existence in itself refuted the Whig claim to speak in the name of the nation. By organising a challenge in parliamentary elections and in municipal politics, and by addresses, they attempted to expose what they saw as the true character of the Whigs – as a party in the sense of a factional conspiracy against the wider and better interests of the nation. In turn they were denounced as dupes of the Court by the Whigs. Although parties actively existed, a two-party system did not.

V THE WHIGS

Whig strengths and weaknesses can only be understood if the rise and fall of the party is constantly related to the fluid, rapidly changing political situation.[23] At first, in early 1679, almost everyone was susceptible to the appeal for unity in the face of the papist menace, but from the formal introduction of an Exclusion Bill in May opinion became divided, and party organisation had increasingly to be substituted for spontaneous or instinctive support. Later, after the dissolution of the Oxford Parliament in March 1681, the Whig tide went out as quickly as it had come in, with no prospect of fresh elections and another Parliament to act as a focus for Whig activity. Whig strength depended on their achievement in restoring a popular dimension to politics that had been missing since 1660, and in creating a general awareness of political issues – what we would call political consciousness. But this was always a precarious achievement, and in the end all but a hard-core lapsed into inactivity and a tacit acceptance that Exclusion had been defeated. This was not so much because of repression by the administration, but rather the result of Tory propaganda which convinced almost everyone that Shaftesbury was driving the nation towards the catastrophe of a new civil war.

The first Whigs did not long survive the death of the man who was largely responsible for their emergence, and for their identification with the policy of Exclusion. Shaftesbury owed his primacy to his ability to understand the interests, prejudices and moods of the people. Elderly and ailing, physically puny and in constant pain, he possessed unlimited confidence in the rightness of his judgement, and a strength of personality that led men of all social classes and varying degrees of political sophistication to accept him as their leader and guide. He was no fanatic, but there is a cold arrogance, a total commitment to extreme policies and a refusal to consider compromise, a determination to go on to the bitter end although defeat stared him in the face, that makes him perhaps the nearest approach in English history to a major doctrinaire demagogue, a Maximilien Robespierre.

Shaftesbury is an a-typical figure in our history, and for this reason his character and motives have largely eluded all his biographers.[24] If he is remembered at all (and the post-1688 Whigs were only too anxious to forget him) it is as Achitophel in Dryden's celebrated poem – the most effective of all deliberately planned character assassinations.[25] Born into a substantial gentry family, ennobled after the Restoration and a holder of high offices for over a decade (culminating in the lord chancellorship), he switched abruptly but irrevocably to opposition politics in 1673. This was not, as most contemporaries at first believed, a tactical change of attitude designed to recover his lost places, nor was it an expression of petulance and disappointment. Shaftesbury's transformation into an organiser and leader of opposition had something of the force of religious conversion; it was as if his unregenerate previous career as a minister and courtier had never existed. He did not become a reformist. The Country opposition from 1673 tried to enact 'good laws', strengthening habeas corpus, preventing electoral malpractices and trying to give the Dissenters limited toleration, but Shaftesbury concentrated on an all or nothing line. His objective was to obtain the dissolution of the Cavalier Parliament, which must be followed by frequent Parliaments.[26]

Frequent Parliaments meant frequent elections, and they would transform the character of English politics. Management on Danby's scale would become impracticable. Ministers and MPs would be unable to ignore opinion. Shaftesbury certainly wanted to regain office, but as minister he intended to behave not in the role of a royal servant but as the 'tribune of the people'. When he was appointed lord president of the reorganised Privy Council in 1679 he was careful not to do or say anything that would weaken his links with the politically conscious Whig rank and file. Shaftesbury is one of the relatively small group of politicians in English history who knew that they were destined to save England, but in his case it was from an internal menace, not an external enemy.

Shaftesbury established the case for Exclusion. National security could be obtained only by blocking the hopes of the conspirators against the Protestant religion and the liberties of the nation, by means of a bill excluding the heir presumptive, James, Duke of York, from the succession.[27] Exclusion was from the start Shaftesbury's policy, and it was he who insisted on concentrating all Whig energies and efforts on securing its enactment. Not only did he reject any alternative forms of security – limitations to be placed on the powers of a Catholic sovereign, the banishment of all Catholics, the nomination of a Regent to govern, leaving James only the title of king – but he also regarded any diversion of effort to obtain piecemeal reforms as a mistake. Although good in themselves (and the habeas corpus amendment act did pass) cumulatively such reforms might weaken the case for Exclusion. As with the dissolution of the Cavalier Parliament, it was a question of all or nothing for Shaftesbury.

Exclusion represents the first of a number of panacea policies that have, with varying ultimate success, evoked widespread popular support.[28] As an issue it was admirably suited to a new, mass party, having above all the great merit of simplicity. The policy itself, its consequences and advantages could be easily explained to a largely uneducated public, whereas the rival policy of limitations was complex and difficult to understand.[29] Furthermore Exclusion could be embodied in a single, short bill, but limitations would have required great skill both in parliamentary draftmanship, and in steering through both houses a very detailed set of proposals which could have been easily wrecked by amendments or delaying tactics. Exclusion also had the enormous advantage of appealing to many of the most deep-rooted assumptions and passions of the time; fear of popery, suspicions of the Court's absolutist intentions, anxiety that Parliament's existence was itself threatened, the belief that the ill-intentioned were banded together in an active conspiracy.

Shaftesbury's decision to stake everything on obtaining Exclusion shaped the whole character of the first Whigs. It was introduced at an early stage in May 1679, and for the next two years it acted as the bond of party unity. At first when it was launched Shaftesbury persuaded his followers that sooner or later Charles would give his consent, although for appearance's sake he was currently pretending to be hostile. By this means Shaftesbury enlisted many moderates before they realised that Charles would never willingly concede the bill, but would have to be coerced; consequently many found themselves publicly committed to a far more extreme measure than they would knowingly have accepted, but they could not retract with ease or honour. Exclusion also provided Whig propagandists with a theme that appealed to the urban masses who, as some contemporaries complained, were converted into 'statesmen', that is made politically conscious by their mobilisation, through petitions, as participants in the political process. In London and many large towns (for example Coventry, Taunton and Oxford) they were also systematically organised to give the Whigs control through successes in municipal elections.

By concentrating on Exclusion Shaftesbury persuaded a very heterogeneous following, who would have disagreed on any broader scheme or programme of legislation, to forget their own special interests or aspirations until the bill had passed.[30] He also used a common demagogic device by insinuating that, once the bill had been passed, it would become practicable to satisfy the demands and interests of each group or section, although it is difficult to see how he could have done this, when such wide differences separated the London radicals from the Country gentry, and the frondeurs who surrounded Monmouth. But Shaftesbury was fully aware of the critical situation in which he needed all the strength he could mobilise. At any moment either natural causes or (more likely) a papist assassin could remove Charles, and so plunge the country into total confusion. He can be criticised on moral grounds for his cynical but ruthless exploitation of the stories of Oates and the other informers about the alleged Popish

Plot, even more for his concoction of a bogus Irish Plot in 1680, which was intended to provide new sensations for the public, but Shaftesbury (unlike most of his trusting followers) can have had no illusions that the odds were not against him and his party.

Even though Exclusion was doomed to defeat, the Whig cause was so interwoven with several distinct, existing causes that its revival after 1688 is easily explained. It incorporated the former Country groups of peers and MPs in the Cavalier Parliament. Their opposition had usually been based on spontaneous 'heat and humour' rather than on systematic attention to business. On occasion this opposition had defeated ministerial moves, but it lacked the organisation and personal stamina to maintain continuous pressure at Westminster on the ministers. It had very limited electoral opportunities, and little in the way of organisation to rally support in the country. Nevertheless the Country opposition had tried to defend the integrity and independence of Parliament against the Cabal and Danby, and most of its supporters went on to accept Exclusion, because it similarly embodied the principle of parliamentary sovereignty – in refutation of the Tory claim that no statute (even though it had the King's assent) could deprive James of his indefeasible right to the succession.[31]

Whig electoral triumphs in 1679 and 1681 showed that the party had a firm power base in the corporations, which sent a majority of members to Westminster. General Whig principles emphasised the role that the nation, through representative institutions, should play in ensuring that government was administered in accordance with the law. At the local level there was a difference between the JPs in the counties, who were all nominated by the King and frequently purged for partisan purposes by ministers, and the elected officers of corporate towns. Many large towns possessed their own entirely separate bench of magistrates, all elected officers, while many medium-sized places had magistrates who were in practice autonomous from the county bench. Politically, towns valued independence from the domination of either aristocratic magnates or the local gentry, who tried to install dependants or clients in offices. The Crown also posed a potential threat. Danby had occasionally threatened action against the charters on which municipal rights depended, used lords lieutenant to over-awe elections and ordered town magistrates to enforce unpopular laws, particularly those against the Dissenters, but in practical terms he had achieved little beyond raising alarms.[32]

The main area of conflict between corporations on the one hand,

and royal ministers, country gentry and Anglican clergy on the other,
related to the Protestant Dissenters. The latter looked first to the
Country opposition and then to the Whigs for relief in the form of statutes establishing some kind of toleration, and repealing the penal
laws. Clearly, as the Anglican clergy constantly alleged, most Dissenters supported Exclusion in general and voted for Whig candidates at
elections. But it is a simplification to describe the Whig party as relying on dissenting support;[33] rather, as their legislative inaction
showed (only one relief measure was passed through both houses),
the Whigs took them for granted. The Dissenters could bring little influence to bear on the leadership of the party, and very few Whig peers
and MPs were practising Dissenters, even on an occasional basis.
Nearly all Whigs were sympathetic to Dissenting grievances, but they
consistently gave a much higher priority to political than to religious
questions. For many it was enough to call for Protestant unity, and
attack the Anglican clergy who obstructed it. It was only within the
corporations that Dissenters, as distinct from their sympathisers,
played an active and important role. Although in most towns the Dissenters constituted only a numerical minority, their cause had
become associated with that of municipal autonomy. Enforcement of
the penal laws against urban Dissenters, if prolonged, damaged local
commercial and industrial activity, inflicting losses on the employees,
associates, customers and creditors of Dissenting businessmen and
artisans. It is significant that the initiative for enforcement of the
penal laws almost invariably came from men outside the local business community – from rural gentry and the clergy – and that enforcement usually required the use of paid informers.

The most important of all corporations, the City of London, was a
special case. All contemporaries accepted the established historical
view that its opposition to Charles I had been a decisive factor in the
political crises of the 1640s. Consequently Charles II and his ministers were always careful to maintain very close supervision over its
affairs.[34] Despite this London became the principal Whig stronghold.
During 1679–80 the Whigs gained control of its government by the entirely constitutional means of winning elections for sheriffs and lord
mayor, and obtaining a majority of seats in common council. This is
not surprising; it was in London and its suburbs that political excitement reached its greatest heights, partly because the Whig press
flooded the capital with its polemical productions. Petitions first took
in London, whose example was then quoted in encouragement of

provincial imitations.

In London, as in the country generally, there were some significant differences from the situation in Pym's days of the early 1640s, which was always being cited by Tories. The role of the clergy had entirely altered. Few of those in Anglican pulpits sympathised with the Whigs, although many (especially in London) refrained from denouncing them (for fear of alienating their congregations) until the Tory reaction had set in. Dissenting ministers were surprisingly inconspicuous. Secondly, neither in London, where it would have been easiest to make an attempt, nor in the provinces, did the Whigs attempt to use violence. There was some talk at the time of Shaftesbury's 'brisk boys' from Wapping, and even a modern touch when it was alleged that a monster football match would be arranged, as a cover for the assembly of an insurrectionary mob of young men who would then march to seize the Tower. In reality the Whigs were confident until March 1681 that they would achieve Exclusion by constitutional methods, and their more sophisticated techniques were concentrated on the task of supporting their party within Parliament. Only when it became clear that Charles had no intention of calling another Parliament, and that he was determined to destroy the Whig hold on the government of the City, did Shaftesbury and some activists begin seriously to consider the use of extra-constitutional methods.[35]

VI THE TORIES

The commonest error about the original Tories is to describe them as the dependants, or the creation, of Charles and the Court. A clear distinction has to be drawn between the pensioners and 'pointblank voters' who had been organised in the Cavalier Parliament by Danby, as the basis of his working majorities, and the Tories who rallied to the King in the late summer of 1679. The Tories were royal auxiliaries who helped the King, but they were not beholden to him. Only a few held offices in the central administration, fewer still owed their election to Parliament to royal influence or assistance. Nor were the majority clients or dependants of the great officers of state, or of aristocratic magnates. From the start there was an important Country element among the Tories, mainly of independent gentry who retained their suspicions of the constitutional and financial integrity of the Court, and distrusted some of the new ministers, but became steadily more alarmed at increasing evidence of the extremism and intransigence of Shaftesbury and his followers.

In the spring of 1679 the unity, cohesion and confidence of the Court had been shattered by Danby's dismissal and imprisonment, the failure of most of his followers to gain election to the new Parliament, Charles's decision to send James into exile abroad and, at the end of April, the surprising establishment of a new privy council of thirty members, including several opposition spokesmen, and with Shaftesbury as lord president.[36] Toryism when it developed as a reaction to the introduction of Exclusion in May 1679, represented a fresh start. It was not a continuation of the now disorganised, demoralised and leaderless bloc of courtiers on whom Charles had previously relied.

From the start there was a double paradox about the Tory party. Its ideal was that of passive loyalty, of unquestioning obedience to legitimate authority and trust in the benevolence of the monarch. Yet by 1679 few men with a reasonable knowledge of the recent past and some insight into current politics, could wholeheartedly trust Charles when he declared that he was unshakably opposed to Exclusion. James, despite his unfortunate conversion to Catholicism, appeared to be far more straightforward and trustworthy – although in the long-term by his switch of alliances in 1687–8 he was to prove far less reliable than his notoriously cynical brother. Secondly, Tories did not believe in the kind of party activity in which they had necessarily to engage in order to contain the rampant Whigs. But a succession of defeats in the autumn elections of 1679 showed the Tories that gentlemen who relied on their local interest and family influence were being over-powered by superior Whig organisation.[37] There was no alternative but to imitate Whig techniques, so Tory clubs were established, addresses or 'abhorrences' canvassed to counter Whig petitions, and a vigorous Tory press came into existence. But many Tories were half-hearted, because they did not really believe that what they were doing was desirable and entirely legitimate.[38]

The earliest and most enthusiastic Tories included a high percentage of the parochial clergy, who believed that the rise of the Whigs was putting the church in danger. Since they could not trust Charles, and had reluctantly to acknowledge that James's conversion was irrevocable, they knew that they had to defend the church by their own efforts. All clerical incumbents now had votes in county elections, and they made themselves conspicuously unpopular by their practice of voting *en masse* against Whig candidates. They also provoked frenzied

attacks by trying to instigate action by magistrates against the Dissenters, as early as 1680, and by their scepticism about the truth of the
Popish Plot.

The basis of lay Toryism can be found in traditional principles of
Cavalier loyalty, but these had been rather too blatantly exploited by
Danby for his own purposes. Moreover his cynical preference for
colourless lieutenants, who would never be able to threaten his primacy, meant that he had no obvious or recognised successor. Tory
leadership was provided in the earliest stages by a group of politicians
with very dissimilar backgrounds. These were a number of comparatively young office-holders, known as the Chits; Laurence Hyde,
Edward Seymour and Sidney Godolphin were the most prominent.
At Westminster they worked with a number of experienced MPs who
had been prominent in the Country opposition against Danby; Sir
William Coventry, Sir Thomas Littleton and Sir Thomas Clarges.[39]
The bond that united them consisted of alarm at the direction in
which Shaftesbury was leading his followers, and it was the ominous
similarity of events to those that had produced the civil war that reawakened loyalist sentiment in the country. 'Forty-one is here again'
was the Tory cry in response to the mounting pressure which the
Whigs were exerting on the King in the second half of 1679. Tories denounced their opponents as old rebels, or the descendants of rebels,
who seemed to be indifferent to the dangers of exacerbating popular
passions and prejudices in order to achieve power. Genuine fears of
the Whigs precipitating another destructive rebellion, all the more
powerful in an age that believed that history repeated itself in a cyclical pattern, provided the Tories with their main argument to counter
the Whig line on the combined danger from Popery and absolutism.

The Tories claimed to represent the soundest section of society, the
owners of land, and claimed that the Whigs made deliberate use of the
'dregs of the people'. Although greatly exaggerated for propaganda
purposes, there was an element of truth in this assertion. In the
autumn elections of 1679, and again in 1681, Tory candidates spon-
sored by a majority of the gentry and all the clergy were repeatedly
routed by Whigs, who were supported by only a handful of the gentry,
but had the votes or voices of the overwhelming mass of the freeholders or urban voters. The Tory gentry similarly resented the erosion
of their precious local influence caused by the increasingly assertive
and independent behaviour of Whig-led corporations. With a few
exceptions (such as Norwich) the Tory efforts to gain control through

organising municipal elections did not succeed, and their consequent lack of success in the Parliamentary elections of 1679 and 1681 weakened their challenge to the Whigs in the Commons in 1680–1 and at Oxford.

Electoral failures did not mean that the Tory position was weak, as it would be today. Tories provided Charles with a majority in the Lords, which rejected Exclusion in November 1680 by more than two to one. Tories were installed in the lieutenancy, controlling the militia, and the commission of the peace, administering justice in the counties, from which all Whigs and their sympathisers were dismissed. A local monopoly of this sort was greatly valued in the seventeenth century, giving the Tories prestige and confidence. Naturally they used these offices for partisan purposes, resuming prosecutions of Dissenters during the summer of 1681, and using grand juries in 1682 and 1683 to make presentations of former Whig activists as factious men who constituted a threat to the public peace. When Charles began to take legal action against the charters of corporations, the Tory gentry worked to persuade corporation officers to surrender them without offering a defence, and Tories were available to fill vacant offices themselves, or ready to nominate associates and clients.

The most notable Tory victory was won in London, where control over the government of the City had been gained before the charter was declared legally forfeit in 1682.[40] This was a reward for long and careful political work which involved the opening of loyal clubs, a systematic scrutiny of the roll of electors and the removal from it of identifiable Whigs, and close and continuous attention to aldermen and common councillors. Once won over, or persuaded to stand for corporation offices, it was essential to bolster the confidence and determination of men who might otherwise feel isolated and vulnerable in a previously Whig-dominated city, and could be intimidated by personal threats or a business boycott. The Tories used intimidation themselves, surrounding the polls for the crucial sheriffs' election in 1682 with men from the train bands, and prosecuting persistent opponents in the polls for riot. They also harassed the Dissenters and their protectors. But by 1682 the Tories had gained a mass following in London, and were on the point of achieving an almost complete victory in the propaganda war. In rough, crude, knock-about daily journalism no Whig could rival the combative Roger L'Estrange, who tirelessly repeated the charge that the Whigs were rebels, and cunningly and effectively aroused popular envy and hatred against the Dissenters. He also used his official powers to take legal action against Whig publishers and printers.

Eventually the successes, energy and enthusiasm of Tory journalists became an embarrassment to the government. Similarly the activities of popular Tory partisans in larger towns, particularly London and Bristol, were judged to be undesirable by ministers. With the Whigs crushed after the revelations of the Rye House Plot of 1683, and the trials that followed, there was no longer any need for popular support. Polemical publishing and political organising were perpetuating an atmosphere of excitement, and encouraging a state of political consciousness that was abnormal. Moreover these urban Tory activists, like their eighteenth-century radical successors, were not only hostile to the Dissenters but were also resentful of the oligarchical families on whom the ministers preferred to rely. Like their Whig opponents the radical Tories, few of whom enjoyed any political connections with men of influence, could flourish only in an atmosphere of crisis.

The Rye House Plot provided new grounds for accepting the theses of passive obedience and the absolute inadmissibility of any form of resistance to a legitimate ruler, which were constantly preached by the Anglican clergy. Most Tories accepted the arguments that peace and stability could only be secured by an unconditional acceptance of royal authority and trust in the good intentions of ministers. The Tory gentry were satisfied by possessing a monopoly in local administration. Most of the Tory rank and file were contented, some by gaining offices and control in the corporations, but more generally by economic prosperity. The last years of Charles's reign were a time of commercial expansion, reasonable harvests and extremely low taxation – a sharp contrast to the miseries of the years of 'Personal Government' under Charles I (1629–40). It is significant that there was no response to Halifax's tactical manoeuvres when, for personal reasons to buttress his ministerial position, he called for a new Parliament, even though Tory control over many corporations made it probable that it would contain a predominantly loyal Commons.

The passive loyalty of the Tories was to mislead James, with disastrous consequences for him. Although they were not conscious of the fact until November 1685, Tory loyalty was implicitly conditional. Most Tories saw themselves as supporters, in the heraldic sense, of the Crown but not as its dependants. They again demonstrated their loyalty, both at Westminster and in the counties, during the crisis caused by Monmouth's rebellion. But when James subsequently refused to modify his demands that Parliament accept an expansion of the army, and the inclusion within it of Catholic officers, the Tories reacted sharply.[41] Courtiers complied with royal demands, but the Tory peers and MPs stubbornly refused to do so. Despite intensified pressure by James in 1686–7, and wholesale ejection from local offices and corporations, the Tories showed themselves to be more united and resolute in blocking James's policies than were their old Whig rivals. Royal moves against the church, culminating in the trial of the Seven Bishops, and the campaign of 1687–8 to pack a compliant Parliament that would legislate as directed by the King, forced the Tories to operate again as a party.[42]

VII

This survey of the first years of the Whigs and Tories shows that they existed and functioned as parties intermittently, at times when elections were being prepared or contested. The rival factions within the Cavalier Parliament – the Court and the Country opposition – cannot be described as parties, because politics were largely contained within the restricted arenas of Whitehall and Westminster, and there was little opportunity for any involvement of the enfranchised section of the nation, let alone the masses. But when elections did occur, at irregular and unpredictable intervals, they were all the more intensely competitive because they were concerned with issues of the greatest magnitude.

Naturally neither Whigs nor Tories regarded their opponents as politically legitimate; there was no sense of a two-party system. Tories saw themselves as upholding political, religious and social order against the activities of a *côterie* of demagogues, who were inciting the masses to violence and rebellion. Whigs thought of themselves as champions of the liberties, properties and true Protestant religion of the nation, which were threatened by papist conspirators and absolutist ministers; they condemned the Tories as the willing instruments, or at best the dupes, of these conspirators. It is a mark of the extraordinary foolishness of James's policies that he succeeded in uniting against himself two parties who had previously been so fundamentally hostile to each other.

3. Law, Courts and Constitution

JENNIFER CARTER

I

FOR the law and constitution there are two crucial questions about the Restoration. First, what exactly was restored in 1660, and how far did the experience of the 1640s and 1650s influence constitutional and legal developments between 1660 and 1688? Second, how much was 'settled': were important legal and constitutional questions defined in a satisfactory and lasting way, or was the so-called Restoration Settlement so transitional that it was to be distorted in the 1680s and swept away in 1689? Certainly there were ambiguities in the settlement which helped to ensure that constitutional harmony and political stability were not achieved until long after Charles II came to his father's throne in 1660, but in all the conflicts that followed there was no further resort to civil war, and even in 1688 there was no general collapse of government. What gave government this durability? Why did the centre hold through two changes of dynasty (in 1689 and 1714), and why did local administration, law keeping and tax gathering continue to fuction even in face of revolution and invasion in 1688? Was there more 'finality' in the Restoration Settlement than there might seem at first sight, or was it simply a fear of civil war and anarchy that kept conflicts at the political level and made 1689 such a conservative revolution?

Traditional interpretations of the Restoration Settlement have tended to stress its shortcomings, and the continuity of conflict between the Crown and its opponents, with Parliament taking up in the Restoration period the unfinished business of seeking effective curbs on royal ministers, finance, military control and the King's right to decide foreign policy.[1] Against this view Caroline Robbins has expressed most concisely the argument that 'the Restoration represented a constitutional settlement at least as important as the

Glorious Revolution. . . . The flight of James II and its effects radically
changed the affairs only of Scotland.'[2] Modern reassessment of the
Stuart monarchy, and accumulating evidence of a tendency towards
successful absolutism in the 1680s, have shown that whatever else was
settled in 1660 there was room left for a considerable development of
royal power.[3] On the other hand, the more extreme solutions to the
problems of government that had been tried in the 1640s and 1650s
were not revived, and the Revolution Settlement reaffirmed rather
than upset most of the Restoration Settlement.

A first analysis of the Restoration constitutional settlement makes
it look like an almost complete counter-revolution. Restored with
Charles II, or within two years, were the monarchy; the two houses of
Parliament as formerly constituted; the Church of England; much of
the old legal system; the traditional ruling classes; even (in large
measure) the pre-war distribution of landed property. Save that most
decisions taken in the law courts were allowed to stand (12 Cha. II, c.
12) everything else that had happened since 1642 was blotted out of
constitutional memory. All this was counter-revolutionary, and, as
Christopher Hill has said, anti-democratic.[4] The political nation
wanted to return to familiar ways after years of war and instability,
and after tasting military rule. Modern historians generally agree
with Bishop Burnet that in 1660 many people wished the King back
'so matters might again fall into their old channel'.[5] Given this mood,
and the deliberately low-key and conciliatory Declaration of Breda
which typified Charles II's personal attitude, and set the tone of the
first stages of the Restoration, few changes were made to the laws as
they had stood when the civil war began in 1642. In 1661 Parliament
repealed the act of the Long Parliament excluding Bishops from the
House of Lords, and amended the law on ecclesiastical jurisdictions.
(13 Cha. II, St 1.c. 2 ; c. 12.) It also settled one pre-war quarrel in the
King's favour by declaring him indubitably and exclusively head of
the armed forces. (13 Cha. II, St 1. c. 6.) In 1662 the act of attainder
against Strafford was reversed. (14 Cha. II, c. 29.) In 1664 the Triennial Act was refashioned, reiterating the principle that Parliament
should meet at least once in every three years, but neither providing a
procedure for its assembly should the King fail to issue the necessary
writs (as the 1641 Act had done), nor prescribing a maximum life of
Parliament (as the 1695 Act was to do). (16 Cha. II, c.1.) Thus were
the old constitutional landmarks set up again with few alterations.
Yet they were not set up quite as before.

II

In several important ways Charles II's position differed from that of his father. First, changes accepted by Charles I before the outbreak of the civil war were now permanently incorporated in the constitution. Of these the most significant was that the King could no longer raise taxes without the assent of Parliament; almost as far-reaching in its effect was the abandonment of the prerogative courts. Second, the twenty years of constitutional and legal experiment before 1660 had not vanished without leaving any trace, and Charles II was the heir of Cromwell as well as of Charles I. That inheritance was complex, tending in some ways to weaken and in other ways to strengthen the position of the Crown. However strong the pull of tradition, and however persuasive the arguments of the divine right school of theology and politics, attitudes to the monarchy could never be quite the same again after 1649, and all that the death of Charles I implied. Equally, the failures of the recent past to produce a system of rule permanently acceptable to Englishmen were a powerful lesson. The Restoration monarchy also inherited from Cromwell's time improved methods of finance and military organisation, and an interesting example of government interference in municipal politics and the running of the counties. More debatable are the negative effects of the recent past – how strong were continuing fears of anarchy or of another civil war? Such fears probably reinforced the counter-revolutionary tendencies of the Cavalier Parliament, especially in Anglican attitudes to dissent, and were arguably the main reason for the failure of Exclusion, and a crucial restraining factor at the break-up of the Oxford Parliament. By 1688, however, a minority of nobility and gentry were prepared to assemble in the north to resist James II by force, and others took the risk of joining William on his march from the West to London, while the bulk of the nation gave acquiescence to what was going on. The acquiescence of the many itself may have been partly a product of fear of renewed civil war, but, like the active involvement of the few, it also testifies to the appeal of William's programme which promised to defend Protestantism, English Liberties, and a free Parliament against recent encroachments.

Without settlement there could be no encroachment. The elements of permanence and uncertainty, and the mixture of old and new ideas in the Restoration Settlement, may be illustrated by several different aspects of constitutional practice: notably in regard to finance; the summoning and dismissing of Parliament; suspending and dispensing powers; and control of the armed forces.

One of the most important of these aspects is finance.[6] (See chapter 4 for fuller treatment.) The old idea of the King's 'own' was resuscitated in 1660, alongside the newer doctrine of no unparliamentary taxation. Neither Charles II nor James II attempted to raise unparliamentary taxes, though at the beginning of his reign James II did authorise the continued collection of customs and excise duties before Parliament met – a decision that caused misgivings to the Treasury and Customs Commissioners and four of the judges, and one which though not subsequently challenged by James's Parliament was to be part of the indictment of his rule in 1688–9. Parliament began to flex its financial muscles to influence government policy in Charles II's reign, but in the 1680s a buoyant life revenue made the Crown unexpectedly strong and independent. Constitutionally the first twenty years of Charles II's reign are especially significant because financial necesssity obliged him to appeal repeatedly to Parliament for money.[7] Otherwise the King had little need to call Parliament together often or to keep it sitting long. In James's four years on the throne Parliament was in session for only about two months, and in the last three years of Charles's reign it met not at all. Yet prior to the Oxford Parliament of 1681 (which lasted only a week) the previous twenty years of Charles's reign had seen a very different pattern emerging. Between 1660 and 1680 there were only two years (1672 and 1676) when there was no session of Parliament: in every other year Parliament sat for at least two months, and usually for three months or more.[8] Thus, because of the King's chronic shortage of money, the post-Revolution pattern of regular meetings of Parliament to vote supply was almost anticipated in the first twenty years of Charles II's reign. Moreover Parliament was able to take advantage of the King's financial necessities to interfere with Charles's religious and foreign policy, notably in 1673 and 1678. Appropriation of supply to particular purposes also began to be used by the Commons from 1671, thus making political advantage of Downing's financial expedient of 1665, and a precedent was set by the appointment in 1667 of the auditors of public accounts.[9]

The power to summon, prorogue and dissolve Parliament was indisputably a royal prerogative, limited only by the Triennial Acts of 1641 and 1664, and it was allowable for the Crown to use this

prerogative to its own political advantage. Charles II used proroga-
tions and dissolutions with considerable skill and effect – especially
to kill Exclusion Bills in May 1679 and March 1681 – and James II
silenced parliamentary criticism in the same way. It is notable that
the tactical use of this royal power was not afterwards criticised in the
Bill of Rights, which concentrated instead on free elections, and
otherwise contented itself with the general observation 'that for the
redress of all grievances, and for the amending, strengthening and
preserving of the laws, Parliament ought to be held frequently'. (1
Will. and Mary, sess. II, c. 2.) Neither Charles II nor James II
intended to do without Parliament altogether. Indeed, James spent
enormous effort in trying to secure the sort of Parliament he wanted,
and he seems to have had a respect for the law and for the authority of
Parliament.[10]

The Restoration had been 'just as much a restoration of Parliament
as of the monarchy',[11] and the strength of Parliament's position in
1660 was indicated, among other things, by the fact that the Declaration of Breda referred the really contentious issues of the land and religious settlements to the decision of King in Parliament. Charles II's
Parliaments produced a considerable volume of long-lasting legislation, though admittedly James's one Parliament did not produce
any legislation that remained on the statute book. James II never, and
Charles II only twice (in 1662 and 1678), vetoed bills passed by both
Houses, though Charles might have vetoed two others had they not
conveniently been mislaid before passing through all their stages.[12]
Here again, then, is an undefined area of constitutional practice. The
basic point is that Parliament was indispensable after the Restoration; but the parliamentary calendar was very much subject to the
King's political needs of the moment.

III

A linked area of doubt, providing the biggest constitutional disputes
of the Restoration period, concerned the royal power of suspending
and dispensing with laws already made by the King in Parliament.[13]
The royal power was well-established. Charles II and James II used
both these powers, and in many cases did so uncontroversially, for
instance in granting individual dispensations from the provisions of
the Navigation Act, or in suspending that Act in time of war. In passing the Act of 1668 prohibiting the importation of Irish cattle, the

Commons deliberately termed such importation 'a public and common nuisance' to prevent dispensations being used in this particular case, since it was already accepted legal opinion that dispensation could not authorise an action that constituted a public nuisance – an opinion confirmed by the judgement of Chief Justice Vaughan in *Thomas v. Sorrell* (1674). Even in the economic area, therefore, dispensing could be controversial, and it was far more so in religious matters. Charles attempted to secure an addition to the Uniformity Bill in 1662, which would have confirmed his rights of dispensation, but this was rejected. In 1663 he again failed to get an act confirming 'that power of dispensing which we conceive to be inherent in us'.[14] In effect Parliament would tolerate the use of the dispensing power in non-controversial areas of policy, or even in the sensitive area of religious policy if it was applied only to a few individuals, as for example to the Catholics who had helped Charles escape after the battle of Worcester and who enjoyed dispensations throughout his reign. What was not tolerable was the large-scale use of the dispensing power, to benefit either Catholics or dissenters. It was exactly this relatively large-scale use of the power that James II embarked upon in 1685, when he commissioned ninety Roman Catholic officers in the army in defiance of the Test Act. His use of the power in this way was so severely criticised by Parliament that the session was abruptly ended. Thereupon the dispensing power was tested at law, by the collusive action of *Godden v. Hales* (1686). Admittedly the Bench had been purged before the case was heard, but the arguments for the crown were fairly strong, and all but one judge concurred in Chief Justice Herbert's judgement in favour of the dispensing power. But legal victory did little to help James politically, and the Bill of Rights was afterwards to condemn the dispensing power 'as it hath been assumed and exercised of late'.

Similarly with the suspending power, it was its application to ecclesiastical legislation that proved controversial. In June 1662 Charles II considered suspending the Act of Uniformity,[15] but the judges were unenthusiastic and Charles allowed the matter to drop, attempting instead, equally unsuccessfully, to secure legislative sanction for dispensing. In March 1972 he used the suspending power, when his Declaration of Indulgence suspended the operation of the penal laws in matters ecclesiastical. Once more the judges were hostile to the suspending power, and Parliament even more so. When Parliament next met in February 1673 the Commons passed a resolution that parliamentary statutes in matters ecclesiastical could not be suspended except by Act of Parliament. The resolution did not itself have the force of law, but it made amply clear what the Commons thought of Charles's religious policy, and when he found he could not get the Lords to back him against the Lower House, he was forced to cancel the Declaration because he desperately needed a vote of supply. Parliament passed an Act of Indemnity (25 Cha. II, c. 5) which, though it did not refer openly to the Declaration, was clearly its consequence, and then went on to reverse Charles's religious policy by passing the Test Act. Thus the suspending power was seen to be of very dubious legality, though it was not actually illegal, and it was never properly tested in the courts. Charles's experiences were not a promising precedent, but James issued two Declarations of Indulgence (1687 and 1688). It was against the second that the Seven Bishops petitioned, on the grounds that such a Declaration was illegal. The Bill of Rights was to lay down that the suspending power could only be used with the consent of Parliament. The whole dispute over the dispensing and suspending powers is the clearest case of Charles II and James II pressing their legal rights as far as they were capable of going – and much further than it was politic to go.

IV

Another constitutional problem, with legal implications, concerned the control of military power – according to Kenyon, 'the central problem of the seventeenth-century constitution'.[16] At the Restoration this problem was settled at least at the level of theory, but practical difficulties remained. The Disbanding Act of 1660 implied that the King could keep such forces as he wished, provided that they were not a charge upon the nation; while the Militia Act of 1661 declared that 'the sole supreme government, command and disposition of the militia and of all forces by sea and land and of all forts and places of strength is and by the laws of England ever was the undoubted right of His Majesty . . . and that both or either Houses of Parliament cannot nor ought to pretend to the same'. (12 Cha. II, c. 15 ; 12 Cha. II, St. 1 c. 6.) Thus control of the armed forces, which Parliament had disputed with Charles I, was now clearly stated to be the King's alone. But the practical advantage of this to Charles II was limited in various ways. The priority when the Disbanding Act was passed was to get rid of the existing Cromwellian army, not to create a new one; and the Militia Act – notwithstanding the clear declaration of law in its opening section – went on to deal with the organisation of the militia, not a regular army.

Charles II did become the first monarch to keep a standing army in England in peacetime, but it was only a small force of 'Guards and Garrisons', supplemented in 1684 by regiments withdrawn from Tangier. The King could not afford a larger army than this, and was always short of money even for the navy, so when forces were needed for war on colonial service they had to be paid for by parliamentary votes of supply, and were raised and disbanded as the occcasion demanded. In effect, therefore, Charles could have no more than a token army unless Parliament paid the bill, and Parliament's attitude was suspicious and hostile – only imminent war justified adding to the army. Parliamentary objections were partly practical, in that soldiers were costly to keep and tended to be a nuisance to the civilian population, but more importantly ideological, in that Parliament feared that a large standing army would make the King too powerful. The Commons resolved on 1 April 1679 'that the continuing of any standing forces in this nation, other than the militia, is illegal; and a great grievance and vexation to the people'.[17] As this resolution shows, Parliament did not harbour the same suspicions of the militia as of a standing army, but the Militia Act of 1663 laid down that the King could keep the militia in service for only fourteen days before he had to pay them for them, and in any case the military effectiveness of the militia was small. Between the Restoration and Monmouth's Rebellion the militia was fairly active in a police capacity, but militia units proved untrustworthy and inefficient in 1685, and James II preferred to build up the regular army.[18] The only exception to the general inefficiency of the militia was provided by London, where the trained bands were useful in keeping law and order. In the Exclusion crisis Charles II remained in control of his capital, and during the scares of December 1688 the militia prevented the spread of rioting in London.[19]

James II, enjoying as he did a larger revenue than his brother, plus special parliamentary grants for building up the Ordnance and the Navy, was able to double the size of the army.[20] At the same time he undermined the militia, allowing musters to be neglected, and disrupting the lines of command by his purges of the county lieutenancy.[21] The benefits of these moves were doubtful. Certainly James II made himself so strong militarily that the Revolution of 1688 would not have been possible without outside intervention by armed forces. On the other hand, 'William would not have come over with an army of 12,000 men to fight a king at the head of 40,000 if religious developments had not produced a situation in which the people could be expected to be on his side'; and, however imposing its appearance, the army 'could not be used for wholesale repression or to impose Catholicism, as it was predominantly Protestant and its loyalty to the king was far from unconditional'.[22] Moreover other problems accompanied the creation of the standing armies of Charles II and James II.

Both Charles II and James II appointed Catholic army officers and James added a significant number of Irish troops to the English establishment.[23] The judges backed James II over dispensing the law for Catholic officers, but they were not so happy about military law, and the expansion of the army created considerable vexation over this question. As usual the army was regarded differently from the navy – by the Naval Discipline Act of 1661 Parliament readily allowed the establishment of martial law to support naval discipline at sea, but no similar provision was made for the army, except in wartime or when it was serving overseas when the need for martial law was tacitly admitted. (13 Cha. II, St. 1 c. 9.) Soldiers serving in England were subject to the ordinary law of the land, and the government left cases between soldiers and civilians to be settled in the normal courts. In addition, however, courts martial were employed for military discipline, and in 1686 the King issued Articles of War, embodying a code of military discipline for the army at home, though it was provided that 'no punishment amounting to the loss of life or limb be imposed upon any offender in time of peace'.[24] At least from 1678 onwards deserters were tried in the ordinary law courts, and their punishment could extend to the death penalty, but two incidents of 1687 showed that this procedure was not supported by all lawyers. Early that year Sir John Holt, Recorder of London, refused to convict a deserter; and in April Lord Chief Justice Herbert and Sir Francis Wythens, sitting in King's Bench, would not allow that a deserter who had been condemned at Reading Assizes be taken to Plymouth to be shot before his regiment – for this decision Wythens was dismissed, and Herbert ordered to change places with the Chief Justice of Common Pleas.[25] The problems of military discipline were not solved until Mutiny Acts began to be regularly passed in the reigns of William III and Anne.[26]

These examples – finance, the summoning and dismissing of Parliaments, suspending and dispensing and control of the armed forces

– all have common features. Each case shows an area of ambiguity in the constitutional arrangements of the Restoration, exploited by the crown to enhance its power, especially in the 1680s, though the biggest single advantage gained by the King in those years, his financial independence, was acquired more by chance than by deliberate design. Though opposition was expressed in Parliament and elsewhere to the Crown's growing financial independence, to its suspending and dispensing the statute law, and to its control of a regular army, that did not check the accretion of powers to the monarchy.

There were other areas of constitutional dispute in which the outcome was more mixed. For instance, in the continuing battles about the Crown's right to sustain in office ministers of its own choosing, or Parliament's right to criticise government policy (including foreign policy), the advantage lay sometimes with the Crown and sometimes with its opponents. Impeachments tended not to succeed unless the minister attacked had lost favour with the King as well as Parliament, but there were occasions when the King had to part with a useful servant, or change his policy under parliamentary attack, and perhaps in the long run the important point was that attacks were sustained – sustained in Parliament down to 1680, and, less effectively, in the law courts thereafter. The Crown's opponents had their moments of triumph, but the loyalty of the classes represented in Parliament remained strong, and the opposition could over-reach itself (as it did conspicuously in the Exclusion crisis), so the Crown successfully built up the already strong position it had held since Charles II was restored unconditionally in 1660. The permanence of the Crown's advantage, however, depended on there being a Protestant heir to the throne, since the loyalty of the parliamentary classes was as much to the Church of England, re-established at the Restoration, as it was to the restored monarchy. In Charles's latter years the Catholicism of James, Duke of York, was an obvious strain, but at least he was a middle-aged man and had no Catholic heir until June 1688, so on balance loyalty overcame fears of growing royal power until that point in time. Moreover, despite what the Bill of Rights said afterward, there was only one clear example of the Crown acting illegally in the 1680s, and that was when Charles II did not summon Parliament by 1684, and James II had not done so by 1688: both Kings were thereby in breach of the Triennial Act, though in 1688 James was actively preparing for Parliament to meet.

V

Law reform had been an important issue during the English Revolution, but views differ both about what was achieved in the 1640s and 1650s, and about how much of that achievement was lost at the Restoration. Thus Holdsworth stresses continuity through the century, and argues that if regard is paid to reforms actually accomplished rather than to those merely projected, very few reforms of the 1640s and 1650s were not confirmed after the Restoration. Similarly Donald Veall sees the reforms of 1640 to 1660 as 'important enough to determine the future character of the English legal system', and the Restoration as a less successful reaction than it seems. Alan Harding, on the other hand, calls the Interregnum 'a lost opportunity' which 'condemned English Law to years of incompleteness and improvisation', and states that 'what the Protectorate did achieve by way of legislation was erased from legal memory at the Restoration'. Where Veall and Harding agree is in emphasising the conservatism of lawyers and property-owners as an obstacle to law reform. The conservatism of the profession is also a major conclusion of Michael Landon's study of the Whig lawyers in politics from 1678 to 1689; and A. F. Havighurst concludes his scrupulous examination of the conduct of the judiciary in Charles II's reign: 'The valid criticism . . . is . . . that, in an age of intellectual curiosity and scientific inquiry, their notions of law were so narrow . . . The judges were not responsible for the inadequate machinery of the law and the narrow rules of procedure which they inherited, but they were responsible for their intelligent modification to meet changing conditions. They did little about it.'[27]

Symbolic of conservatism, and a small but significant retrogressive step, was the alteration at the Restoration of the language of the law courts. Since 1650 English had been the language of the courts, but one of the earliest acts of the Restoration was that which continued this reform only up to 1 August 1660. (12 Cha. II, c. 3.) From then until 1733 the English law courts reverted to using Norman French and law Latin in formal documents and records, thereby putting the layman in court at some disadvantage. At the trial of Sir Harry Vane in 1662 the court ruled that the indictment must be read to the prisoner in English 'for it is the substance and not the form to which he must reply'.[28] In this particular case the decision to read the indictment in English was less a concession than a means of baffling the prisoner, since Vane repeatedly and unsuccessfully asked to hear the indictment in Latin, so that he could attack it on technical grounds.[29] The usual practice was reversed in the case of the Seven Bishops, for when the Clerk of the Court began to read the information in English the Solicitor General asked that it be read in Latin instead, and this was done, despite the protest by Bishop White of Peterborough that the Bishops did not understand law Latin.[30] More seriously disadvantageous to those on trial for treason or felony was that they did not see a copy of the indictment before the trial; they were not allowed the services of counsel except on points of law and they could not put their witnesses on oath. In these ways procedure in court enhanced the harshness of the law, and Jeffreys was ahead of his time in thinking these established practices unfair.[31]

It would be naïve to look for much leniency in Restoration law or in legal procedure in political cases, given the revolutionary character of the recent past and the political strains of the 1680s. Kenyon fairly emphasises the lack of vengeance in the Restoration Settlement itself, when the Act of Indemnity and Oblivion (1660) (12 Cha. II, c. 11) pardoned almost everyone except the regicides, and imposed for three years special fines for reflecting, by speech or writing, on any man's conduct during the past twenty years. (These fines were set at £10 if the offender was a gentleman, £2 if he was below that rank, to be paid to the party aggrieved.) This was indeed a remarkable attempt to draw a veil over the past.[32] For the future, the Act for the Preservation of the King's Person and Government (1661), (13 Cha. II, St. 1 c. 1) besides confirming the existing law of treason, also imposed penalties on those who declared Charles II a papist or heretic, and those who maintained that the Long Parliament had not been dissolved; or that any oath taken in the past to acknowledge a change of government in church or state had binding force; or that Parliament alone could legislate. Another Act of the same year (13 II, St. 1 c. 5) forbade the submission of petitions to King or Parliament by more than ten persons. The existing law of treason, dating from the reign of Edward III, had already been extended by judicial construction before the civil wars. At the Restoration the additions to it made during the Interregnum fell away, but the process of extension by judicial construction went on, reaching the point in the *Trial of Algernon Sidney* (1683) when the prisoner was convicted for opinions expressed in an unpublished manuscript found in his study – a verdict reversed by statute after the Revolution.[33] A less political case of 1668 shows equally well how far judicial construction could carry treason. Apprentices who had taken part in a riot, in which brothels were attacked, were held by ten of the eleven judges who considered the case to have acted treasonably. When such an attitude could be taken in the case of rioting apprentices, it is easier to understand the brutality of the trials and sentences at the time of the Popish Plot (when the government itself was not particularly anxious for convictions, but public and political excitement was running high and the security of the state seemed to be struck at), or the Bloody Assizes (when the government was eager to make an example of Monmouth's rebels).

In political cases, and in many aspects of criminal law, Stuart justice was nasty, brutish and short. In some of its worst excesses it was recognised as such by contemporaries – for instance, there was a reaction at the time against the Bloody Assizes.[34] Mostly, however, contemporary opinion seems to have supported both the substance of the criminal law and the manner of its administration. Western has shown how censorship (fierce in intent, if admittedly inefficient in practice) was accepted by contemporaries, although it is one of the parts of Restoration law least attractive to modern eyes;[35] the same could be said of religious persecution. In a turbulent period, lacking an organised police force, property-owners felt that they needed a harsh law for their own protection as much as the King needed it for his. Already the tendency of the criminal law was towards growing severity, with the number of new capital offences created by statute beginning to grow, and judicial interpretation broadening the definition of crimes like burglary. The severity of game laws, and of the poor law, add to the impression of the propertied classes trying to protect themselves against the rest of the populace – though in all of this it has to be added that there was usually a great gap between the letter of the law and its enforcement.[36]

Alongside these trends, however, are some indications that the cause of law reform was not quite dead. The most significant development was that of equity jurisdiction, principally in the Court of Chancery, but also in the Court of Exchequer, where the number of bills filed in Charles II's reign was double what it had been in Charles I's.[37] In Chancery, the first earl of Nottingham 'did much to make English law serve society'.[38] Chancery took over from the ecclesiastical courts jurisdiction over wills, and was involved in the economically important development of the land law, controlling mortgages and trusts.[39] Abolition of feudal tenures at the Restoration removed one check on the extension of trusts, and two other pieces of legislation which also helped forward the process of reform in this branch of law were the Statute of Distribution (1670) concerning the property of those who died intestate, and the Statute of Frauds (1677) which formalised the procedure for creating trusts, and required wills to be written and witnessed. (22 and 23 Cha. II, c. 10 ; 29 Cha. II, c. 3.)[40]

In a few areas legal procedure was also improving in the Restoration period. One improvement was in the gradual refinement of the law of evidence, making hearsay inadmissible.[41] Another was the continuation of earlier seventeenth-century trends towards the evolution of subjects' remedies against royal officials by means of the writs of *certiorari* and *mandamus*.[42] A third was in the use of habeas corpus as a check against arbitrary arrest, though this development required help from legislation. Already by the time of the Restoration, the writ of habeas corpus had a special status in the popular mind as a protection of the citizen's liberty, and it was an important part of day-to-day criminal procedure, being the accepted method by which a person committed by local justices could appeal to King's Bench for bail, and providing a means to review pre-trial proceedings. But there were defects in the procedure. For example, it was not clear whether the writ could be issued in law vacations, or whether it could help prisoners moved from one place of custody to another. The Commons discussed bills to improve the procedure in 1668, 1669–70, 1673–4, 1675 and 1676–7, before the bill of 1679 finally passed by the most slender majority (if the old story is true that it passed in the House or Lords only because one fat lord was counted as ten). Essentially the Act of 1679 (31 Cha. II, c. 2) attempted to remedy existing procedural problems, and to ensure at least a speedy trial, and it made Parliament's suspicion of the judges clear by prescribing punitive personal damages against any judge who delayed the issue of the writ in vacation. Of course the Act applied only to criminal cases, and it did not meet all the problems of the time, as for example the demanding of excessive bail, which was one of the judicial actions of the 1680s singled out as illegal by the Bill of Rights. Nevertheless, the improvement of the habeas corpus procedure must be accounted a significant reform.[43]

The Restoration legal system differed in one important respect from that prevailing for most of Charles I's reign. The main prerogative courts had been abolished by statute in 1641, and were not revived under Charles II. The jurisdiction of Star Chamber had been 'clearly and absolutely dissolved, taken away and determined', and so had the similar jurisdictions of the Council of the North and the Council in the Marches of Wales, the Courts of the Duchy of Lancaster and the County Palatine of Chester. (16 Cha. I, c. 10.) The Court of High Commission was likewise abolished by statute. (16 Ch. I, c. 11.) The Court of Requests was not formally abolished, but it withered away after 1642. At the Restoration no attempt was made to bring back any of these lost jurisdictions, except that the civil jurisdiction of the Council of Wales was revived (it remained controversial and was abolished in 1689), and a form of ecclesiastical jurisdiction was re-introduced in July 1686 (the Ecclesiastical Commission was highly controversial, but probably not technically illegal).[44] In 1660 the work of abolition continued with the act ending royal rights of purveyance, military tenures and the Court of Wards. (12 Cha. II, c. 24.) Removal of the Court of Wards completed the demise of the 'feudal law', the destruction of which had been one of the objects of law reformers, and it underlines the victory of common law over prerogative.

There were two major consequences of the disappearance of the prerogative courts. First, the pre-war rivalry of common law and prerogative was firmly settled in favour of the common law and the whole future development of English law thereby affected. The history of the Admiralty jurisdiction neatly illustrates this generalisation. Before the war the practical need for a branch of law and a court system to deal with commercial and maritime cases was already producing growing business for the High Court of Admiralty. Conflicts of jurisdiction between the common-law courts and the Admiralty Court were settled in Council. A Long Parliament Ordinance of 1648, renewed during the Commonwealth, helped forward the development of Admiralty jurisdiction, and, as Yale says, 'the very survival of the Court testifies to the strength of demand'. But after the Restoration, all attempts to get legislation to establish the Admiralty jurisdiction failed – in 1662 and 1663, in 1670 and in 1685 – mainly because of the professional divide between common and civil lawyers, and the jealousy felt by common lawyers towards their civilian brethren. When Admiralty jurisdiction was eventually established by Statute in the nineteenth century 'The commercial law of England had long been in the hands of the common lawyers'.[45] As this example also shows, the victory of common law over prerogative was equally a triumph of common lawyers against civilians. The civilians had never been a large group (Brian Levack estimates that common lawyers outnumbered them by ten to one in the reigns of James I and Charles I), but they had enjoyed considerable status, and a growing importance in the pre-war period, when they were the branch of the legal profession most closely associated with the monarchy and the established church. After 1641 their decline continued to the mid-nineteenth century.[46] Another result of the ascendancy of common law was that the English system was confirmed in its isolation from the Continental and Scottish systems, and the separate legal system of Scotland had to be specifically safeguarded by the Union Treaty at the time of the Anglo-Scottish union of Parliaments in 1707.

The victory of common law was not in itself detrimental to the Crown – it has been well said that there was a strong common-law case for royal power; and in the later, as in the earlier Stuart period, most constitutional cases heard in the common-law courts were settled in the Crown's favour.[47] Where the important difference came was in the day-to-day administration of the law. The Court of Star Chamber especially, but the Privy Council and other courts also, had in Charles I's reign been used to bring royal policy to bear upon the legal system. Judges going on assize circuits were summoned first to the Star Chamber to hear what policy they should take with them into the provinces. Local magistrates could be disciplined by Star Chamber or the Council. The composition of juries could be influenced by central government through these mechanisms. This whole apparatus of local control was greatly weakened by the loss of the prerogative courts. Charles II and James II had, therefore, to lean more heavily on those parts of the legal system which they did control – notably the judiciary. Much has been written about the judges of the Restoration period, and especially about the degree of their subservience to the Crown. Holdsworth associates the deterioration in the quality of the Bench in the seventeenth century, as compared with the sixteenth century, not only with increasing political pressure upon the judges until the Revolution of 1688, but also with the collapse of the system of education at the Inns of Court in the 1640s. By about 1684 'Westminster Hall might be said to stand upon its head',[48] because the best available legal talent was no longer found on the Bench. The last big trial of the period, that of the Seven Bishops in 1688, mainly because the judges trying the case were so obviously inferior to the defence counsel has been called 'grotesque'.[49] By their decisions in the political and constitutional cases of the 1680s the judges identified themselves with the claims of the Stuart monarchy, and some of their controversial decisions did not last – for instance

James's dispensations though supported by the verdict in *Godden v. Hales* were condemned by the Bill of Rights; and the verdict given against Oates in 1685 was also implicity criticised there, while Oates himself received a royal pardon from William III. More importantly the judges laid themselves open to distrust of the same sort that had grown up against Charles I's judges before the civil war, which both took away from the public standing of the judiciary and diminished its usefulness to the King.[50]

After the Restoration, Charles II's initial appointments to the Bench were respectable, and he even re-employed judges who had served during the Interregnum – six who had been in office at the Restoration were subsequently reappointed, as were three others who had retired earlier. Judicial appointments down to 1668 were made during good behaviour, and when the first serious clash between the King and judges came, over the Declaration of Indulgence in 1672, Charles could only prevent Sir John Archer from acting as Chief Justice of Common Pleas, he could not conveniently dismiss him from office. Havighurst suggests that the retirement in 1676 of Sir Matthew Hale (for ill health, and not on political grounds) marks a turning point in Charles's reign. Until that time royal coercion had been slight, and the quality of the Bench high; thereafter royal pressure increased and the character of those appointed to high judicial office generally declined.[51] Both Charles II, and more especially James II, sought compliant judges, put pressure on those in office and dismissed those whose opinions did not fit in with royal wishes. At this time the tenure of judges became particularly insecure; Charles II removed eleven of them in the eight years to 1683, and James II removed twelve in the four years of his reign.[52] With the threat of dismissal always in the background it was obviously hard for judges to come to sound decisions, especially in politically sensitive cases, and difficult too for the Crown to find adequate replacements to fill so many high judicial offices. On the other hand the very number of dismissals made by Charles II and James II shows that subservience to royal wishes was not automatic, and there were occasions when the judges as a body gave advice that the Kings did not want to hear – as they did to Charles II over his proposed suspension of the religious laws. Moreover, if royal displeasure was the worst of their problems, the judges also had to fear public vilification, and parliamentary criticism backed by the threat of impeachment. After Chief Justice Scroggs had presided at the acquittal of Wakeman in 1679 he was pursued by a mob and had a dead dog thrown into his coach. He was attacked by Oates and Bedloe before the Privy Council in January 1680, and later that year he was one of four judges recommended for impeachment by a Commons Committee.[53]

The characters and courtroom behaviour of Scroggs and Jeffreys have attracted much unfavourable notice, especially compared with the high standards set after the Restoration by Sir Matthew Hale. Hale had served as a judge under Oliver Cromwell, but he was promoted by Charles II and became Chief Justice of King's Bench (1671–6). He was universally respected as much for his character as for his legal distinction – in his eulogistic *Life and Death of Sir Matthew Hale* Burnet credited him with many virtues, including even kindness to animals.[54] By comparison Sir William Scroggs, Lord Chief Justice from 1678 to 1681, was 'rough' indeed, and he is most often described as a timeserver, though he was a bold and courageous man who regarded himself as independent. His worst period as a judge was during the Popish Plot trials of November 1678 to February 1679, which afforded too much scope to his violent anti-Catholicism. Even then, however, Scroggs seems to have steered his own course, rather than responding to political pressure from the King, the politicians or the public, but in the end Charles had to retire him in April 1681.[55] George Jeffreys, Lord Chief Justice in 1683 and Lord Chancellor from 1685 to 1688, represents the worst in Stuart judges – not because he lacked legal talent as was often alleged, but because of his bullying tactics in court, his vindictiveness and opportunism. At the Revolution he may indeed have become 'the scapegoat because of his friendlessness',[56] but there were plenty of reasons for contemporaries disliking and repudiating him, and modern attempts to whitewash his character have not succeeded. What should be emphasised, however, is not the personalities of the judges, or even the varied stresses to which they were subject, but rather the nature of their office at this time. They were still royal servants rather than independent judges. They were involved in administrative tasks, and often used as advisers by the Privy Council and the House of Lords. Obviously they were expected to be vigorous upholders of law and order, but more than that they were expected to preach loyalty at the assizes – though the Star Chamber charge had lapsed, the judges still received royal instructions before going on circuit, and when on circuit they collected information about the political state of the country. James II was simply going a little further than usual when he used the judges on circuit as electoral agents in 1685.[57]

'The autocratic bad temper of many judges after the Restoration, particularly at assizes, was largely occasioned by the difficulty of handling ignorant and partisan juries, especially now that they could not be disciplined by Star Chamber.' In Holdsworth's long view of legal history it may be fair to argue that the jury system did even more than habeas corpus to protect subjects' rights but at this date 'the position of the jury, as neutral judges of fact, had not yet been stabilised, and if the jury could not be persuaded to accept the judges' verdict as to fact they must be coerced.'[58] In 1667 and 1668 complaints were made in the Commons against Chief Justice Kelyng and Justice Tyrell for intimidating juries and punishing them when they brought in verdicts contrary to the direction of the court. Kelyng's spirited defence of himself before the Commons gives a vivid glimpse of the pig-headedness of local jurymen – in one of the cases at issue a Devon jury brought in a verdict of manslaughter, instead of murder, against a supervisor who had beaten an apprentice so severely that the boy died.[59] After hearing Kelyng the Commons took no further action against him, but did resolve that fining and imprisoning juries was illegal. A bill to secure the independence of juries was brought in but failed to pass. Two years later, a legal precedent was established whereby juries secured immunity from punishment for bringing in verdicts contrary to the judge's direction. In *Bushel's Case* (1670) Lord Chief Justice Vaughan declared that judges could not punish jurymen for their verdict unless there was evidence of criminal collusion. He ruled that a jury could come to a decision from its own knowledge of the facts of the matter, though it should be generally guided by the evidence heard in court. It was for this old-fashioned reason, rather than in conformity to modern ideas that a jury should be impartial, that Vaughan ruled as he did. This ruling prevented the punishment of juries by fine or imprisonment thereafter, but it did not put a stop to the judges' bullying tactics, and it meant that from now on there was even greater temptation for those concerned to influence the composition of the jury in advance of a politically sensitive trial.[60]

Contemporary opinion assumed that jurymen ought to be persons of some substance, and in certain types of case the jurymen were required to be at least £20 freeholders (16 and 17 Cha. ii, c. 5.).

Because of the genuine difficulty of recruiting such persons in and around London, where most properties were leased or let, there were complaints that Middlesex juries often contained non-freeholders, but problems of this sort were of little account compared with the blatant attempts made by sheriffs to find juries sympathetic to the Crown, or, if the sheriffs were supporting the opposition, juries that were like-minded. Keeton declares that 'There has never been a period of English history when the art of jury packing was practised so extensively'.[61] One of the objects of the remodelling of municipal corporations in the period after 1681 was to try and secure reliable juries, as well as reliable local magistrates. During the Restoration period there were many examples of bad juries, but also of juries which returned brave verdicts in difficult circumstances. For instance, the Middlesex jurors who cleared Shaftesbury in 1681 and acquitted the Seven Bishops in 1688, were acting in sympathy with popular and opposition opinion, but against the known wishes of the King. Conversely the jurymen who acquitted Wakemen in 1679 had to flee from their homes in fear of the mob.[62]

If juries could be packed, so too could the Commission of the Peace, and that more easily. In this period there were two major purges. The first was a purge of Whigs and substitution of Tories after the Exclusion crisis, and the second a purge of Tories when James II was building an alliance of Whigs, Dissenters and Catholics to help produce the kind of Parliament he wanted. The scale of these operations was impressive: for instance in 1687 James II put into the Commission 455 new JPs, and in 1688 more than 795 (out of a total of 1197).[63] Charles II's remodellings seemed to have been fairly successful at least politically. The government gained ground by the promotion of loyalists and the discountenancing of opponents, and it also became easier to enforce the laws against religious non-conformity which had often been slackly administered in the past.[64] James II had less success. By 1688 thirty-three per cent of the deputy lieutenants and nineteen per cent of the JPs were Roman Catholics, but there was considerable resentment against the promotion of Catholics and Dissenters among the traditionally loyal ruling classes in the counties.

The practical effects of such large-scale changes on the legal and administrative work of the magistracy must have been detrimental. Even before the purges an amateur magistracy could not be relied upon for consistency or efficiency in legal or administrative work, and the disappearance of Star Chamber had weakened central control and direction. Already, at the Restoration, the Commission of the Peace had become more aristocratic, and this had not improved its competence, while the quorum had not been a minimal safeguard of efficiency since the early seventeenth century.[65] Changes in the Commission of the Peace could be counter-productive in both political and practical terms, therefore, and the same applies to the similar changes in the lord lieutenancy and the commissioned ranks of the militia. A few strategic changes of lord lieutenant were useful, to discipline opponents and promote friends of the Court, but wholesale changes such as those embarked upon by James II after his closeting of the leaders of opinion in the counties in 1687 were likely to be counter-productive. The disruption caused by these changes made it harder for the militia to be mustered to oppose the invasion of 1688, but more significant was the political backlash produced. Carswell's analysis of the support for James's policies, based on the replies given by the magistracy to the Three Questions, is 'that although James had a not inconsiderable body of support, he had something like two-thirds of the landowning classes against him, and half of these were not afraid to say so'.[66]

VII

Similar though not identical conclusions may be drawn about the campaign to remodel the municipal corporations. Charles II began a concerted effort to secure control of the membership of the corporations in 1680, using when necessary the legal tool of the *quo warranto*. Partly by these means he secured a remarkably loyal Parliament to meet his brother in 1685. James II's efforts at remodelling the corporations were even larger in scale: whereas Charles had granted or regranted 58 municipal charters in the last four years of his reign, James's score was 121.[67] Modern historians take seriously the chances of success which this campaign had, although in the event it was not put to the electoral test in 1687 or 1688, and defeat was virtually admitted by the restitution of London's charter and a few others in October and November 1688.[68] However there was also a price to pay in disruption of local government in these towns, where the result of repeated remodellings might be to produce warring factions within the corporation.[69] The large-scale use of *quo warrantos* is also remarkable as another instance of the monarchy using a legal power to support unpopular policies to an unwise extent. William's promise of a free

Parliament was one of the most attractive items in his programme, and no government after the Revolution tried the crude electoral tactic of wholesale removal of corporation charters and remodelling the membership of corporations.

James II was not setting out on a hopeless quest when he sought to persuade the ruling classes that there was no alternative for them but to accept his policies, nor was his attempt to call a new world of towns into the political balance against the traditional preponderance of the landowners foredoomed to failure – except for one thing it might have succeeded in getting him the sort of Parliament he wanted. What spelt failure was that James's tactics were intended to serve a religious policy which most influential people found unacceptable. The gains made in monarchical power since the Restoration were not universally resisted until they were combined with this policy, and with the appearance of a Catholic heir to the throne in 1688, who would carry the policy on into the future.

There are interesting parallels and contrasts between the situation of Charles I in 1642 and James II in 1688. Charles could not continue governing without Parliament because he had neither independent financial means nor any army, and he could no longer depend upon the co-operation of the locally-influential classes, so basic law and order and the ordinary processes of government were beginning to break down in the provinces.[70] James's position at first sight seems much stronger. He had money and an army, and though there may have been growing non-co-operation with his policies in the country, there was no total collapse of government – at the local level law and order held up pretty well (even in face of the Irish scares after James's flight) and tax-gathering and other functions of government continued; while at the central level an informal committee managed to carry on the government in December 1688, after James attempted to paralyse the processes of government by throwing the Great Seal in the Thames. As much as his father, however, James in the end needed the co-operation of locally important people, both for the continuation of ordinary government at local level and to support his policies nationally. By 1688 his policies were seen by these people as an encroachment on the established position in church and state.

The most obvious way in which James was interfering with the established system was by his strenuous attempts to secure toleration for his co-religionists, but he was seen also as pressing his legal claims too far (especially in his use of the dispensing and suspending power) and as undermining Parliament by his electoral tactics. Less explicitly formulated, though deeply felt, was the idea that James's policies were an attack on the traditional ruling classes – the nobility in particular, but the gentry, urban élites and office-holders as well. What these groups were doing in 1688 was resisting the centralising tendency of the Stuart monarchy, just as in somewhat different circumstances they or others like them had resisted similar tendencies on the part of Charles I and Cromwell. Their Revolution was not a popular movement, but it was one that commanded acquiescence – just as in 1660 the Restoration had been carried through with popular sympathy.

4. Financial and Administrative Developments in England, 1660–88

HOWARD TOMLINSON

Thomas hobbes referred to Charles II's Restoration as a revolution, in the astronomical sense that it was a return to the established cyclical pattern, 'a circular motion of the sovereign power, through two usurpers, from the late King to this his son'.[1] As far as the restoration of the King's government in 1660 was concerned this was an accurate reflection, for the trappings of the Commonwealth State were dismantled and the system, methods, many of the men and most of the institutions – with the notable exceptions of the Star Chamber and High Commission, the Council in the North and the Court of Wards – of the old monarchy were restored. It would be foolish, however, to suggest that the Interregnum had little effect on the Restoration government. Not all the innovations had worked effectively and some of the impressive administrative changes of the Commonwealth and Protectorate period – the establishment of committees under the Long Parliament and the Rump, the use of the devices of excise and monthly assessment as important features of the tax system, and the institution of higher salaries and the curbing of excessive fee-taking[2] – were not permanently instituted. Nevertheless they cannot be dismissed as being of little consequence.

The reforms were to have a profound influence and, together with the impact of Dutch finance, French administrative enterprise (notably admiration of the French system of management by Secretaries of State) and war, were to be the main determinants of the more durable

For Notes to Chapter 4, see pp. 214–18; for Bibliographical Notes, see pp. 200–1.

financial and administrative developments between the Restoration and Revolution. These developments may be briefly summarised: the permanent establishment of the Treasury and the creation of a new revenue and credit system; the slow decline of the Privy Council; the consequent extension of the role of the Secretaries of State and the growth of independent departmental administration and the emergence of new conditions of service and more rational administrators. Of these the financial developments were the most crucial, for it was the newly constituted Treasury Commission of 1667 that inspired and enforced many of the changes in the subordinate departments of state, and it was the increased yield of the Crown revenues – especially in the 1680s, when the Crown's net income rose from an average of about £1,377,000 per annum 1681–4, to no less than £1,954,000 in 1687–8[3] – that financed the advances in the size and expertise of Restoration government.

I

In 1660, the new Lord Treasurer, the pious but uninspiring fourth earl of Southampton, inherited a defective system of Treasury management, a confused and inefficient method of tax collection and credit techniques that were outdated compared with the best continental models. One of the chief problems was the lack of control over Crown revenues. Too often revenues were diverted from the Crown's receivers directly into the hands of the Crown's creditors, thereby bypassing the cumbersome procedures of the Exchequer – a body that had been re-established in 1654 as the central institution of finance – undermining its credit and increasing the opportunities for speculation and delay. Allied to this problem was that of tax collection. Unlike the Exchequer, which, with the exception of the provision that tallies were to be inscribed in English rather than Latin, had been largely unreformed during the Interregnum, there had been some advances made in the collection of revenue in the 1640s and 1650s. In the field of indirect taxation, for example, both the customs and to a lesser extent the excise, a tax first levied by Parliament in 1643 and one of the most important financial legacies of the civil war and Interregnum, were collected directly through officials appointed by the government. This experiment was not an unqualified success, and in the customs, at least, was beginning to break down in 1658–60 as a result of the violent political upheavals of those years. The decision to continue direct collection of the customs and excise in 1660–2, with only slight modification of the existing arrangements, resulted in a poor yield and was confirmation of the inadequacy of the Interregnum arrangement.[4]

While there was an attempt during the years of the Protectorate and Commonwealth to collect taxes more efficiently by the extension of government control, there were no similar innovations during that time in the system of national credit – a further reason against overstating the progressive character of governmental finance in the Interregnum. Indeed the funding of a national debt, and the whole idea of national credit upon which funding depended, was unknown in England in 1660, although such a scheme had been successfully tried in Holland by De Witt in 1655.[5] English Exchequer officials simply relied on the time-honoured credit instruments of loans, whether by professional financiers, corporations or individuals, advances made by revenue farmers or ordinary taxpayers and payment tallies.[6] Such antiquated credit techniques inevitably limited the Crown's financial capabilities, for there was no security for a creditor that his debts would be honoured, and little incentive for the small investor to lend money to an importunate government. As Sir George Downing, the dynamic Secretary to the 1667 Treasury Commission and the instigator of the credit revolution of the 1660s, observed on the eve of the war with the United Provinces, the Dutch believed that the English could not sustain a fight for 'you are not so good husbands of your money nor do you lay it out so carefully and with that advantage as they'.[7] Twenty-five years later such criticisms would have been less than just, for by the Revolution a profound change had been effected in the central direction of the revenue and the creditworthiness of the Crown. Three broad areas of reform may be recognised: the creation of the modern Treasury, the firm instigation of direct collection of the major branches of the revenue and the adoption of a new instrument of credit that was to become the mainstay of the financial revolution under William III.

Central to all reforms was the establishment of an authoritative body of Treasury commissioners after Lord Treasurer Southampton's death on 16 May 1667. The decision to put the Treasury into commission was not without precedent, but the type of men the King appointed to act as commissioners was a quite definite departure from tradition. For with the advice of the Duke of York, Charles II decided to appoint to office three 'rougher hands' without aristocratic pretensions – Sir Thomas Clifford, Sir William Coventry and Sir John Duncomb. This policy was in direct contradiction to the established custom that the senior Treasury commissioners should be sober men of good pedigree to give authority to a department that (in Clarendon's words) 'had much to do with the nobility and chief gentry of the kingdom'. Clarendon would have named existing holders of the highest offices, who apart from having no financial expertise, would have had little time available to give to Treasury business. Nevertheless it was soon quite clear that the appointment of 'ill-natured' men who were 'not to be moved with civilities' would be of advantage to the King's service. These particular men, moreover, were young yet experienced enough to prosecute a vigorous programme of reform in place of the previous administrative inertia of the Court. It was in vain that Lord Chancellor Clarendon protested against the social inadequacies of the officers designate, and although he succeeded in persuading the King to add to the board the names of the surviving Chancellor of the Exchequer, Lord Ashley, and the duke of Albemarle as a figurehead, authority could and did effectively remain with the 'rougher hands' who made up a legally constituted quorum. The addition of Sir George Downing as secretary made it quite certain that the new commission was to be a landmark in the development of the modern Treasury.[8]

The two main achievements of this commission concerned the strengthening of the Treasury's financial authority *vis-à-vis* the other agencies of government and the regularisation of Treasury bookkeeping methods. The demand for the recognition of Treasury status was a conscious effort on the behalf of the commissioners to assert the Treasury's inherent powers as the centre of government finance. Under Southampton these powers were latent; during his tenure the Treasury was little more than a subordinate financial agency, dominated by the Privy Council, with little initiative over revenue matters and even less control of expenditure. Within days of taking office, however, the 1667 commissioners attempted to reverse this position. A stream of assertive instructions were issued, governing their control of revenue and expenditure at the expense of King, Privy Council, Secretaries of State, Exchequer and other departments. Before any money warrant was signed by the King, their lordships were to be informed so that they could report to him 'as to the matter of fact and as to the condition and present state of the revenue'; the King was enjoined to 'sign nothing for secret service but what really is so', and to prevent the Secretaries of State from issuing or signing any warrant relating to the revenue; the Lords of the Privy Council were reminded that it had been the custom for the words 'pray' or 'desire' rather than 'direct' or 'order' to be used in any communication with the Treasury; moves were made to stop the granting of places for life or in reversion; and the Exchequer officials, especially those officers in the Upper Exchequer concerned with the audit of accounts, were urged to attend to their business diligently and to round up recalcitrant revenue collectors and delinquent departmental accountants.[9] These minutes were not mandatory, but their authority was established when many of them were enshrined and extended in successive orders of the King in Council.

There were at least four orders of fundamental importance. The order of 17 June 1667 laid down the rule of 'specific sanction', which authorised the Treasury to regulate departmental expenditure – even though the King's formal warrant had been issued enabling the departmental treasurer to spend a general sum of money, the Treasury commissioners had (and still have) the discretionary power to determine specific items of expenditure. In order that the Treasury would have up-to-date information as to the state of credit in any one department, treasurers of the spending departments were to submit weekly certificates of their receipts, issues, revenues and debts. A similar order was also applied to the receivers and farmers of the major revenues regarding their receipts and rent payments, so that at the end of any week it was theoretically possible for the commissioners to compute the extent of the Crown's liabilities, and this provided a basis for the weekly disposition of funds.

On 1 November 1667, several months after the issuing of the 'specific sanction' rule, the initiative of the Secretaries of State was limited in Treasury matters – an order that was underlined in the ruling of 31 January 1668, which again curtailed the Secretaries' jurisdiction. But that ruling was of much wider import than this, for it not only confirmed, at the Secretaries' expense, the Treasury's right to control virtually all revenue matters, but also provided that all warrants imprested to departmental treasurers should be first countersigned by the commissioners. Furthermore it was written 'fair on a board and hung up in the Treasury Chamber' as a constant reminder of Treasury supremacy. It was complemented by the order of 12 February 1668 allowing the Treasury discretion as to whether to bring financial business before the Privy Council.[10] The new-found power of the Treasury was confirmed by the elaborate Treasury schedule of 20 October 1668, a minutely detailed report on the anticipated revenue and liabilities of the King.[11] The careful apportionment of the King's revenue and the dire warning of the crisis at hand serves as evidence of the Treasury's discipline and authority at this time. Its independence, too, is revealed by the fact that the report was made directly to the King rather than the Privy Council, and that it became the basis of the final settlement on 23 November 1668, thereby by-passing the recommendations of the Privy Council retrenchment committee.[12]

The organisation of the extant records is further confirmation that 1667 was a historic turning point in the Treasury's development. As a Public Record official explained in 1842, when he was investigating the mass of Treasury papers, with the advent of the 1667 commission 'a new system began, which hath subsisted, without essential variation, to the present time'[13] – a system that evolved in response to the administrative demands created generally by the exercising of a greater control over revenue and expenditure, and particularly by the extension of the system of Treasury orders registered in course upon the King's ordinary revenues (see below). Sir Philip Warwick, the former secretary to Southampton, had found it necessary to keep only four different types of ledger. With the accession of Sir George Downing – and it is to Downing that we must primarily give the credit for this remarkable rationalisation of Treasury method – there was a proliferation of book-keeping. Distinct registers were kept of every aspect of Treasury business,[14] the most important and successful being that book pre-eminent among Treasury records, the *Journall* kept by Downing 'for registering the brief notes he should take for framing any orders upon or pursuing other their Lordships' directions'.

It was in 1667, then, that the Treasury came of age; the appointment of the 1667 commissioners marked a decisive watershed in Treasury history. This does not, of course, imply that the Treasury had gained complete control over all matters relating to the Crown's revenue and expenditure within a few months of the elevation of the 'rougher hands'. Such a proposition is demonstrably false. The major branches of the revenue were still within the grasp of revenue farmers over whom the Treasury had little direct control once the initial bargain had been struck – contracts could be revoked, but the actual process of money collection remained, for the time being, outside Treasury hands (see p. 1). On the expenditure side it was still within the King's power to dispose of his revenues as he saw fit, the

commissioners being responsible simply for the financial consequences of that decision. Even when the apportionment had been
made, the Treasury's power of supervision was somewhat curtailed
by the effectiveness of their authority. The commissioners might re-
mind the King of the proverb that 'he who will not stoop for a pin will
never be worth a pound',[15] they might repeatedly cajole the departmental treasurers about the necessity of frugality and they might even
appoint their own watchdogs within the departments, but this did not
mean that the King or the departments would not overspend. The
King could never be brought to book for his extravagance, and individual treasurers were only irregularly called to account by the Exchequer. What was established in 1667, therefore, was a new and
unprecedented degree of discipline over the King, Privy Council, Secretaries, Exchequer and spending departments, rather than absolute
or necessarily effective control. Thereafter subsequent assertions of
Treasury authority – notably by Danby (1673–9) and the Treasury
commissioners (1679–84) – were in essence *reassertions* of a position
that had been mapped out in 1667–8.[16]

The second outstanding change in fiscal administration under the
restored monarchy was the abandonment of the system of farming in
three principal branches of the King's revenue – the customs in 1671,
the excise in 1683 and Hearth money a year later – and the closer
supervision of direct taxation. For the three indirect taxes, tax offices,
each with salaried staffs but largely under Treasury control, were
created to supervise direct collection. These central hierarchies of revenue officials were not new. Similar organisations had been established during the previous periods of direct collection, and skeletal
staffs of revenue officers were sometimes maintained even when the
taxes were being farmed. Therefore the new Customs Office, rebuilt
after the Fire by Sir Christopher Wren, as well as the Excise and
Hearth-money Offices of 1683–4 – consisting essentially of a central
board of control (in the case of the customs and excise), receiver-
generals to manage receipts, comptrollers for certifying accounts,
other officials to impress the will of the central office upon the localities, secretarial and domestic staffs and local collecting officers[17] –
were based on structures that already existed in part. Both the Customs and Excise commissioners leaned heavily on the existing organisation of the farmers in the localities; in the Excise Office a degree of
central supervision had been maintained throughout the period of
farming, so that the 1683 establishment was based on the personnel of

the head office that had been built up since the Restoration; and the Hearth-money Commission of 1684 was based on and amalgamated with that of the Excise, although a distinct central organisation was created to administer the tax.

The point to establish is not the novelty of these tax offices but their permanence. Once it had been finally resolved to abandon tax farming, the essential superstructure of these offices remained unaltered for the greater part of the eighteenth centuty.[18] As Professor Edward Hughes has insisted, the significance of these fiscal changes under Charles II was that 'the work was never gone back upon'.[19] The decision to abandon the farming out of the customs, excise and Hearth-money taxes did not represent a conscious policy decision to improve revenue yield, but rather was a consequence of the failure of the farming system at a time of financial crisis. In 1671, for example, the move was made to administer the customs directly only at the last minute, after attempts to find suitable alternative methods of collection had failed. Similarly excise farming was abandoned in 1683, firstly because of the growing friction between the existing farmers and the responsible officials over such questions as defalcations and 'running cash'; and secondly because in a period of credit shortage no financial group was capable of making a sufficiently attractive proposition to ensure the continuance of the farm.[20]

Nevertheless, once the idea of farming had been dispensed with, the revenue yields were sufficiently attractive to ensure the continuance of direct collection. For the consequence of abandoning the farming of the customs, excise and Hearth-money – as distinct from the reasons for their abandonment – was increased administrative efficiency and an upsurge in net returns. In the first full year of the Customs Commissioners' administration (1671–2), for example, there was a net return of £420,000, the highest yield since the Restoration; in the subsequent years of the 1670s the annual average net customs income exceeded this figure and in the 1681–8 period the average net yield was over £550,000 per annum. The figures for the excise and Hearth-money taxes tell a similar story. The gross value of the excise amounted to an average of more than £680,000 per annum in the five years succeeding direct collection (1683–8), compared with an average of about £565,000 per annum in the previous three years under farm (1680–3); and the net yield of the eight Hearth-money collections in the Michaelmas following direct collection (1684) to Lady Day 1688 averaged about £216,000 per annum, which contrasts with a return of approximately £157,000 per annum in the ten previous collections under farm.[21] With all three taxes, customs, excise and Hearth-money, there were several factors at work which may have accounted for the increases of the 1680s – the favourable trade boom, the good harvests and the increase in population and new buildings of those years, for example – but the increased efficiency of the central officers seems to have been at least as equally important as any of them. Whatever the relative merits of each, had the farming of these three major branches of the revenue continued, there must be some great doubt as to whether the Exchequer would have benefited as handsomely.

The machinery for the collection of direct taxes was not quite as sophisticated as that for the ordinary revenue. This was a result of their intermittent use – direct taxation was not a regular form of taxation in this period, twenty-one direct taxes being authorised by Parliament, 1660–88 (the majority of them in the 1660s), compared with the annual grants *post* 1688. It might be expected, therefore, that the administration of direct taxes was not only grossly less efficient than that for the customs, excise and Hearth tax, but also inferior to that in the post-Revolutionary period. Neither of these statements, however, is wholly true. For the post-Revolutionary direct tax office had its counterpart in Charles II's reign, and this appears to have had a significant influence on the efficiency of direct tax collection. As early as the summer of 1665, agents for taxes were appointed to supervise the collection of the new rates on land voted to meet the emergency of the Dutch wars. They soon decreed that the large sums produced by the Royal and Additional Aids should be transported to London *in specie* 'in His Majesty's own carriages and under good guards', in order to mitigate 'the want of returns by bill of exchange'. From this rudimentary beginning an Exchange Office was established in the summer of 1667 to organise a system for the return of tax receipts by bills of exchange instead of *in specie*, an incidental effect of this being to restrict the freedom of the local Receivers-General and bring them more directly under central Treasury control. The office was retrenched in 1670, but thereafter similar organisations were intermittently reconstituted to administer the 1671 Subsidy and the Assessments of 1673 and 1677. Thereafter a skeleton agency was permanently maintained to bring in the arrears when there were no current direct taxes to collect. Again it is dangerous simply to equate increase of yield with improved administration. It does seem, however, that the striking increase in both the rate of collection and percentage yield of the 1673 and 1677 Assessments ' 'as due mainly to the increased powers of the Receivers-General, and their use under firm royal direction.[22]

The third important fiscal development – the creation of the system of loans upon 'credit Orders repayable in course' – was one of the most significant legacies of this period. The credit order was devised by Downing and, with the backing of Coventry and Arlington, first introduced in the Additional Aid, passed in October 1665. This was a remedy for the severe credit shortages caused by the limitations of the anticipation tally, which had been over-extended beyond the yield of the Royal Aid of that year, and the confusion resulting from the unwillingness of moneyed interests to lend to the Crown at a time when the Plague created uncertainty in credit operations. The Additional Aid's key appropriation and borrowing clauses may be outlined, for they were to become the standard devices of post-Revolutionary financial measures: the tax, appropriated solely for the purposes of war, was to be paid directly into the Exchequer, without diversion; registers, open to public inspection, were to record the receipts and issues of money and the listing of payments 'in course' (in strict rotation according to receipt of loan); and three distinct kinds of negotiable credit were created – Treasury Orders (promises-to-pay when the tax was collected) allocating funds to departmental officials for ordinary cash issues, Orders to tradesmen for the repayment of goods supplied for the war and Orders for the repayment of cash loans at a parliamentary guaranteed interest rate of six per cent.[23]

It was intended that the new clauses should break the monopoly of the goldsmith-bankers as government lenders, and be sufficient inducement to attract ordinary citizens to advance money, now that there was a firm parliamentary promise that repayment would be made without hint of favouritism. The measure was not as successful as had been hoped, as the time was unpropitious for the raising of any kind of credit. In addition strong opposition manifested itself in the persons of both Clarendon, who saw the Act as an invasion of the King's prerogative of discretion, as smacking of republicanism and as likely to ruin his influence with the bankers, and Treasurer Southampton, who ignored its provisions. Nevertheless, by dint of widespread canvassing, Downing succeeded in raising nearly £200,000 in loans, and the principle was applied to the remaining parliamentary grants for the war; in 1667–8 it was extended to the major branches of ordinary revenue. It was this extension, however, that was the main cause of the breakdown of the system. The issues of fiduciary Orders to departmental treasurers as a form of paper money was only kept in check by the fact that they were tied to a specific parliamentary fund – Orders could not be issued in excess of that fund. After 1667–8, however, there was no limit to the extent of their use, and fiduciary Orders were issued with abandon, beyond the monetary base of the system.

As the Treasury commissioners so clearly saw in their report to the King of 20 October 1668, the royal revenues were quite unsuitable for large-scale credit operations: ' . . . the great anticipation under a devouring interest lying upon the Excise and Customs . . . subjects your Majesty's occasions to the will of others, whilst your Majesty is to depend upon loans'. The loans, however, became increasingly difficult to obtain – the bankers found it more profitable to purchase Orders rather than lend to the King – and the inevitable result was the 'Stop of the Exchequer' of 5 January 1672, when repayments and interest on the 'unalterable course' of Treasury Orders were suspended because of the dead weight of outstanding orders, amounting to over £1,000,000 on the ordinary revenue. The Stop did not, however, quite result in the 'death blow' of the system as W. A. Shaw claimed. The Orders credited on the unimpeachable source of the direct taxes continued to be honoured, and appropriation and borrowing clauses were applied to all the subsequent direct taxes of the period, with the exception of the eighteen months' Assessment of 1673. The credit order system as applied in this limited fashion, therefore, continued throughout the period, survived the Revolution and linked the fiduciary Order of 1667–72 with the similar Exchequer Bill of 1696, which was to become the standard financial instrument after 1688.[24]

The financial developments of the Restoration period were thus crucial to the Revolutionary epoch. The fundamental prerequisite was the consolidation of the Treasury's power. Once this had been established it was possible to instigate a system of direct collection of the major branches of the revenue, and to develop a credit instrument that – while not being immediately successful – was to have immense consequences for the future. When these reforms are considered together, and in relation to such fiscal expedients as the experiments in percentage taxation in the Poll taxes and 1671 Subsidy, and the attempts to fund the post Stop debt, the relevance of the title 'financial revolution' to the period after 1688 may well be questioned.[25] For most of the essential features of this 'financial revolution' – the notion of a

National Bank (the Exchequer rather than a private institution), the securing of Treasury supremacy and the institution of a modern system of debt management – had been attempted, with greater or lesser success, prior to the invitation to William of Orange. It was the wars against the Dutch rather than those against the French that were instrumental in creating the conditions for fiscal change in the late seventeenth century.

II

The Clarendonian theory of financial control – reliance on a lord treasurer and an exclusive group of bankers over whom the monarch might exercise discretionary powers – had its counterpart in the Clarendonian theory of government by Privy Council. Clarendon believed in entrusting administration to a sworn body of privy councillors, who might protect the King's prerogative by resisting the undue encroachments of both Parliament and favourites. Such councillors were to be a select band of men, chosen by the King, who would add dignity to the proceedings of royal government. This sacred institution, according to Clarendon, 'hath the greatest authority in the government next the person of the King himself, to whom all other powers are equally subject'. Through the presence of the great officers of state, the Council would be in touch with all aspects of government and would bind them into a single administrative unit.[26] This ideal, however, was never fulfilled. Even under Charles I, the full Privy Council did not possess these exclusive powers – by the 1620s policy decisions were referred to a small inner ring of councillors, and as the Council became larger both standing and *ad hoc* committees were formed as adjuncts to the main Council.[27] This process was to continue in the period after 1660.

There is little doubt that a select group of courtiers was at hand in the late seventeenth century to advise the King: contemporaries certainly acknowledged the existence of a 'cabinet council',[28] which the King consulted over important matters of policy. It is equally probable that this body was derived from the Privy Council, that it was composed, as Roger North observed, of 'those few great officers and courtiers whom the King relied on for the interior dispatch of his affairs', and that it began to have formal meetings – usually on a Sunday at Windsor or in the senior Secretary's office at Whitehall – in this period if not before.[29] It is more difficult, however, to trace the evolution of this select group of advisers, and even if we accept the argument that at least two Privy Council standing committees – the 1668 Committee for Foreign Affairs, and the 1679 Committee of Intelligence 'for the opening and considering all advices as well foreign and domestic' and the Committee of Foreign Affairs which evolved from that body[30] – were rudimentary Cabinets, the use of the word 'cabinet' should be strictly qualified. As Professor Godfrey Davies has conceded, 'there was no formally recognised chief or prime minister, there was certainly no unanimity, and there was no definite principle on which members were selected beyond the recognition, in practice at least, that certain office-holders ought to be included'. Still less was there any connection between the 'cabinet council' and dominant opinion in the House of Commons.

It serves little purpose to relate the Restoration 'cabinet council' with these later developments. Indeed, Professor Plumb has reminded us that the attempts of Turner and others to describe a coherent system of cabinet government over several reigns has caused the utmost confusion. Even the post-Revolutionary cabinet councils were markedly different from those of this period, for they were formed to deal with such specific emergencies as the King's absence from England, they had little overt connection with the Privy Council and a much closer relationship with Parliament and they met with regularity from 1695 onwards.[31] Prior to 1688, however, cabinets were not of such decisive importance in policy-making – it was not a continuing force in government, and both Charles II and James II could and did ignore its advice when it met. Charles II mistrusted the 1679 Committee of Intelligence, when Shaftesbury was a member, and it is doubtful whether he was much influenced by its advice even after Shaftesbury's fall; under James II the Cabinet was virtually in eclipse, that monarch preferring to take important decisions in a camerilla with no formal status, consisting of himself, Sunderland and Roman Catholic advisers like the Jesuit, Edward Petre and Lords Arundel and Powis. The cabinet council may have become, in the words of Roger North, 'a formal council', but it certainly did not have 'the direction of most transactions of the government' throughout the period.

Other standing committees, quite apart from the committee of foreign affairs or 'cabinet council', were also formed in this period. Although they had less influence than the 'cabinet council' – the jurisdiction of which extended to both 'foreign affairs' and those

'concerning the temper of the kingdom', which matters were discussed (and sometimes decided) before being considered by the Privy
Council as a whole – they certainly relieved the main Council of
numerous administrative duties. And in the long run this was to have
a more decisive effect on the Privy Council's power. There were two
key reforms of these standing committees in this period. In 1668 the
standing committees that had been established at the Restoration
were reorganised, the King 'reflecting that his councils would have
more reputation if they were put into a more settled and established
course'. Four committees were appointed – for Foreign Affairs 'as is
already settled' (the Cabinet Council); Naval and Military Affairs 'so
far as they are fit to be brought to the Council Board without inter-
meddling in what concerns the proper officers'; Trade and Plantations; and Petitions, together with 'regular days and places for their
assembling'. Eleven years later these committees were retrenched and
four others were nominated in their stead – for Intelligence (as we
have seen), Ireland, Tangier and Trade and Plantations. It is in these
later years of Charles II's reign that the standing committees were
most active. Thereafter, however, they tended to wane.

James II ordered that all the standing committees of the Privy
Council should be revived, although it is probable that before the end
of the period committees of the whole council began to take over their
functions, because of the failure of attendance at the individual standing committees, each of which tended to be dominated by the same
privy councillors. This same tendency may be seen in the special *ad hoc*
committees – usually temporary bodies, appointed to deal with specific problems. In the 1660s such committees were frequently appointed, over seventy having been established (1660–8). From 1679–85,
however, nineteen were nominated, and James II appointed only five
in the four years of his reign, problems formerly being dealt with by an
ad hoc committee increasingly being referred to a committee of the
whole council.[32]

Despite the fact that the influence and activities of Privy Council
committees – of all types – decreased in James II's reign, for the major
part of the period they were a constant factor in government. It is
therefore pertinent to ask how far had they limited the scope and
power of the Privy Council by the time of the Revolution, and, more
importantly, to what extent had that institution declined as the hub of
the King's administration?[33]

The consideration of affairs in Cabinet Council prior to their

coming before the full Privy Council was bound to have limited the
Privy Council's power – the presence of the sovereign and the important office-holders at these meetings made it possible for their
decisions to be put into effect immediately without the intervention of
the Privy Council. It should not be assumed, however, that the Privy
Council was completely superseded by the Cabinet Council in this
period. If we understand the Committee of Intelligence to be an inci-
pient Cabinet in this period, the register of the meetings of that committee shows that the initiative for some of its actions came from the
King in Council, and that many of its decisions were referred to its
parent body, which was meeting more frequently than the Intelligence Committee in the 1679–81 period.

The lack of other formal Cabinet records for the period makes it difficult to determine whether the Privy Council came under the dominance of the Cabinet Council at other times. Nevertheless it appears
that it was not until after the Revolution that the Privy Council was
more strictly subordinated to the Cabinet's will. In this period it was
the other committees that presented a more real threat to the Privy
Council, because they were more exclusively concerned with administration, and it was the gradual accumulation of administrative functions of government outside the confines of the Privy Council that was
ultimately to sap its strength. Many important questions were certainly taken out of the hands of the Council by the *ad hoc* committees –
in 1679–86, for example, numerous committees were appointed to deal
with such matters as the Popish Plot and the reviewing of commissions of the Peace – and a considerable amount of the work of the
Privy Council was done in standing committees; this trend was not
reversed by the merging of these committees into a committee of the
whole Council. Nevertheless it is important not to exaggerate the
independence of these committees. Committees were summoned by
order of the Lord President of the Privy Council (or the Secretary of
State); when any alteration was made to their composition it was signified in Council, and no important paper could be referred without
its being at first read at the Privy Council, with the exception of matters relating to the Foreign Affairs Committees. The committees,
therefore, were responsible for much of the day-to-day work of the
Privy Council, but the majority of them had a limited authority of
their own and could be over-ruled by the senior body.

The extent of the Privy Council's decline, therefore, should not be
over-emphasised. In this period it was certainly not an all-embracing

council of control, as Clarendon had wished it to be. Its influence in foreign affairs was negligible in this period, the Council simply being used as a formal means of approval for the King's policies, and, as we have seen, it had little control over financial matters. In both spheres the power of the Privy Council declined in this period: the effectiveness of the Privy Council's action over the sale of Dunkirk in 1662, for example, may be compared with its total lack of influence over the 1683 evacuation of Tangier; and the activities – albeit futile – of the 1667 Privy Council Retrenchment Committee may be contrasted with the few, inconsequential orders relating to financial matters in the later Privy Council registers. There was, therefore, a decrease in the amount of foreign and financial business coming before the Privy Council. None the less the Privy Council remained important for several reasons. Firstly, the Council was an ideal place for the Crown to gain support for any given policy: the majority of the councillors were loyalists, and it was a wealthy and influential assembly. As Turner has written 'in respect of this formal sanction the Privy Council was never superseded and its work was indispensable'.[34] Secondly, the Council was, in Ogg's words, 'the central clearing house of the administration',[35] responsible not only for compartmentalising government business, but also for conducting a good deal of administration on its own account. It is necessary to take only a glance at the Privy Council registers in order to appreciate the amount of administrative work with which the Council was concerned – orders for the raising of troops, proclamations prohibiting the export of iron ordnance and circular letters to the lords lieutenant enjoining strict enforcement of the Corporation Act, were all within its purview. Finally, the Council was of vital importance at a time of supreme national crisis, as in the Interregnum of 1688, when the Privy Council helped preserve the public peace (11–21 December), between the flight of James II and the meeting of the House of Lords.

Against the wishes, then, of both Clarendon and (for very different reasons) Shaftesbury and his supporters in Parliament – who in 1679 successfully pressurised the King into streamlining the Privy Council in an attempt to make it an effective instrument of government[36] – both Charles II and James II failed to use the Privy Council as a policy-making body. Charles, as Clarendon suggested, had 'rather esteemed some particular members of it than was inclined to believe that the body of it ought to receive a reverence from the people or be looked upon as a vital part of the government',[37] and James went

outside its select ranks for counsel. By the end of the period it had
even given up the pretence of having a part to play in policy, and
bills were no longer read in Council before the King passed them, at
which, Edward Southwell reported, 'the Privy Council were glad . . .
because it might not seem to lie on them the advising not to pass any
bill'.[38] Notwithstanding this evasion of responsibility, its role in
government should not be ignored, even though it was slowly losing
ground in policy-making to the Cabinet and in executive action to the
Secretaries and developing departments of state.

III

The increase in the scope of the Secretaries of State, on the French
model, was also a move away from Clarendon's ideal scheme of
government, for it meant a further limitation of the Privy Council's
jurisdiction. The Secretaries were becoming both more influential
within the Council and more independent of it. By 1660, if not before,
the Secretary of State was as important in the running of the Council
as the Lord President – an office which had been in abeyance
(1660–79) – and could perform all his important functions, including
those of summoning, presiding and vote-taking.[39] In the counsels of
the state, however, the Secretaries were becoming more important
than the Lord President, because of the increase in their discretionary
powers and their standing on the numerous Privy Council committees. Their discretionary powers are clearly illustrated in Secretary Jenkins's letter to Earl Conway of 5 October 1681, when Sir
Leoline refers to a Privy Council debate over the propriety of selling
Prince Rupert's new cannon invention to France:

> My Lord Privy Seal . . . was pleased to fall upon the Secretaries of
> State for that they did not communicate to the Council those mat-
> ters of importance that the peace of the Kingdoms and the repose of
> Christendom did depend upon . . . . Thereupon I took the liberty
> to assert that it was the duty of the Secretaries so to manage those
> correspondencies that his Majesty should direct, that he should
> have a constant and punctual account of it, but that they were not
> at liberty to carry any part of their intelligencies to the Council
> unless his Majesty directed it specially so to be done; that I for my
> part had always governed myself by that rule because I thought it a
> duty that lay indispensably upon me. My Lord was pleased to reply

that Mr. Secretary's answer was such an answer as never was offered by a Secretary to a Privy Council before; however, that he could not find fault with the answer for it was constant to the practice of later years.[40]

Morever, in many Privy Council committees – certain of which actually sat in one of the Secretaries' offices – their presence was indispensable. One or other of the two Secretaries were on forty-three of the fifty-four committees appointed (1660–64); the Secretaries were a vital force in colonial committees of this period; and they were *ex officio* members, forming with the Lords President and Keeper one of the quorum of three, of the 1668 and 1679 standing committees. So the Secretaries could be influential in the cabinet councils, as well as the administrative bodies of the time. Indeed this could scarcely be otherwise because of their control of intelligence and the extent of their knowledge of foreign and domestic state business.[41]

Ultimately, however, the Secretaries' position depended on their intimacy with the King. There were certainly dominant Secretaries in this period like Arlington (1662–74) and Sunderland (1679–80, 1683–8). But their power did not depend on their office – which indeed could be a positive handicap as it was to Sunderland in 1683 when, although politically of much greater importance than his colleague, Jenkins, he was the subordinate Secretary for more than a year because of the convention that the sitting Secretary should be promoted to the senior Southern department whenever a new appointment was made – but on their relationship with the King. Their power may be contrasted with that of Trevor, Williamson and Coventry, who had little influence on policy.[42] The Secretaries' importance *vis-à-vis* the Privy Council was increasing, their work-load was multiplying, their office was gradually acquiring a more public character – in terms of the establishment of salaries, continuity of tenure and business organisation[43] – but Secretaries were still dependent on the King's pleasure, as Sunderland found to his cost in December 1680, when he was dismissed for voting in favour of Exclusion.

The development of the Secretaryships of State was paralleled by the growth in importance of the offices of Secretary at War and Secretary to the Admiralty: although the advance of these two offices was much more rapid than that of the older-established Secretaries of State, they never entirely lost their personal character in this period. Nevertheless the Secretary at War was certainly emerging from being the mere personal assistant to the chief of the forces, to an extremely important military executive officer, with direct control over recruitment, the granting of leave, the provision of quarters and the issue of clothing. One of the key instruments of this transmutation was the warrant issued on 27 September 1676 which gave the Secretary authority over appointments, convoys and quartering. This warrant also changed his status from a military to a civil officer by making him answerable to the King rather than the commander of the forces. Another reason for the Secretary's advance was the long tenure in office from 1683 to 1704 of William Blathwayt, who before the period was out had begun to build up an office independent from that of the Secretary of State's staff, although the Secretaries of State still transacted much military business.[44] The evolution of the place of Secretary to the Admiralty was closely related to the emergence of the office as Secretary at War. The title, Secretary to the Admiralty, only appeared at the Restoration and, like the position of the early Secretaries at War, the earliest occupants of the post of Secretary to the Admiralty – Sir William Coventry, Matthew Wren and Sir John Werdon – were personal secretaries rather than Crown servants. Pepys's career as Secretary to the Admiralty (1673–79, 1684–88), like Blathwayt's service at the War Office, did much to establish the departmental nature of the post, its public character being confirmed when Pepys was appointed by letters patent in 1684. The three great advances made during Pepys's tenure of office – the regulation of business, the classification of records and the accommodation of a permanent staff – ensured that there was a stable organisation to initiate and co-ordinate naval affairs. Indeed Pepys's influence was such that he often acted as a third Secretary of State.[45]

The war departments of state were beginning to acquire a more disciplined organisation. In the Navy Board and Ordnance Office – responsible for the servicing and gunning of ships and the military forces, rather than the higher reaches of administration – detailed instructions were instituted, settling the duties of each officer. Neither set of instructions was completely original, but they were a marked improvement on those that had been issued previously, although the excessive system of checks and balances written into each meant that they did not necessarily improve performance. Both departments, too, were acquiring more specialised functions. The Armoury and Tents and Toils Offices were amalgamated with the Ordnance Office in 1670 and 1685, and in 1683 a naval sub-department for victualling was established under the direct control of the Navy Board.[46]

Closely allied to these developments was the growth of organs of government with jurisdiction over trade and plantations and the increase in England's diplomatic and consular representation abroad. The Restoration period, with the 1660 Navigation Act, the establishment of Carolina, the capture of New York, the acquisition of Tangier (until 1683) and Bombay, the attempt to create a dominion of New England, and the reorganisation of the East India Company and the founding of the Hudson Bay and Guinea Companies, was a formative one in the emergence of the English colonial system. From 1660 to 1672 two separate councils with parallel functions, the one dealing with trade, the other with plantations, were established to administer this growing colonial Empire. Thereafter the business of trade and plantations was fused and administered by one body, from 1672–5 by a separate council and from 1675 by a Privy Council committee. The Privy Council had a degree of control over trade and plantation affairs for the whole of the period through the committee of the Council for Foreign Plantations, established 4 July 1660 and continuing in existence as a consultative body alongside the other councils until 1675, when it was reconstituted as the ruling body. But the real work of colonial administration was conducted outside the formal Privy Council, especially by the end of the period when all questions relating to trade and plantations were automatically referred to the relevant committee. The 1675 committee of trade and plantations was essentially an independent body, the forerunner of the autonomous Board of Trade and Plantations, established in 1696.[47] The cost of the diplomatic and consular services doubled in this period although as far as the former is concerned it is doubtful whether Charles or the country got value for money. The consular service, however, took on a more national character, rather than being simply an agency of the trading companies or groups of influential merchants, appointments to over thirty different consulates being made in Charles II's reign.[48]

As important as these institutional changes were the crucial adjustments made to the character of government in Restoration England. Many of the conditions of a modern civil service, which had been tried out in the Commonwealth and Protectorate period, were gradually instituted after the Restoration. In a few offices – those of the Secretary to the Admiralty and the Treasurer of the Ordnance, for example – salaries from the public funds were replacing fees, thereby freeing officials from dependence on any particular type of business and making them more aware of their general responsibilities. The abolition of fees probably only occurred in isolated instances and there was by no means a complete reform of the fee system. Indeed, in some departments like the Exchequer and Secretaries of State's Offices, the payment of fees was to remain an established practice throughout the following century.[49] In any case, with the inadequate resources at the government's disposal, complete abolition across the board would have been impossible – the Crown could not possibly have afforded to have paid realistic salaries as compensation, and many doubted the efficacy of a reform of a practice which in the short run saved the Crown an enormous amount of expense, and was not necessarily a bar to administrative efficiency.[50] Others like James II, however, believed that the payment of a good salary would make officials 'value their employments and not subject them to a necessity of base compliances with others to the King's prejudice, by which to get one shilling to himself he must lose ten to the King'.[51] And there is certainly evidence that attractive salaries were paid in many public offices – by the end of the period all the great officers of state had an annual income well in excess of £1,000 and a senior departmental official could aspire to a salary of several hundred pounds[52] – which may have had the effect of limiting excessive fee-taking.

There was a more radical overhaul of the tenures of patent offices in this period.[53] An analysis of office-holding during Charles II's reign shows that steps were taken during the period in office of the Treasury Commissioners (1668–72), to alter the tenures of officers from life to 'during pleasure' (*durante bene placito*), and to limit the granting of reversionary interests. Under the Treasurership of Danby there was a return – for reasons that were entirely political – to the old practice of granting life and reversionary interests, but this was abandoned during the Treasury Commission of 1679–85. Such reforms were restricted to those officers who were paid directly by the Exchequer, and no attempt was made to alter life tenures in Chancery, although even here there was a noticeable decline in the issue of reversions at this time. Nevertheless this did mean that the reform was carried through in a number of departments – in the Ordnance, the Mint, the Works, the Privy Council staff and certain branches of the Household. And even in the Exchequer, that doggedly antiquarian department where certain offices were virtually hereditary, tenures during pleasure were introduced, although unlike most of the other departments they did not remain a permanent feature.

The consequences of these reforms were immense. Life tenure circumscribed the Crown's freedom of choice, for like tenure 'during good behaviour' (*quamdiu se bene gesserint*), it was made explicitly binding on the monarch making the grant and on all his successors. It therefore made it extremely difficult, although not impossible, for the Crown to dismiss an incompetent servant or one of 'dubious' religious faith. Tenure during pleasure, on the other hand, enabled the Crown to terminate an interest at will without proof of misconduct. This type of tenure, moreover, was in no way binding on future monarchs, enabling a review of the administration to be made at the beginning of each new reign. An official's personal stake in his office was thereby lessened, and he could not legitimately reason that his proprietorial rights were being invaded if he was displaced, as the life tenant Sir Edward Sherburne claimed after his dismissal as Clerk of the Ordnance in 1688 because of his Roman Catholic faith.[54]

The gradual demise in the tradition that certain offices were a form of property may have resulted in a decline in the selling of offices, which became less valuable and marketable commodities once they could be held only during pleasure. Certainly, in two of the offices where tenures were successfully changed – the Ordnance and the Privy Council Offices – there was a marked decline in sales of offices as the period progressed.[55] If certain offices, moreover, were no longer valued as property, there was no excuse for the outgoing office-holders to take their clerks with them once they left office. Indeed to compensate for the growing insecurity of tenure among the senior officials, who were increasingly susceptible to political dismissals, there was a positive need for their subordinates to remain at their posts to preserve a continuity of expertise in government. The growth in security of tenure for all clerks, except those against whom misbehaviour could be proved, enabled a defined system of promotion to develop among the clerical establishment in a wide range of departments.

Accompanying these changes was the emergence of a new type of administrator whose solution to problems was based on a rational judgement from a compilation of available evidence. Pepys is the most famous example of a royal official who adopted a more rational stance in the face of the practical problems of government, but he is by no means an isolated figure. Sir Christopher Wren, Charles Davenant and William Lowndes are three Restoration administrators who were imbued with scientific ideas, and there were many others. This more intellectual and systematic approach to administration, based as it was on admiration for the French model, and on current ideas of political arithmetic and natural philosophy, must inevitably have had a beneficial effect on governmental efficiency.[56]

IV

The extent of these developments should not be over-estimated. The modern professional civil service as we know it today is a product of the nineteenth rather than the late seventeenth century. In this period there was little concerted attempt to end the appointment of deputies or pluralists; sinecures were prevalent; appointments were not made on merit alone; there was no systematic pensions scheme; there was no clear distinction between public and private credit, and inadequate supervision of the lower reaches of administration resulted in many office-holders taking undue profits at the Crown's expense; departmental records were in many cases looked upon as private property; and a cumbersome system of administrative co-ordination led to inefficiencies as the disastrous mobilisation of James's fleet in 1688 proved. The administration still retained many Household characteristics. It was small – the Treasury's permanent domestic and clerical staff in the 1680s numbered less than twenty, and many important departments, like the Admiralty, could still be housed in private dwellings; it was part-time – the Privy Council meetings in James II's reign, for example, averaged less than one a week; it was peripatetic – the King's Court, and, therefore, the Privy Council, 'cabinet-councils' and decision-making bodies, perambulated regularly between Whitehall, Hampton Court, Windsor and Oxford. Administrative efficiency still depended to a large extent on the King's personal involvement – he still took an active part in meetings of the Privy Council and its committees, and the Treasury; he was responsible for summoning and presiding over the cabinet-council; and he had personal control over the appointment of his senior office-holders.

Nevertheless the King's government did not remain static in Restoration England. Indeed, as we have seen, it was a period of dynamic changes. These changes were not completed until comparatively modern times, but they were of fundamental importance to the health of the body politic, for few of them were reversed. They underpinned the 1688 Revolution, and although they were extended under William III and Anne, the later developments – in finance, in Cabinet and departmental government and in rational administration – owed a great deal to the advances of this period. If there was an administrative revolution under the Stuarts, its origins are as likely to be found in Restoration as in Revolutionary England.

5. Restoration England and Europe

J. L. PRICE

I

FOR a brief moment under Cromwell England had emerged from its insular self-absorption to play with conviction the role of a major power in Europe, yet during the Restoration period it failed to do so with any consistency and, indeed, for much of this time either subordinated its foreign policy to that of France, or retreated once again into an almost exclusive concentration on its internal political problems. The reasons for this relative impotence lie partly, of course, in the endemic political instability which the rest of Europe had come to regard as characteristic of the country, though conversely the very nature of the foreign policies of Charles II and James II served to a certain extent to exacerbate these internal difficulties. There were, however, other problems which help to explain the failure of English governments during this period to develop a clear and consistent foreign policy. In particular, for many years after 1660 the situation in Europe was difficult to assess, and it was thus not easy to determine what policies might best serve England's interests. On another level, what these interests were was far from indisputable, nor was it as yet clear in what sense the King's foreign policy should serve them.

After the Peace of Westphalia in 1648 the old pattern of international alignments, which had opposed the Spanish and Austrian Habsburgs together with their predominantly Catholic allies against France, the Dutch Republic and their chiefly Protestant allies, was beginning to break up, and it was to be thirty or forty years before a new and stable pattern was to emerge clearly, which would set the resurgent power of France, together with a few Catholic allies, against a European coalition led by the Emperor, the Dutch Republic and, belatedly, England. In between came a period of uncertainty during which the increasingly apparent decline of Spain, the equally apparent emergence of French power and the last great surge of Ottoman aggression set a series of problems for European statesmen. It was difficult for many years to assess the relative powers of the various states, and consequently alliances and alignments were tentative, as those in control of foreign policy explored a changing and uncertain situation.

The extent of Spanish weakness was at first not clear, and traditional anti-Habsburg attitudes did not disappear overnight. Cromwell and his advisers in 1654 still saw Spain as '. . . the greatest enemy to the Protestant in the world, and a nation of great council, and harder to be dispossessed of any accesse of greatness',[1] and their later alliance with France against Spain was an expression of this already anachronistic view. In fact it was Spanish weakness, not strength, which was to set some of the major European problems after 1660. The case of the Austrian Habsburgs was less clear. Although in retrospect it is evident that 1648 also marked the end of Habsburg hopes of increasing the power of the Emperor in the Holy Roman Empire, this was not immediately obvious to many German princes, and indeed throughout this period Austrian power remained difficult to assess.

It has been argued that even Louis XIV and his advisers, aggressive and self-confident as they were, feared Habsburg revenge initially at least.[2] Both the French border with the Southern Netherlands, so uncomfortably close to Paris, and that with the Empire seemed vulnerable to attack, and as far as the latter was concerned it could only be the Emperor that they feared. Yet the situation seemed very different from Vienna. Leopold I and his ministers were much too conscious of the number and variety of the menaces to the Austrian lands to consider aggressive action seriously. In the 1660s Sweden could still be regarded as the arch-enemy, well-placed to threaten Silesia and Bohemia from its base in Western Pomerania. Poland too was a constant cause for concern, susceptible as its court and nobility were to French influence. Moreover, although absolutism had been firmly enforced on most of the Austrian lands, in Habsburg Hungary this process was only beginning, and the concern of the nobility for their privileges combined with the Hungarian Protestants' fears of persecution to make unrest almost endemic throughout the 1660s and 70s. Looming largest of all, however, and a constant restriction of Austrian freedom of action, was the Ottoman threat. After a long period of quiescence, the Ottoman Empire had begun its last great attack on Christian Europe with its invasion of Crete in 1645. The war of 1661–4 with the Turks was a reminder that Leopold hardly needed of the danger of becoming too involved in Western Europe when he had so dangerous an enemy in his rear.

As early as 1640, the Austrian diplomat, Lisola (perhaps significantly a native of Franche-Comté which bordered on France), had singled out France as the main enemy of the balance of power in Europe,[3] but it was long before this point became self-evident, particularly as the Fronde revived the belief that France was likely to be kept weak by 'intestine divisions'.[4] However, in the 1660s it rapidly became clear that the French monarchy had eliminated all effective challenge to its authority, and that France was taking over from the Habsburgs as the greatest power in Europe. This dramatic change in power relationships led to some rapid reassessments. As early as 1663 Frederick William, the Elector of Brandenburg, reacted angrily to evidence of French overbearance with the characteristic, if hardly seriously meant, statement: 'Rather live under the protection of the Turks than in servitude to France',[5] where the choice of the word servitude seems particularly significant. By 1667 the English ambassador in Brussels, Sir William Temple, had become deeply concerned by the military power of France, and his assessment of possible developments was alarming if not alarmist:

> For if the French shall carry Flanders, as they very well may in another campaign, by the weakness and disorders in the government here (Brussels); the Dutch are sensible that they must fall to be a maritime province of France, upon the best terms they can. The Empire will expect to see them soon at the Rhine, and thereby masters of four electors; and what a condition England will be left in by such an accession of maritime forces, as well as provinces, to such a power as France is already, is but too easy and too melancholy a reflection.[6]

However such an extreme view was far from universal in the 1660s, and it took a series of aggressive moves by the French – most dramatically the attack on the Dutch Republic in 1672 – to convince the governments of Europe of the magnitude of the problem posed by France.

Similarly, in the Dutch Republic the *raadpensionaris*, Johan de Witt, was faced with the difficult task of rethinking his ideas on the European situation. While in the 1650s he had still seen Europe in terms of two rival blocs – Habsburg against Franco-English – in the following decade he had to discount Spain as a significant force, and also became sceptical about the ability of the Austrian Habsburgs to intervene effectively in Western Europe, particularly when they were at war with the Ottomans as they were in the early 1660s.[7] This near-elimination of the Habsburgs left, in effect, France and England to be considered, and both set the Dutch major problems. As the leading economic power in Europe, the Dutch were the object of an English resentment which had already led to war in the 1650s, and was likely to continue to make relations between the two powers problematical.[8] On the other hand, France was both a political and an economic threat to the Dutch Republic. If the French, as was now clearly their aim, were able to acquire by war or diplomacy the Spanish Netherlands, then they would become not only an uncomfortably powerful neighbour but also a danger to Dutch prosperity. If France gained Antwerp it was hardly conceivable that the Dutch blockade of the Scheldt could be maintained, and that city might rise again as a direct rival to Amsterdam and London. That the French government was indeed jealous of Dutch economic success was underlined by the tariffs of 1667, aimed specifically at Dutch trade. The Dutch dilemma was that they had to oppose French expansion, but could not hope to do so successfully without substantial aid. The obvious source of such aid was England whose interests were also involved in keeping France out of the Southern Netherlands – or so the Dutch thought.

II

In this uncertain European situation England itself was one of the most unpredictable factors. In the first years of the Restoration English foreign policy was subject to wild oscillations: first an aggressive war against the Dutch Republic, then alliance with the Dutch against France, and then an alliance with France against the Dutch. Such instability was seen as characteristic of English policy: in 1668 De Witt remarked acidly to Temple that he did not know for what reasons, 'but since the time of Queen Elizabeth there had been only a continual fluctation in the conduct of England, with which one could not concert measures for two years at a time'.[9] After 1674, on the other hand, England failed to play an active role in Europe, and it was through this inactivity as much as by its earlier aggression that it influenced events in Europe during this period.

Obviously, the inconsistent course of English policy was in part the result of the internal difficulties facing Charles and James. Although Charles enjoyed reasonably good relations with Parliament in the early years of his reign, from about 1674 distrust of his intentions together with financial difficulties made any active foreign policy impracticable, while James concentrated on his domestic policy to such an extent that he seems hardly to have given serious consideration to foreign affairs at all.[10] Moreover, besides the difficulty of assessing the European situation, and thus of determining the proper course of English policy, English governments were hampered throughout this period by a certain insular ignorance of European conditions, and by poor intelligence.

Although Charles, James and many of their advisers had had firsthand experience of Europe during their exile, this knowledge of pre-1660 Europe was not perhaps the best training for a proper appreciation of the problems which were to arise later. Also, in many cases exile seems to have been a school of prejudice rather than understanding. Those ministers who had not shared the trials and experiences of exile were, more often than not, in possession of only an imperfect understanding of conditions outside England. Chosen for their skills in domestic politics, such men as Danby and Sunderland were probably even more taken up by these matters than the sovereigns they served; both showed a distinctly limited comprehension of European realities and both, understandably enough, tended to judge foreign policy by its effects on internal politics rather than by the extent to which it promoted or protected English interests. Danby, for example, although he had been on the conventional tour to France and Italy in his youth, never left England again after his return in November 1650.[11] Despite his high office, his ideas about foreign policy remained 'still very much those of the average country gentleman' and in 1677 Temple found it necessary to point out how anachronistic his proposals for a renewal of the Triple Alliance were.[12] Such misapprehensions seem to have been all too typical of English politicians. Even Secretaries of State came into office ill-informed about European affairs and conditions and it would appear that the quality of the intelligence they received was not such as to counteract this disadvantage.

Perhaps even more serious was the problem of determining what the proper aims of a foreign policy were. Contemporaries of such widely contrasting characters and political orientations as Johan de

Witt and Louis XIV agreed on the proposition that every state had more or less fixed interests:[13] the problem was to decide on what they were. De Witt and Louis can be used as examples of two very contrasting approaches to this problem: the French king could see in the Dutch pursuit of what they considered their vital economic, and particularly mercantile, interests only the influence of self-interested merchant pressure-groups; and the Dutch, De Witt in particular, were inclined to underestimate the personal and dynastic elements in the foreign policies of monarchies. England at this time fell somewhere between these two extremes, and many of the inconsistencies in English policy can be attributed to an uncertain oscillation between the pursuit of English political and economic interests and the more personal policies of the Stuart kings, for the two could not be relied upon to coincide. The distinction between these two elements is made with particular clarity by Temple in his discussion of his reasons for supporting the English attack on the Dutch Republic in 1664: both Court and Parliament, he wrote, 'favoured war . . . and it was not easy to think any should better understand the honour of the Crown than our Court; or the interests of the nation, than the house of Commons'.[14] Such an apparent congruence between the imperatives of 'the honour of the Crown' and 'the interests of the nation' was not to be repeated very often in the years that followed.

Besides the difficulty of agreeing on the proper objectives of foreign policy, there was the problem of finding appropriate means to achieve the ends once they were determined. In particular, contemporary economic thinking was liable to suggest means which we, with the advantage of hindsight and of economic theories which are at least more advanced than those of the seventeenth century, can regard as unlikely to achieve the ends in view. Colbert in France, for example, shared the belief of English ministers that warfare was a proper weapon to use to undermine Dutch economic supremacy in Europe,[15] though quite how trade routes could be conquered remains unclear. Such thinking, however, was instrumental in bringing about the first major English initiative in this period – the Second Anglo-Dutch War.

In the early years of Charles II's reign there was no great urgency about the determination of foreign policy. The English government could afford to bide its time and keep its options open between a pro-French or a pro-Dutch line. France appeared a potentially attractive ally and at this stage seemed to represent no particular threat to

English interests, while the Dutch, although seen as a major block to English economic advance, were certainly not an aggressive power, in military terms, at this time. The rest of Europe could be expected to regard England as a valuable possible ally: the naval successes of the first Anglo-Dutch War had been impressive, and the part played by English troops in the Flanders campaign probably even more so to a Europe which, the Dutch apart, had little understanding of naval power. However, the situation in Europe in the early 1660s put no pressure on the English government to define its position. Apart from the distant war between the Austrian Habsburgs and the Ottoman Empire, the continuing war in Crete, and the last feeble Spanish attempts to prevent the establishment of Portuguese independence, Europe was at peace and only the ill-health of Philip IV of Spain hinted at the possibility of there being serious problems for Europe in the near future.

III

England soon began to create problems for her neighbours, as it was to do for the remainder of our period. The Dutch in particular were sensitive to clear signs of English hostility arising out of economic and colonial disputes, but were perhaps even more disturbed by the difficulty of predicting what the English would do. Already in 1664 De Witt was complaining of difficulty of dealing with the English who '. . . are used to direct their actions at all times not by reason and justice, not even according to their own interest, but only by their caprice or their greed',[16] as he tried to decide whether England was really moving towards war with the Dutch Republic. It is perhaps a significant comment on English policy, that this rational statesman with an exceptionally cool and businesslike appreciation of the international situation misread English intentions, deciding that they did not desire war; but England did continue to put pressure on the Dutch with attacks on Dutch bases on the West African coast, on New Amsterdam, and finally on a Dutch merchant fleet in European waters in January 1665.

The second Anglo-Dutch War is one of the few English attempts at an active European policy in this period, and when considered more than superficially it is a somewhat puzzling one. Certainly Parliament, and particularly the Commons, was putting pressure on Charles to extract trade concessions from the Dutch, and Feiling has argued that the war '. . . sprang from those national antagonisms which defy the most pacific of governments. Feuds and conflicts accumulated for half a century were pressing for solution, and to solve them without recourse to arms would have asked, on either side, a rare magnanimity coupled with absolute power. But magnanimity could not be expected from mercantilism, and both Charles II and de Witt depended for political existence on mercantile support.'[17] However, as Feiling himself says these 'national antagonisms' and 'feuds and conflicts' had been in existence for a long time by 1664 and had only led to war once, and they were no more acute at this time than they had been before. Similarly, after 1674, although such problems continued unabated and with no significant Dutch concessions, war between the two countries was avoided. Moreover, it is far from clear what those in favour of the war hoped to gain that had not already been obtained at the end of the first Dutch war ten years earlier. As Ogg has pointed out, Charles II did not want war, and neither did Clarendon or Southampton; the East India Company was far from convinced that war was the most appropriate way to further its interests though they provided part of the *casus belli*, and the apparently bellicose Downing in The Hague only pushed for the exertion of pressure because of his conviction that the Dutch would make concessions rather than fight.[18] Although there certainly were influential pressure groups who hoped for concrete benefits for themselves, and for perhaps rather less well-defined advantages for their country, from war with the Dutch Republic, perhaps another element in the situation should receive more stress than it does in most accounts – poor and misleading intelligence. English agents insisted that the Dutch would not in the end fight, but would make important concessions to English demands if put under sufficient pressure. In Downing's words: 'Go on in Guinea, if you bang them there they will be very tame.'[19] Yet the evidence was there that the Dutch were prepared to fight if necessary; they had been preparing their naval forces throughout 1664, and had sent a squadron to West Africa in the autumn. Finally they were provoked into declaring war in February 1665.

The second Anglo-Dutch War was an attempt to achieve economic ends by non-economic means. Far from being the logical conclusion to long years of economic and colonial rivalry, it was rather an ill-conceived attempt to compensate for the continued inability of the English economy to compete effectively with the Dutch. Those who believed that Dutch trade could in some sense be conquered were perhaps misled by drawing an analogy with colonial trade: in this sector the conquest of forts and factories, backed up by naval force, could and did lead to the conquest of the trade to certain regions and in certain colonial goods, as indeed the Dutch themselves had amply demonstrated in the East Indies earlier in the century. Such policies were to prove ineffective when the target was the complex and ubiquitious Dutch trading system in Europe itself. The war was a failure not just because England lost (or failed to win), but rather because war was not an appropriate weapon in this particular battle. In the following years, as the English economy strengthened, the pressures from merchant groups for war against the Dutch Republic lessened rapidly, despite the continuation of those rivalries and conflicts which had apparently made war inevitable before.

In the event England gained little if anything from the war, and its most important effect was to present Louis XIV with a favourable opportunity to pursue his claims to parts of the Spanish Netherlands, as the two powers most likely and most able to oppose him were neutralised by being at war with one another. Philip IV of Spain had died in 1665 and Louis laid claim, by right of inheritance through his wife, to territory in the Netherlands. His lawyers provided an armoury of entirely spurious legal arguments to back his claim, but more important was Louis' decision to enforce it by a full-scale invasion of the Spanish Netherlands in the summer of 1667. This French campaign was a disturbing revelation of French power and Spanish weakness. The Spanish forces in the Netherlands were exposed as completely inadequate to put up any effective resistance to the French, and the government in Madrid seemed incapable of action. Only intervention by other powers, it seemed, could check France. Leopold I was in an unenviable situation: although the Dutch and English had made peace at Breda in July 1667, the chance that they would immediately join forces against France seemed remote and Leopold, concerned as always with the possibility of an Ottoman attack and faced with the problem of endemic political and religious unrest in Hungary, was only too aware that he lacked the military strength to face France on his own. Influenced by a powerful group at the Viennese court which was obsessed by its perhaps-exaggerated idea of French power, the Emperor came to an accommodation with France over the division of the Spanish empire if, as was expected, Charles II of Spain should die without children, in the secret partition treaty of January 1668. This allotted to France the Southern Netherlands, Franche Comté, Navarre, Rosas, Naples and Sicily in Europe, as well as the Philippines.

It was the splendid prospects opened up to him by the treaty with the Emperor that induced Louis to agree to moderate terms at Aachen to end the war with Spain.[20] However, in the eyes of most contemporaries it was not this secret treaty but the much trumpeted Triple Alliance which halted France. This alliance also signed in January 1668, initially between England, and the Dutch Republic, later extended to include Sweden, was another of those sudden, dramatic shifts in English foreign policy which Europe had come to expect, and it appeared to have been instrumental in persuading France of the necessity of accepting reasonable terms. This misapprehension about the effect of the Triple Alliance contributed to that, possibly unrealistic, respect for English power which was to be the common property of European statesmen, with the notable exception of the French, for the next twenty years. The terms that Louis XIV accepted were, in fact, based on those he had already proposed the previous September; nevertheless French moderation made a great impression in Europe – it appeared that Louis feared a combination of the two maritime powers.[21]

De Witt had, in fact, been understandably reluctant to exchange friendship with France for such an uncertain ally as England, but Dutch fears of French ambitions in the Southern Netherlands, combined perhaps with the belief that checking the French in this area was so evidently a vital English interest that the alliance would be durable, led the Dutch to accept the English proposals. The next few years were to show that De Witt's fears had been all too justified.

IV

During the decade which followed the shape of European alliances slowly began to become clearer and firmer. The relative moderation of the terms Louis was willing to accept in 1668 did not still the fears which had been aroused by the revelation of French military might in 1667–8. The occupation of the duchy of Lorraine in 1670 was far from reassuring, but there followed the most dramatic event of the period, the French attack on the Dutch Republic in 1672, the near-success of which made apparent the magnitude of the threat posed by France not only to the Dutch and to the Spanish Netherlands, but to the

Empire as well. Whether this was a false impression is another matter; the rapid progress of the French armies in the early summer of that year suggested that Louis XIV really had the military power to match his ambitions.

In this period also an important religious element was brought, or reintroduced, into international relations. To the fear of French political domination were added fears for the future of Protestantism. Increasingly Louis XIV came to be seen as the champion of an aggressive and intolerant Catholicism, and not only because of his treatment of French Protestants. Again the attack on the Dutch Republic was instrumental in giving credibility to such ideas – it was seen not only as a step towards political domination in Western Europe, but also as the first move in a campaign to undermine the position of Protestantism in Europe. The inclusion by the French of freedom of worship for Dutch Catholics in the demands they made on the Dutch in 1672 could only exacerbate such fears. Given the ambiguities of English policies, the Dutch Republic was the foremost Protestant power, and if the Dutch were decisively defeated which state could replace them as Protestant champion? The Elector of Brandenburg certainly saw the Dutch as the bulwark of European Protestantism,[22] and after 1672 religious considerations became increasingly important in the determination of his foreign policy, and he was not alone in thinking this way. After 1672 it was much more difficult than before to ignore the problem which a powerful and aggressive France posed for the rest of Europe, whether as a threat to the independence of neighbouring states or to the security of the Protestant faith.[23]

Yet in this period, when not only governments but also broader sections of educated society, especially in the Dutch Republic and Germany, were becoming increasingly aware of the dangers of France, the English government first allied their country to Louis XIV, and then pursued a policy – if indeed policy is not too positive a term – of neutrality, which was more or less benevolent towards France. Immediately after the signing of the Triple Alliance, Charles II began to negotiate with the French, and by the treaty of Dover in May 1670 agreed to join the French in an attack on the Dutch Republic. Charles's motives for this swift reversal of policy remain, typically, obscure, though the French subsidy which this treaty brought him was obviously a considerable attraction. Also his sympathy for absolute monarchy on the French pattern, while not as marked as that of his brother, must have played a part, as must his sympathy for Catholicism – however muted that was to remain. Moreover the King and the pro-French faction at court led by the Duke of York were either insensitive to or unconcerned by the growing power of France. If French subsidies and the beneficial effects of participation in a successful war against the Dutch could strengthen Charles's position at home and lessen his dependence on Parliament, then from his point of view allowing France to establish itself strongly in the Low Countries was an acceptable price to pay for these political advantages.

In retrospect, the dangers of such a policy to English interests seem almost self-evident: if France had conquered the Dutch Republic could the Spanish Netherlands have avoided the same fate for long, and would not this have been a serious blow to English interests? In defence of Charles's policies, it has been argued that the defeat of the Dutch would have given England unchallenged maritime supremacy, at least in the short term, and that

> The attack on the Dutch, therefore, was . . . a perfectly legitimate development in English policy. Its execution did much to diminish indirectly the menace of Dutch rivalry, and so helped to make possible the great commercial and maritime expansion of England in the last decades of the seventeenth century.[24]

The economic argument is a familiar one, and is even less convincing in this context than in the case of the second Anglo-Dutch War. Certainly the French finance minister, Colbert, intended the war to accomplish the economic annihilation of the Dutch – though quite how he envisaged this in practical terms is far from clear – but it has been pointed out that he achieved more by the use of protective tariffs than through six years of war.[25] The war was even less in line with England's economic needs, for it would seem that it was just in this period that Dutch economic supremacy was beginning to weaken and the English economy starting to reveal its strength. Certainly it is around this period that Dutch merchants began to complain of a decline in their trade, or at least in its profitability, and English merchants to show more confidence.[26] It is perhaps significant that the declaration of war in 1672 was not accompanied by the same degree of anti-Dutch feeling as that which showed itself in 1664–5, and the remaining animosity towards the Dutch was soon overshadowed by fear of France.

In sum it can be argued that to consider that the wars against the Dutch Republic were instrumental in bringing to an end its economic dominance is only to echo contemporary misapprehensions. 'To suppose that British economic supremacy was based on naval strength or directly connected with Dutch decline, is to fall into the mercantilist fallacies common during the period.'[27] On the other hand once peace had been made with the Dutch at the Treaty of Westminster in 1674, English trade was able to make rapid progress. It was in this period of neutrality that English merchants could take advantage of the continued Dutch involvement in the French war and make significant inroads into the Dutch trading network, particularly in Northern Europe.[28] Further, France was herself no mean commercial rival, and the policies devised by Colbert to hit at Dutch trade, especially the tariffs of 1667, were probably equally damaging to the English economy.[29] Though less successful the English representatives at the negotiations which led up to the Treaty of Nijmegen in 1678, which finally brought the war between France and the Dutch Republic to an end, were as insistent as the Dutch that the tariffs of 1667 should be abolished. So even if we ignore the strategic and political dangers brought by the French alliance, it cannot be said to have made much sense with regard to England's economic interests.

v

For England the war entered into so confidently in the spring of 1672 had already gone sour by the following September, with the promise of territorial gains or commercial concessions from the Dutch fading rapidly.[30] Although Charles II was far from reluctant to withdraw from a war which now seemed to offer little to himself, his government or his country, he felt tied to Louis XIV, not least because he feared that Louis would reveal the secret clauses of the Treaty of Dover, which included Charles's declaration of his intention of embracing Catholicism, with all that might have been thought to imply, if England made a separate peace. However the King was not wholly in control of the situation: Dutch agents were working on members of Parliament and on public opinion in general, and by the autumn of 1673 there was general condemnation of the French alliance in the Commons, inspired to a notable extent by fears for the future of Protestantism.[31] Such pressure forced the government's hand, and a separate peace was signed with the Dutch in February 1674, on terms which conceded nothing of importance to England.

The combined Franco-English attack on the Dutch Republic was probably the greatest mistake of Louis's reign. It forced on the Dutch, who had tried under De Witt to follow a policy of friendship with France, the unwelcome role of leading opponent of the French. In the longer view, as Zeller pointed out, Dutch friendship or even neutrality would have been invaluable to France in the long struggle with England that was to come.[32] Moreover the near-catastrophe of the summer of 1672 brought William III to power in the Dutch Republic, and the *stadhouder* was to be more uncompromising in his unswerving opposition to France than the Dutch regents (the urban oligarchs who had dominated Dutch politics under De Witt), with their acute awareness of economic interests, had been or could ever be. In the years after 1672 William III was the dominant, though not all-powerful, voice in the determination of Dutch foreign policy, and the cost of his relentless anti-French policy was one that the Republic could ill afford to pay. The Dutch were indeed placed in an unenviable situation by the French aggression of 1672: after this experience, however much they felt unable to bear the burden of consistent opposition to France, they were in the main persuaded that even less could they afford to ignore the continued threat which France represented to the very existence of their state.

The Dutch dilemma was to a considerable extent of English creation. For William III and his grand pensionary, Fagel, it was axiomatic that it was in England's interest, no less than in the Republic's, to oppose the growth of French power, and therefore they hoped and expected that England would join them against France. Moreover they were convinced that only with English aid could France be effectively checked. Yet even after major French advances in the Southern Netherlands the English government resisted pressure to enter the war on the Dutch side. While the Dutch were faced directly with the French problem, England was not immediately threatened by France, whatever the country's long-term interests may have been.

In this context it is intriguing to note how generally it was agreed that England had the power to play a decisive part in the war. This belief seems in part to be a legacy of the misapprehensions about the effects of the Triple Alliance. Fagel argued in 1676–7 that English intervention would force the French to accept any terms which Charles dictated,[33] and this attitude seems to have been a common view among the allied ambassadors gathered at Nijmegen. Given

England's poor performance in the war of 1672–4 and her internal
political difficulties – which by this time were beginning to appear endemic – this assessment of English potential seems remarkably opti-
mistic, and it is perhaps fortunate for England's European reputation
that, after 1674, neither Charles nor James ever put the matter to the
test. The French attitude to England may well have been more realistic: although Louis XIV was always ready to buy English friendship,
he was never prepared to pay very much for it, and showed little sign
of any great respect for English power under the later Stuarts. He
remained confident, with some justification, that he could neutralise
England by alternating subsidies to the King with intrigues with the
various opposition groups[34] – a policy which in retrospect seems to
have worked remarkably well and cost relatively little.

After signing the peace treaty with the Dutch in 1674 England
retreated into insularity, and its influence on developments on the
continent was the effect of inaction rather than any positive policy.
For the rest of his reign Charles II resisted heavy pressure, especially
from Parliament but also from an emerging public opinion acutely
concerned with the twin threats of France and popery, to turn against
France. Although Charles was undoubtedly to some extent sympathetic to France, and was certainly insensitive to the dangers inherent in
French expansion in the Netherlands, and indifferent to French
encroachments in the Rhineland, this passive policy was to some
extent forced upon him. There is a great deal of force in his complaint,
made in 1677, that even if Parliament was prepared to vote the necessary supplies for the preparations for a war against France, it could
not be relied on to provide enough for the successful prosecution of
such a war. Interestingly he drew an explicit parallel with his
grandfather's experience in the Palatine war of the 1620s.[35] Moreover
even before the turmoil of the Popish Plot and Exclusion crisis, Parliament was being worked on by French, Dutch, Imperial and Spanish
agents which did not make it easier to deal with.[36]

Charles did make two excursions into European politics which at
the time at least seemed important. In December 1677 in response to
pressure from Danby and Parliament, an agreement was reached
with the Dutch Republic to impose moderate terms on France by
joint action. Louis XIV in fact accepted reasonable terms at the
Treaty of Nijmegen in August 1678, and it appeared that the success of
the Triple Alliance had been repeated.[37] Nevertheless, just as the
Triple Alliance had not been the reason for French moderation in

1668, the Anglo-Dutch treaty was not the cause of Louis XIV's reasonableness in 1678. For behind the cover of his public policy Charles II had continued secret negotiations with France, and in May 1678 he agreed to remain neutral in return for a payment of six million *livres*, so it was not fear of England which brought Louis to terms. Again in 1682 it appeared that English intervention had been decisive when, in response to representations from Charles, French troops were withdrawn from Luxemburg. (Not that the English king was concerned about Luxemburg, but he was in a dilemma as his public treaty obligations to aid Spain clashed with his secret agreement with France to remain neutral, in return for subsidies. Publicly he had to stand by his commitments; privately he appealed to Louis to get him out of this difficulty.) Certainly William III and Fagel believed the English intervention to have been decisive,[38] and later historians have assumed that Charles's threat to call a Parliament explains Louis's otherwise puzzling behaviour.[39] However it now seems more likely that the French king withdrew from Luxemburg to avoid giving the appearance of aiding the Ottomans in their imminent attack on the Austrian lands, in order that he would be in a better position to profit from the expected defeat of the Emperor.[40] It was not through such superficially effective interventions that England influenced Europe in this period, but through her real inactivity, which was so favourable to France.

Nijmegen, on the surface at least, was a French triumph. The anti-French coalition had been broken, and the Dutch had been induced to sign a separate peace despite the opposition of William III, which meant that potential allies would in future be reluctant to rely on them. Not that there was any doubt as to William's firmness of purpose, but the limits on his ability to control Dutch policy had been made clear. France had made appreciable territorial gains, and had demonstrated the strength and effectiveness of both her armies and her diplomacy. On the other hand Louis had failed to crush the Dutch Republic, and the war, for a time at least, had brought into being a European coalition against France. Most of Europe, and in particular the Emperor, had been convinced of the necessity of opposing French expansion.

Certainly, the short-term consequences of the peace were favourable to France. The collapse of the coalition, English neutrality and Dutch reluctance to be exposed once again with only inadequate support to the power of France, allowed Louis to go ahead with his *réunions* policy, which by the exploitation of legal niceties brought him considerable territorial gains in Alsace and Lorraine, and the annexation of Strassburg. The Ottoman invasion of Austria in 1683 allowed Louis to occupy Luxemburg again, and the Emperor was compelled to recognise, provisionally, the French gains of these years at the truce of Regensburg in 1684. But after this point the overall situation began to turn against France. The Ottomans were dramatically and decisively defeated under the walls of Vienna, and the Regensburg truce allowed Leopold to begin the reconquest of Hungary which was to strengthen the Austrian position considerably.

VI

Moreover the religious motif in international relations which had already sounded clearly in 1672 was to become increasingly important in the 1680s. Two events combined to intensify Protestant unease – the Revocation of the Edict of Nantes and the accession of James II, a confessed Catholic, both in 1685. The reaction to news of the Revocation was especially strong in Germany, where reciprocal toleration was seen as the indispensable basis of stability, and Louis's intolerance was the contradiction of lessons hard learnt during the Thirty Years War and a threat to the religious clauses of the Peace of Westphalia.[41] In the Dutch Republic it brought a religious argument to the support of William's intransigently anti-French policy, and the Elector of Brandenburg, after a flirtation with France in the hope of securing his position against the Swedes in Pomerania, was shocked into once more giving religious considerations priority.[42] The accession of a Catholic king in England seemed to assure France, if not of active English support, then at least of continued benevolent neutrality. It was also seen by Protestants as a threat to their faith – and not only in England. This heightened sense of Protestant insecurity helped to clear the way for the coalitions which would check France after 1688, much to the benefit, ironically, of Leopold I, the persecutor of Hungarian Protestants.

During the last years of his reign Charles chose to accept a French subsidy which allowed him to avoid calling a Parliament. The Crown's policy changed little under James II: although it would be wrong to see him as a client of France, his concentration on domestic politics, and his lack of concern over the possible consequences of French expansion, gave his foreign policy, or lack of it, a pro-French appearance.

The failure of English governments before 1688 to join in the struggle against France upset the plans of William III for an effective coalition against France, and disturbed an emerging public opinion in England which saw the ambitions of Louis XIV as endangering both England's political interests and the security of its religion. But was this policy of neutrality in fact a betrayal of English interests? It can be argued that there was no real danger of France being able to achieve the sort of successes feared by Temple. The frontiers of Europe – or at least of Western and Central Europe – remained remarkably stable from the fifteenth to the late eighteenth century, and in retrospect it seems unlikely that Louis XIV, any more than the Habsburgs before him, would have been able to upset this structure by making major territorial conquests. Certainly, despite her apparent strength, the gains made by France in this period were relatively minor, and no harm came to England's interests despite her neutrality. Indeed, the refusal to become embroiled in Continental wars may have been very beneficial for the development of the English economy in these years. Not that we can give Charles or James the credit for such reasoning, but the policy they pursued for their own interests may well have served their country better than they knew.

In a dynastic sense, at least, Charles and James were right in their attitude to France. The danger for the Stuart monarchy came from a very different quarter, from William III and the Dutch. One of the consequences of William's invasion was that England was brought out of its insularity to take its place at last in the great coalitions against France.

6. Trade and Shipping

GORDON JACKSON

THE reigns of monarchs do not figure prominently in studies of the economy. Only conspicuous spendthrifts and dynastic warmongers interfering with the normal processes of getting and spending excite the attention of students tracing industrial evolution or trade expansion. However some reigns do acquire a certain economic distinctiveness, and of these none in English commercial history is more notable than the Restoration monarchy. It followed a generation of political uncertainty and military activity, and more than a generation of economic stagnation. The colonies were in disarray and the allegiance of their people in doubt. Dutch merchants and shipowners were everywhere driving out the English. With the European economy on the upturn after the long recession of the first half of the century, the Restoration was the point of make or break for English trade. If England could re-establish control over her old trades and extend new ones she might survive and even flourish. If not, there was every chance that, with her paucity of raw materials and poverty of manufactures, she would remain one of the poorer countries of Europe. In fact the decisions of government and initiatives of merchants after 1660 encouraged an unprecedented, transforming growth in commerce that allowed her more than to hold her own. While it would be wrong to imply that this transformation was completed in the quarter century after 1660, this was the crucial time when England entered upon her modern commercial relationships. The period ended abruptly not because of the Revolution but because war in Europe halted economic growth in the mid-1680s. Not until the mid-eighteenth century did England again enjoy the growth rates experienced under the Restoration.

I

This transformation after 1660 had its antecedents in a series of inter-

For Notes to Chapter 6, see pp. 220–1; for Bibliographical Notes, see p. 202.

locking changes taking place over the previous century. In the sixteenth century exports were largely woollen cloth, and because the
English never learned to process it properly – dyeing was a subject of
enquiry pursued by the newly founded Royal Society in 1662 – they
were compelled to send it to their traditional market in Antwerp for
finishing in the Netherlands. Because the shortest sea crossing was
safest, it went chiefly from London; the cloth exports of other ports
were in decline. How long this situation could have lasted is a matter
for conjecture: it was certainly no formula for growth. Since all countries had their own woollen industries, nicely balanced by comparative advantages, any enlargement of English exports was circumscribed on the one hand by the superiority of the finer quality
cloths made on the Continent, and on the other by the poverty of the
market for poorer quality cloths and the impossibility of significant
price reductions. In such circumstances exports could be augmented
only by non-economic means, and this, more than anything else, fos-
tered the concept of trade war.

In fact the problems of the woollen trade were overtaken by war of a
more orthodox kind which brought diminishing demand, while constant troubles in western Europe eventually encouraged the English
to make direct contact with their final customers in the north and
south. The Muscovy Company (founded in 1555) opened up trade
with Russia via the White Sea, the Eastland Company (founded in
1579) adventured to the eastern Baltic, and the Levant, Barbary and
Africa Companies (all founded in the 1580s) explored the possibilities
of the Mediterranean and West Africa. England's long reliance on
foreign middlemen was already curtailed in the 1580s when Antwerp
was sacked by the Spaniards, blockaded by the Dutch and abandoned
by the merchants. The English chose not to tie themselves wholly to
the new entrepôt that emerged in Amsterdam, but rather to continue
exploiting the direct trades in which they enjoyed a greater competitive advantage.

They were able to do so largely because of changes taking place in
textile production. Though they were not good at finishing woollens
they had, with the help of Flemish immigrants, quickly perfected the
manufacture of 'New Draperies' which, though variously named
(bays, perpetuanas, says, serges), were chiefly worsteds of lighter
weight and greater variety of colour and texture than woollens. Beginning around Colchester, they spread quickly in the early seventeenth
century through East Anglia and the West Country, easily competing

(with West Riding kerseys) for the cheaper end of the woollens market. Above all they were especially suitable for warmer climates and sold well in southern Europe and the colonial empires. Since these New Draperies relied heavily on the longer staple wool that was a fortuitous by-product of enclosure (better-fed sheep produced longer wool), and since England had a quasi-monopoly of such wool, she had at last exportable textiles that stood a chance of advancing in competition abroad.[1] Recent estimates suggest that the value of New Draperies rose by about three-quarters in the first four decades of the century, and more or less made up for the decline in woollens during the depression in Europe. In 1640 they accounted for perhaps forty per cent of London's textile exports. However, while New Draperies had great potential, England was still dangerously dependent on textiles as a whole, which made up almost ninety per cent of total exports, and on north-western Europe.[2]

Trade with new regions was associated also with new imports. Timber was valued as a commodity in great demand as English timber was used up, and it was too bulky to go through an entrepôt efficiently. But other goods were initially received as a by-product of the export of New Draperies. In the more difficult areas, where paper payments could not be secured, it was necessary to accept semi-luxuries such as cotton and silk, dried fruit and drugs. Many articles of common consumption under the Restoration were very recent introductions, implying a burgeoning distribution network in London and the provinces and, to sustain it, a growing number of people with a taste for new goods and money to indulge it. It is a pity that the significance of Nell Gwynn's more respectable occupation is so often eclipsed by the glamour of her more lucrative pastime: there had always been royal mistresses, but orange sellers were a product of a much newer trade!

The new semi-luxury trades of the south and the vital timber trade of the north obviously had a great contribution to make once England had settled down to a spell of peaceful development. But the lustiest infants in the nursery of trade were the plantations and the East India Company. Across the Atlantic the English had, in the wake of the more adventurous Portuguese and Spanish, established a string of small colonies – 'plantations' – which enthusiasts such as Hakluyt had promised would produce 'all the commodities of Europe, Africa and Asia, as far as we were wont to travel, and supply the wants of all our decayed trades'.[3] Newfoundland was important from the start for its cod fishery, but the other plantations were agricultural, and heartily disliked for draining away people without producing gold. Tobacco proved to be their salvation, to the disgust of James I and the pleasure of his people. Some 20,000 pounds were exported from the mainland plantations – Virginia and Maryland – in 1619, when it was selling in London for between £1 and £2 per pound, and around 1,000,000 pounds per annum in the 1630s when the price had fallen to almost as many pennies.[4] The West Indian islands could not produce for this figure and turned to sugar in the Civil War, stimulated by Dutch expertise and capital. The value of tobacco and sugar was undisputed at the Restoration. The question was whether they could be made to benefit the Mother Country.

The East Indian trade was far more attractive to the casual observer, who expected the East India Company (founded in 1601) to secure the profitable spices for which Europe still craved. In fact the direct trade was brief, for the Dutch, who had recently seized the trade from the Portuguese, cleared the English pioneers from the spice islands by force. The English withdrew to India, where they established a factory at Surat, on the west coast, and opened a small trade in North Indian goods such as cotton muslin, indigo and saltpetre. It was unpopular among those who regarded export of bullion with disfavour, but sufficiently prosperous to encourage the establishment of another factory, at Madras on the east coast, in 1639. Here, with the acquisition of some six square miles of territory, was the feeble beginning of British India.

The new trades outlined above did not spring up of their own accord: they were created, painstakingly, by a new breed of merchants, by men of broader vision, sharper initiative and greater credit. Foreign middlemen may in the past have taken the profits, but they also took the risks and provided the capital. Trading though an entrepôt had been simpler than trading at a distance. The new merchants had to find their own suppliers and markets. Instead of receiving credit from producers they often had to extend it to them, especially in the plantation trades. They had to arrange payments and so became involved with the international payments system that was slowly emerging. And they became involved, through loans to government, in matters of high finance. In every aspect of trade and its organisation men were acquiring experience in a world of growing complexity, and needless to say they reaped their reward. In Elizabethan times there had been a handful of prominent merchants. In early Stuart times there began the consolidation of the greatly expanded mercantile community that figured so prominently in Restoration England.

II

Their success rested in no small measure on long-term changes that had occurred within the domestic economy. A major factor was the rising output of agriculture. After almost a century of shortage, England achieved a grain surplus around 1650. The switch from import to export relieved the balance of payments, while corn laws in 1670 (to encourage exportation and discourage importation) and 1672 (to give bounties for exportation) prevented prices from falling too low and cutting the income of landowners, farmers and labourers. Since this increase in output was achieved with little increase in a rural population hard hit by epidemic, emigration and the lethal magnet of London, there was a marked improvement in productivity which meant, in effect, more money for individuals to spend on domestic manufactures and imported goods. For many people this was the first opportunity to purchase goods beyond their basic needs and immediate environment, a matter of great importance when overproduction in the plantations brought the price of colonial 'luxuries' within their reach. New commodity trades and new consumers grew up together.

Improvements in agriculture were inextricably linked with the massive growth of London, which both depended on and encouraged them.[5] The capital had long enjoyed a large share of the country's commercially-based consumption. It was the focus of an expanding network of food and fuel supply routes that greatly stimulated internal and coastal traffic. Butter, cheese and corn came overland from southern England and coastwise from the eastern ports, which revived under the new stimulus in the seventeenth century. Coal came from the Tyne, which was also a centre of bounding activity: c.420,000 tons per annum in the 1660s and 510,000 tons in the 1680s. Cattle came on the hoof, around a million a year. In return imports were distributed from London to the provinces, the outports being more involved in exporting than importing. Indeed, any discussion of trade must bear in mind that an expanding trade between countries was more than matched by an expanding trade between counties. England was her own best customer. Coal, salt and metals were distributed from limited areas of production. Wool was moved from the grazing regions to the textile regions, and textiles were sent everywhere. It has been suggested that after tremendous growth in the coal and general distribution trades in the first half of the century, over half of England's shipping was involved in the coastal and fishing trades at the Restoration.[6] At that date there were almost 700 miles of navigable rivers to encourage cheap transport to and from the leading ports, and the next three or four decades saw a considerable extension, as well as the beginnings of road improvement and the introduction of four-wheeled farm carts, scheduled carriers and stage coaches.

The growth of internal trade created a body of wealthy middlemen in London and the provinces whose expertise and accumulated assets made a valuable contribution to commerce in general. They eased the flow of resources to London to serve its interlocking functions in port activities, manufacturing, building, the law and administration. The Restoration Court was itself an attraction: London became fashionable. The nobility and gentry arrived, bringing their money. 'In London', Sir William Coventry wrote c. 1670, 'they spend all their revenue. In London they borrow what money they spend above their revenue . . . both borrower and lender agree in bringing the money to London where the borrower (by spending it) takes the best care he can it shall return no more into the country.'[7] It was, of course, an exaggeration – Londoners still ate, sat by fires and dressed in worsteds – but it makes the point: London had attracted sufficient of the country's people and wealth for its consumption pattern to be the determining factor in the import trades. Had the people and the wealth remained in the provinces the whole future of England would have been different.

Compared with the assets of the landed class, the wealth of the merchants was not particularly impressive in 1660. What was impressive was their share of the country's liquid assets. These came partly from profits on trade and partly from the agricultural sector, drawn by the high interest rates that were thought to be hampering commerce in the 1660s. The Lords' Committee on the Decay of Rents and Trade in 1669 voted twelve to one in favour of a legal maximum of four per cent interest,[8] but their advice was wisely rejected. Cheaper money would certainly have assisted trade, but interest rates could only come down when available funds were more in tune with demand. In this respect it has been argued that commercial expansion was hampered by the rebuilding of London after the fire, but money spent on property still went into circulation as someone else's income, and some trades – especially that in timber – were greatly encouraged. While high interest rates put English merchants at a slight disadvantage compared with Dutch, they did at least ensure that the latter provided some of the funds required by the former. 'A great part of the money used in trade and for the rebuilding of London is Dutch money', a member of the Council of Trade told the Lords' Committee in 1669.[9]

The highest rates of interest and the largest fortunes were not in fact generated in trade, but in government finance when taxes fell short of expectation and wars required borrowing (and offered rich pickings to contractors). The Restoration was the age of great financiers rather than great merchants: 'At the top, the great merchant was more likely to exploit the weaknesses of the public administration and to milk the taxpayer ... than to risk his capital in commercial ventures.'[10] Nevertheless, once attracted to London, capital entered the pool of liquidity that was available for more mundane investment. There was a limit even to government borrowing, which in any case received a setback in 1672: 'the famous stop upon the exchequer almost blasted their very root', it was said of the newly emerging bankers.[11] None the less they continued to emerge and by the end of the century there were some forty of them in the city. The main point is that while money may have been more expensive in London than Amsterdam, there was a reasonable supply of funds available after 1660.

III

The first half of the century had been, for England, a period of apprenticeship. But the master was still firmly in control. At every step English hopes had been countered by Dutch triumphs: it had been Holland's half-century of greatness. She had long dominated the trade of western Europe and continued to do so; she mastered the new whaling trade and eastern trade in the 1620s, she smashed Spanish sea power in the 1630s and she wormed her way into the English plantations in the 1640s. In general her ships and seamen were, from long experience, both better and cheaper. Her merchants offered longer credits and accepted lower profits than English merchants. Above all it was experience that counted. 'The Dutch master us in trade', the Lords' Committee on Decay of Trade was told in 1669; 'We always begin young men here; there it holds from generation to generation.'[12]

Others saw Dutch superiority in terms of brute force, and traditional friendship between the two Puritan powers was not enough to ease the strain of long-standing rivalry. The first Anglo-Dutch war of 1652–4 sprang from the knowledge that progress could only be made in the face of Dutch superiority with government support. For the time being the growing troubles of the Protectorate discounted advantages that might have derived from the war, and it was left for the Restored monarchy – or its merchants – to build on the foundation already laid.

It was abundantly clear in 1660 that England's full potential as an industrial and trading nation could not be achieved without protection, and that her shipping could prosper only in a closed market system. Henceforth the government would do its best to understand and satisfy the needs of trade. 'The King', Lord Clarendon said in August 1660, 'doth consider the infinite importance the improvement of trade must be to this kingdom, and therefore his Majesty intends forthwith to establish a council for trade.'[13] Councils and committees of trade and plantations became a regular if intermittent part of the administration, illustrating the government's concern with supervising trade in the interests of native manufactures and shipping. Regulations could be justified on political grounds, and therefore appealed to those without any particular interest in trade: they would, through the Customs, provide the best source of revenue, they would bring the recalcitrant plantations to heel and they would support the navy.

The matter of the revenue was an ancient tradition and needs no elaboration, but the coercion of the plantations was of new and absolutely vital importance for trade under the Restoration. No amount of plantation produce would secure self-sufficiency, or earn profits through re-exportation, if there was no way of ensuring its arrival in England. Yet in 1660 the plantations were at worst in rebellion, and at best enjoying a trade free from metropolitan interference. When, for instance, the first Restoration despatch was sent to Barbados – the leading sugar island – it was not even known who was governor.[14] During the civil war the Dutch had gained a foothold in the tobacco colonies. It was their expertise and capital that installed the sugar industry (even in England the refineries were operated by Dutchmen), and it was their shipping that served the transatlantic trade and took it, wherever possible, direct to Europe. Such activity ran counter to the very concept of plantation, which enshrined the nationalist rivalries of Europe. Plantations existed solely for the benefit of the Mother

Country: the West Indies were no different from the West Riding, and in this respect the expulsion of foreign merchants from the plantations in the 1660s was a logical sequel to the expulsion of the Hanse merchants from England in the 1580s.

Concern for shipping regulations came with the realisation that for a maritime and colonial country power resided in navies, and navies depended intimately on merchant shipping. There was no permanent, fully-manned Royal Navy until the nineteenth century. In war, merchant ships became armed transports or were laid up, while their crews were 'pressed' to serve in the royal warships. The encouragement of native shipping and a large 'nursery of seamen' lay at the heart of the Navigation Laws for almost two centuries.

The question of legislation arose immediately in 1660 because the Restoration nullified the Navigation Acts of 1650 and 1651. The former had been the first real statement of an imperial theory: that Parliament had the right to control the trade and shipping of colonies 'planted at the cost and settled by the people, and by the authority of this nation, which are and ought to be subordinate to and dependent upon England . . .'. Foreigners were excluded from plantation trade, and foreign ships allowed only by licence. The 1651 Act went further by excluding foreign ships entirely from plantation trade and third-party ships from European trade. Moreover, not even English ships were allowed to import goods from entrepôts. That the Act was aimed at improving naval power, rather than trade, is clear from the fact that trade actually suffered under these restrictions, but in practice there was much avoidance of the Act in home waters and little possibility of enforcing it in colonial waters. While the 1651 Act represents the beginning of legislation, it is the Restoration Act which really marks the beginning of the 'Navigation System'.[15]

The 1660 Act – 'for the increase of shipping and encouragement of the navigation of this nation, wherein under the good providence of God the wealth, safety, and strength of this kingdom is so much concerned' – repeated much of the 1651 Act.[16] In simple terms, goods were to be carried to and from plantations exclusively by English ships of which the master and three-quarters of the crew were Englishmen, and foreign merchants were to leave the plantations before 1 February 1661–2. To encourage shipping in the newer trades, financial penalties in the form of aliens' dues were inflicted on goods from Russia, Spain, Portugal and Turkey, and on certain enumerated goods such as naval stores, dried fruit and potash from any source, when not carried in English ships. Finally the Act reiterated the earlier total ban on imports unless brought from places 'of their said growth, production or manufacture, or from those ports where the said goods and commodities can only or usually have been first shipped for transportation'. The only exceptions were goods brought from entrepôts in the East Indies and the Levant, and colonial produce brought from Spain and Portugal.

At this point concern for shipping was reinforced by concern for the revenue and for the wealth-producing trade on which shipping – and power – was ultimately based. Though the very idea of a foreign entrepôt was an anathema, additional clauses were added to the Navigation Bill during its third reading making England the entrepôt for all the important products of the American plantations. Hitherto plantation goods (except tobacco from Maryland and Virginia) could be carried anywhere so long as the shipping code was observed. Henceforth enumerated goods such as sugar, tobacco, cotton wool and dyestuffs might be carried only to England or another plantation, and ships sailing to the plantations had to give a bond which was forfeit if they did not return with their cargoes to England. In this way evasion of the shipping code would be more difficult; England would have her sure supply of raw materials and luxuries at a cheaper rate than foreigners (who would have to pay transhipment charges and duties), and work would be created in the English ports where goods had to be landed. Revenue was raised through import duties, and though three-quarters was returned as 'drawback' on re-exportation, the Exchequer still benefited greatly. It was a wise move in view of the fact that duties on tobacco alone in 1661 were approximately four times as valuable as duties on all the imports from the East Indies, and reasonable in so far as customs duties were not levied in the plantations. To compel American goods to land in England might charitably be regarded as the way the monarchy secured its 'due'.

The fact that profits could be made out of colonial exports indicated that they might just as easily be made out of imports, and to this end a further Act was passed in 1663 to make England the staple for all European goods destined for the plantations. Quite apart from the benefits to merchants, ships, labour and the revenue, sufficient cost would be added to foreign manufactures to guarantee the competitiveness of English products. Finally slaves for the West Indian sugar plantations could be imported only in English vessels. The Navigation System was complete.

It was, however, easier to pass laws than to enforce them, and for the first half of the reign of Charles II there must be doubts about their effectiveness in the colonies, where avoidance was not over-difficult before the establishment of a proper Customs service in 1696. 'In spite of the Act of Trade 15 Car. II,' it was said in a royal warrant to colonial governors in 1675, 'great quantities of European goods have been imported into your colony not being laden in England, Wales or Berwick; to the great detriment of the King's Customs and of the trade and navigation of England.'[17]

Bearing in mind the free-trade inclinations of American merchants, the government systematised the whole process of enforcement in 1673 by placing financial burdens on illegal shipments and so, it was hoped, making it unprofitable to ship direct to Europe. While no one could determine the final destination of plantation exports, it was simplicity itself to levy a 'Plantation Duty' on all enumerated goods exported in ships which had not given bond to return to England, and to require a 'Plantation Bond' from the master to unload in another plantation or England. While there were still loopholes through which the wily master might sail, the 1673 Act went a long way towards securing its object which was, in the words of the earl of Danby in 1675, 'to turn the course of a trade rather than to raise any considerable revenue to his Majesty'.[18]

Such was the system of regulation that was intended to divert the plantation trades through England, and entirely exclude third-party ships. But these were not matters quietly discussed by merchants over their new Port wine. Trade talk was fighting talk, and those advocating the Navigation Laws were equally vociferous in demanding a show-down with the Dutch. The Anglo-Dutch war of 1652–4 had set the pattern of naval battles for command of the European waters through which all Dutch trade must pass. Now it was confidently expected that a vastly improved Royal Navy (with over two hundred ships built by the Commonwealth) would repeat its triumphs.[19] It is of little moment that the war was precipitated in 1664 by English raids on Dutch factories on the African slave coast. Almost any excuse would have done, as the duke of Albermarle freely admitted: 'What matters this or that reason. What we want is more of the trade the Dutch now have.'[20] 'This second Anglo-Dutch war', wrote G. N. Clark, 'is the clearest case in our history of a purely commercial war. It was a war of which the purpose was simply to take by force material places and things, especially ships.'[21] Tactically the war was nothing much to be proud of. A succession of naval battles drew blood, both sides expended a vast amount of money for little advantage and the peace of Breda (July 1667) settled little. Strategically, however, the war marked the turning point in Anglo-Dutch relations. The Dutch accepted England's right to enforce the Navigation Laws, and handed over New Netherlands whose major town, New Amsterdam, had thwarted the initial working of those laws. Renamed New York it eventually became the major centre of English trade on the American seaboard.

Although the second Dutch war confirmed England's position as a maritime power, it was the third war which secured her an irreversible position in international trade. This war, thought by many to be unnecessary, is usually seen as part of Charles II's secret dealings with Louis XIV, whose further aggrandisement demanded the breaking of Dutch power. When France attacked Holland in 1672 England joined in until domestic hostility towards Charles's policy forced his withdrawal in 1674. Thereafter, while the French continued a campaign against the Dutch that was far more exhausting than naval battles had been, the English sailed off to enjoy the commercial benefits of neutrality. Before long it was France rather than Holland that was feared, and the virtual prohibition of trade with France between 1678 and 1685 marks the beginning of a new rivalry that lasted into the nineteenth century.

IV

The first result of the Navigation Acts aimed at the increase of shipping was a shortage of ships! To ban Dutch vessels from English ports, and to hound them from the colonies, was the surest way of halting trade: there were simply no English vessels to take their place in the short run. Yet it was absolutely vital that England should have *more* ships than hitherto. The new plantation trades were bulk trades, and because they were long-distance trades they automatically made greater demands on shipping than short-distance trades. Vastly more shipping space was required to bring £19,000 worth of tobacco from America than to take £19,000 worth of woollen cloth to Amsterdam. Moreover the stock of ships had to increase faster than the total goods carried to allow for the fluctuating and seasonal nature of the new trades, and for the various forms of under-utilisation.[22]

One simple solution to the problem was to buy Dutch ships. Since the registers are lost we have no means of knowing how many ships were acquired after 1660, but it must have been many hundreds. Certainly the authorities were concerned that with so many being purchased the way was being opened for future frauds, and an Act was rushed through in 1662 to prevent the naturalisation of foreign-built vessels after October 1662. It did not, however, prevent their use in trade with England so long as the vessels concerned paid whatever dues were payable by foreign-owned vessels (which were, of course, fully entitled to bring goods from their own countries). What it should have done was to exclude such vessels from colonial trade, but Professor Andrews has shown that they continued to be used throughout the seventeenth century when occasion demanded.[23]

A second solution was to steal ships. It is estimated that between 1000 and 17,000 vessels – more than the entire existing English merchant fleet – were seized during the first Dutch war, 400 during the war with Spain (1655–60), 522 during the second and 500 during the third Dutch wars. Allowing for heavy losses during the Spanish war, there was probably a net gain of something over 1000 ships, mostly Dutch-built, which, together with those legitimately acquired, formed the core of the merchant fleet after 1660.[24] Morever, because Dutch ships were generally bigger than English ones, they made up a disproportionately large amount of the total tonnage. 'It is probably true to say that between 1654 and 1675 foreign-built ships were never less than a third of the total tonnage in English ownership, and that at the latter date they accounted for something like half of it.'[25]

The third, longer-term solution was to build the ships in England. It was easier said than done. Lacking the encouragement of heavy demand, English shipbuilders had ignored recent developments in ship design and were still turning out heavily armed ships well suited to fighting pirates, but very expensive to operate. Dutch builders, serving the bulk trades of northern Europe, had turned to vessels sacrificing speed and armament to cargo capacity. For its measured tonnage the *fluit*, or flyboat, was lighter in construction and therefore cheaper than a typical English vessel; it carried more cargo and was easier to load and unload; and because of its simplified sail pattern it required fewer seamen (even then they were poorly paid and ill-fed by the Dutch). Although there is no statistical proof of the emergence of a thriving English shipbuilding industry, complaints about its shortcomings ceased by the late 1680s, when native-built vessels probably accounted for four-fifths of the greatly expanded fleet. It would be

wrong to see this relatively slow growth in terms of recalcitrant builders failing to produce the required type of ship. Cheap foreign vessels
were available in the 1660s, and it was not in England's interest to pay
dear for what she could get cheap. She would certainly have experienced grave difficulty finding the capital to purchase new ships on the
scale necessitated by the Navigation Acts, even had the expertise been
immediately available. English shipbuilders were fortunate in having
a twenty-year breathing space during which they could organise
themselves to cater fully for national needs.

It is generally accepted that English shipping underwent a rapid
transformation in the Restoration period, both in number and type of
vessel, but the paucity of contemporary evidence permits us to do no
more than hint at the likely orders of magnitude. The best estimates
would indicate something of the order of 200,000 tons in total in 1660
and 340,000 tons in 1686, reflecting a huge achievement on the part of
builders and owners alike.[26] Unfortunately we cannot even guess at
the amount of capital involved. All we can do is repeat the estimate of
Petty, who thought that in 1665 shipping accounted for £3 million
compared with £30 million for the entire national stock except real
estate and coin.[27] It is worth emphasising that, whatever the actual
sum involved, the Navigation Acts put an immense strain on the capital resources of the country by requiring investment in ships that had
previously been hired, perhaps in the long run more cheaply.
Moreover investment in shipping almost certainly increased faster
than the value of goods carried, and faster than investment in manufacturing within the country. It is important, too, to stress the ramifi-
cations of shipping. A large proportion of the non-agricultural
workforce was engaged in employments related to shipping. Gregory
King thought there were 50,000 seamen in 1688, almost as many as all
artisans and craftsmen combined. Even more impressively it has been
estimated that as much as a quarter of London's population
depended on shipping and commerce for its livelihood.[28]

In the final analysis England succeeded less by excluding foreign
merchants and shipping from old trades than by advancing her own
into new ones. It is here that the second aspect of the Navigation Acts
came into play: England had declared a monopoly over her fastest
growing trades. It is, for instance, reliably estimated that the tonnage
of shipping required to service the traditional trade with Holland and
Germany advanced by only five per cent between 1663 and 1686,
whereas southern European and Mediterranean shipping grew by

about a third, East Indian shipping by half, American and West Indian by almost one hundred per cent, and northern European by more than one hundred per cent.[29] While tonnage does not reflect values, it nevertheless gives some rough idea of the way in which trade with the major areas was moving. Tentative evidence of the value and commodity composition of trade may be drawn from the only statistics surviving from the Restoration period – for London alone for 1663 and 1669 – and from the Customs statistics available from 1669, which, even allowing for the growing difficulties of trading with France, may not be too unrepresentative of conditions at the end of the Restoration, when trade growth was halted.

The area with the fastest growing volume of trade was northern Europe: Russia, Scandinavia and the Baltic. The most valuable commodities were flax, hemp and iron, but it was timber that most regularly filled the ships. Without it there could have been very little urban construction in England after 1666, when foreign soft wood, which was both cheap and easy to work, of necessity replaced native hard woods. The merchant who boasted that he owed his mansion to the sugar trade owed it in a far more practical sense to the timber trade! Nevertheless the bulk of the trade was probably indirectly associated with the growth of other trades in so far as it supplied naval stores. It took several hundred tons of shipping to carry the raw materials to build a hundred tons, and while some domestic materials were still available under the Restoration, it was estimated that a two hundred ton vessel contained at least fifty tons of imported materials. Ironically this trade was carried almost entirely in foreign vessels, and not simply because traditional English vessels could not cope with ships' timbers. There were almost no exports to Scandinavia, and it made little sense for English shipowners to employ their limited resources in a one-way trade that made its meagre profit out of importing the commodity with the lowest value to bulk ratio (apart from coal).

Primary products from the north were destined to play a crucial role in the industrialisation of England, but for the moment the most valuable source was the expanding trade with Spain, Portugal and the Mediterranean. Silk (the most valuable of all raw materials) and cotton were brought by the Levant Company from their monopoly area. Almost all the imported olive oil came from the Mediterranean ports, good quality wool and iron from Spain, and almost half the dyestuffs from Asia Minor, or the plantations of

Spain and Portugal via those two countries. Foodstuffs from this region were equally important. Dried and citrus fruits were growing rapidly in popularity, and Spain and Portugal were by far the most important source of wine by the end of the period. To some extent this flood of imports from the south reflected the worsening political relations in the north and, in particular, the rapid decline in relations with France, but it chiefly reflected a differing ability or willingness to consume English exports. Colbert did not like them. The Spanish and Portuguese with their large plantations, the Mediterranean countries, and the Levant with its huge hinterland in Turkey and Persia, could not get enough of them, especially New Draperies, Newfoundland cod and corn. Without doubt relations with southern Europe were more exciting than at any time before or since. Success that came slowly in the north had come quickly in the south, and Charles II had his Portuguese queen to prove it. As she was to be a disappointment to him, so, eventually, enthusiasm for the southern trades declined; but by then other more lucrative trades had overshadowed them.

Catherine of Braganza brought friendship with Portugal, a short-lived factory in Tangier, and Bombay in western India where English interest and influence advanced rapidly under the Restoration. The activities of the East India Company in their various factories rose to national significance, based on an annual investment of c.£100,000 in the early 1660s and £600,000 in the 1680s.[30] Although pepper was a leading import, spices were not the most significant items, and, since the China trade was still in its experimental stage, tea was of no consequence. The bulkiest commodities were actually pepper and saltpetre, but the most valuable were manufactures. Calicoes, which doubled in value during the period, were, after linens from northwestern Europe, the most important manufactured imports, and the East also overtook the Mediterranean as the principal supplier of silk fabrics. This emphasis on manufactures, which emerged as trade grew under the Restoration, was not, however, destined to survive. In 1701 the importation of certain types of calico was forbidden as a protective measure, and shortly afterwards the blossoming of the China trade gave the East India trade its better known characteristics. What did survive throughout the century was the immense problem of the balance of payments. England produced nothing the Indians wanted – or could afford. Initially a trade in woollens was pushed from Surat into northern India with limited success, but such enterprise was impossible when new factories were opened in warmer areas. The sale of

European goods, the President of the Madras factory wrote home in 1676, 'is no furtherance to ye Investments, but the contrary, being things merely obtruded upon them in favour of the English manufactures and a mere burthen and pestering of their godowns' (i.e., warehouses).[31] The necessary export of bullion was commonly attacked by 'bullionists', but it was, of course, beneficial to the balance of payments as a whole: calicoes ranked second only to sugar among English re-exports.

The final contribution to the shifting emphasis of Restoration trade was made by the rapidly developing plantations. Tobacco continued to spread across Virginia and the neighbouring colonies, and imports rose from around seven million pounds in the early 1660s to twelve million in the late 1680s. Various other crops were introduced or exploited, but the most explosive and valuable growth was in sugar production. It did not require the opening up of large areas of territory or the emigration of large numbers of Englishmen. The Company of Royal Adventurers into Africa was chartered in 1660 without slaves particularly in mind, but the easy availability of negroes answered so nicely the demand for labour from the sugar producers that in 1663 it sought and obtained a monopoly of the slave trade.[32] Soon it was providing huge numbers, not only to the English plantations, but also to rival interests in the Dutch, Spanish and Portuguese plantations. By the 1690s the great heyday of the trade was over: henceforth it would be concerned more with the replacement than the creation of a slave population in the sugar islands. While the profitability of the slave trade is often exaggerated, it is the case that England's speedy creation of this portion of her transatlantic entrepôt trade would have been impossible without slave labour. It would have been equally difficult without the rapid organisation of food trades, chiefly carrying Irish produce until the eighteenth century, when the New England colonies took over. Moreover, the whole of the plantations, whether they produced tobacco, sugar, dyestuffs or drugs, still obtained most of the inedible necessities of life from 'home': hence the desire to make England their staple.

In noting change it would be wrong to give the impression that Holland and Germany ceased to be important because their share of English trade inevitably declined as the newer trades developed. Their superior skills provided intricate manufactures which the English could not provide for themselves until well into the eighteenth century, and they were beyond question the major consumers of

English exports. In particular English control of plantation exports only made sense in so far as the surplus could be sold to the richer countries of western Europe, which were taking almost two thirds of re-exports at the end of the century. Nevertheless it was the re-exports *per se* that were the distinguishing feature of the period, not their shipment to Europe.

v

The achievement of the Restoration monarchy and merchants was, then, 'to turn the course of trade'. Protective legislation released the enterprise of merchants already encouraged by long-term developments within the domestic economy. A general quickening of commercial activity had provided new exports, consumed new imports and liberated funds for investment in further production not in England but in the plantations where, in economic terms, the marginal efficiency of capital was greater. Because the goods so produced were cheap and popular they enjoyed a market far in excess of the domestic market. In this way 'English' products expanded greatly, and national shipping expanded to carry them.

For a relatively poor country this was, at that time, the only road to prosperity. As in Holland, English national wealth was able to forge ahead of limited agricultural and industrial production by the simple expedient of diverting investment to commerce, shipping and colonial enterprise. The key features of Restoration trade were therefore the elimination of third-party trade, the concentrated effort to secure trade outside the traditional European entrepôts and the acquisition of new commodities which could be re-exported on a grand scale. By the end of the century almost a third of total exports were re-exports which did not require massive investment within England, but which certainly produced wealth that found its way back into the domestic economy and eventually encouraged growth there, beginning, perhaps, with the switch from imported calicoes to home-produced cottons. It is difficult to imagine any form of investment in England that could have produced anything like the same results as investment in the plantations, in general commerce and in shipping.

Without the Navigation Acts the changes discussed above would have been difficult, but it is also true that the Navigation Acts would have been meaningless had there not been a thriving commercial sector able to take advantage of a monopoly situation. It was most

obvious in London, but the major outports were also the foci of buoyant enterprise after 1660 as Newcastle, Hull, Exeter, Bristol and Liverpool enjoyed a booming trade with the Continent and the colonies.[33]
Although the spur might have been the legal exclusion of the Dutch,
growth in the American plantations, for instance, was English
growth, and trade with the Levant or East Indies really owed little to
the Acts. Expanding Restoration commerce should not be seen
simply as a consequence of the Acts, but as a positive movement for
which protection provided the lever whereby a vulnerable newcomer
could attack the entrenched position of a dominant trading power.
The Acts do not represent a conscious policy to create national power,
as is sometimes thought, but an *ad hoc* reaction to practical problems
that arise whenever new ventures are established against the advantages of old ones.[34] They were not an attempt to capture world trade,
but to share it. If they were a statement of anything, beyond revenue
and navy, it was that the portion of trade allotted to England should
be enjoyed by Englishmen. The Restoration did not see England's
final triumph over Holland, but it did see the shaping of new trends
that were destined to shift the centre of economic gravity from
Amsterdam to London.

7. The Restoration Church

R. A. BEDDARD

I

'NEVER was there so miraculous a change as this', wrote Bishop Duppa of the Restoration, 'nor so great things done in so short a time.'[1] Within a year of Charles II's homecoming the Puritan Revolution had collapsed. By 1663 it had vanished, and its acknowledged enemy, the hierarchical Church of England, raised as if from the grave, sat once more in the seat of authority. To appreciate the about-turn in affairs we need to recollect the general sequence of events. In 1660 the Stuart monarchy was, after eleven years spent in exile, brought back by an apparently united and powerful Presbyterian party in church and state. In 1662 that same party lay shattered, powerless to resist the fast flowing tide of Anglican sentiment that swept the country. The speed and thoroughness with which the episcopalians recaptured the establishment was striking – and all the more so because of the alleged weakness of the pre-war Church of England, and the savage overthrow of episcopacy less than twenty years before. The origin and explanation of this remarkable Anglican resurgence is to be found in the politics of the Cromwellian Interregnum.

Before returning to England Charles II expressed from Breda his preference for religious toleration: 'a liberty to tender consciences'. Yet, while attempting to give a lead to public opinion at home, he referred a final decision on the matter to Parliament.[2] At the time there was no reason to believe that an assembly of landowners would want anything else. They had, after all, been responsible for pulling down the intolerant apparatus of Laudian prelacy in the 1640s. But times had changed, and men's opinions had changed with them. It was here that the King and Lord Chancellor Clarendon seriously miscalculated. They knew nothing of the change of heart which many of them had undergone in the interval. Far from affording the nobility and gentry greater political recognition, the Puritan Revolution had, in its later stages, deprived them of their hereditary influence in the counsels of the nation. Forcibly denied a hearing in Parliament and shut out of Cromwell's artificial polity in the counties, their discontent deepened into hatred. Too late they realised that, in challenging the ancient structures of royal and episcopal authority, they had unwittingly struck at the foundations of their own power. Under the erosive impact of Cromwellian rule and the threat of social subversion, which seemed to lie beneath the popular millenarianism of the sects, their essential conservatism revived.

Not for the first time in the century secular grievance was seconded by religious dissatisfaction. Neither the rigours of Presbyterian discipline nor the confusions of Independency appealed to the moderation of men of property. For all that they had bridled at Archbishop Laud's government of the church, few had ever contemplated leaving the church into which they had been born and baptised. Thus the scene was set for the recovery of the old faith, along with the revival of the old emotions of pre-war society: the love of domestic peace, traditional order and legitimate authority. In the coincidence of their troubles the embittered squires of the Commonwealth and the sequestered priests of the Church of England reached a new understanding, grounded upon their common political advantage. Whereas before they had been at loggerheads, parson and squire now came to accept one another as allies in a single cause – the struggle against usurpation in church and state. Divested of the exorbitant social and economic pretensions which it had acquired under Laud, Anglicanism won the hearts of the upper classes, especially the Cavalier families; not least of all, because the 'suffering loyalty' of the priests gave to their resistance a greater courage and sense of purpose. From this enduring bond of affection sprang that most salient feature of later Stuart politics: the alliance of country squire and high church parson.

II

In Oxford, until 1646 the capital of Royalist England, a knot of faithful priests – John Fell, Richard Allestree and John Dolben – maintained the rites of the Prayer Book, only a few steps from Christ Church, the college from which they had been ejected as students and to which they returned as canons in 1660. Meanwhile they ministered to hundreds of scholars, drawn largely from the *jeunesse dorée* of the Cavalier party.[3] At Westwood, in Worcestershire, Sir John Pakington welcomed Henry Hammond, who, as the church's most inflexible defender of episcopacy, may be accounted the 'angelic doctor' of Restoration Anglicanism with its exalted view of the episcopal office.[4] At Staunton Harold in Leicestershire, the young Sir Robert Shirley, heir to the Devereux fortunes, took in that indomitable Royalist, Gilbert Sheldon, Clerk of the Closet to Charles I, who soon busied himself raising money for the exiled Court.[5] At Easton Maundit in Northamptonshire, Sir Christopher Yelverton, himself a puritan sympathiser, sheltered the aged Bishop Morton of Durham, who repaid his hospitality by timely converting his son, Henry, into a decent episcopalian, 'a true son of the Church of England'.[6] In Devonshire Sir William Courtney responded generously to the 'deplorable condition' to which Dean Peterson of Exeter was reduced by sequestration. He 'forthwith sent his coach for him . . . and told Mr Dean he would take care of him as long as he should live'.[7] In 1660 both were at their stations to greet the return of episcopacy, Peterson in his cathedral and Courtney in the county.[8]

In country houses throughout England the loyal clergy of the Anglican *Diaspora* found positions of trust, as chaplains, tutors and confessors.[9] There they accomplished in adversity what Laud had failed to achieve in prosperity. They enlisted the active support of the important laity of their church. It was from the ranks of their former patrons, pupils and penitents, that the demand for the re-imposition of Anglican Uniformity rose most insistently at the Restoration. Conformity to the doctrine and worship of the church had become, for them, a ready means of identifying those who accepted the traditional order in government and society: an order founded on the rule of law and the rights of property. By 1660 the Church of England had taken on its celebrated role as the vehicle for social and political conservatism in the life of the nation.

The elections to the Convention Parliament in the spring of 1660 demonstrated the ingrained conservatism of the localities. Held on the basis of the pre-revolutionary franchise, they were bound to reflect the authentic, if hitherto repressed, feeling of the countryside and its natural rulers, the squires and magnates. In the counties the landed interest favoured the Cavaliers and their sons; while in the boroughs radical candidates were rejected.[10] In other words, well before the

King's return, the Anglican Royalists, including zealous episcopalians of the calibre of Pakington and Yelverton, were taking over the
House of Commons from their Presbyterian and Independent rivals.[11]
In the Lords events similarly advantaged the Cavaliers. It was this
substantial and growing Cavalier presence at Westminster that
ensured that the Restoration would be unconditional, despite the
opposition of General Monck and 'the Presbyterian party'. So it was
that John Bramston, knight of the shire for Essex and a Royalist who
declared himself 'early for episcopal government', could question the
belief, too willingly received at Court, 'that the King could not come
home but by the Presbyterians; whereas', Bramston maintained, 'it
was the Cavalier party, the loyal gentry, that brought him home in
truth'.[12] The truth was that neither Charles nor Clarendon understood their actual debt to the Cavaliers.

The Restoration was a decidedly contradictory affair, produced 'by
a union of contradictions, by a concurrence of causes', which, as
Clarendon later observed, 'never desired the same effects'.[13] It was
bound to give rise to conflicting hopes, which no alliance, however expedient, between old and new Royalists, between Cavaliers and Presbyterians, could possibly resolve. The making of the church settlement
and, even more, the subsequent ups and downs of the Anglican establishment were to uncover these contradictions and, in the process, to
breed new discontents. The King was restored because, without him,
men of substance could not think how to extricate themselves from the
'world of confusion' into which they had fallen. Their aim in recalling
him was not to gratify him, but themselves. This was obviously true of
the ambitious Presbyterian politicians in London, 'who all trucked for
imployments and honours'.[14] But it was equally true of the self-
regarding, country-based Cavaliers, who promised themselves
security and recompense in the King's return. By admitting Charles
to 'his own', his aspiring subjects – the Presbyterians above, the Cavaliers below – expected the restored monarchy to preserve them in
what they held to be their rightful inheritance.

In the countryside many landowners had adopted the institutional
loyalties of the Cavalier party, to church and king. More telling, for
the future course of church and state relations, was their adoption of
the Cavaliers' sense of political priority. They placed loyalty to their
ancestral church before loyalty to the Crown. Indeed, they had come
to regard their religion as part of their birthright, a personal property
on a par with their estates. It was from this identification of the

Church of England with the rights of private property that the strength of the Anglican establishment derived. Henceforth the landed classes were to take unkindly any action – whether of sectary or papist, monarch or politician – which threatened to undermine the church. After 1662 the church 'as by law established' was cherished as a bulwark against religious fanaticism, arbitrary rule and civil strife. As such it could count on the support of the political nation in general, and of the Cavaliers in particular.

III

The irony was that the same conservatism which restored the King also endowed the restored monarchy with sufficient authority to challenge the settlement which the landowners were to fashion in Parliament. 'To the King's coming in without conditions', wrote the historian, Burnet, 'may be well imputed all the errors of his reign.'[15] Yet, it could scarcely have been otherwise; for, in 1660, the Cavaliers were too trusting and too busy fending off unwanted Presbyterian conditions to impose any of their own. The Restoration had left the religious question wide open. Convinced of the need to promote national unity, as the only foundation on which to build a strong monarchy, King and Chancellor pursued a policy of reconciliation in church and state. The Breda Declaration of 4 April 1660 had expressed the hope 'that henceforward all notes of discord, separation and difference of parties' might be 'utterly abolished among all our subjects'.[16] Charles wished to be ruler of a united people, not merely the leader of a party, and of a defeated party at that. He knew that moderation, not excess, would further his designs. He therefore openly stood for toleration and discouraged those extravagant loyalists who proclaimed the automatic restoration of the Laudian Church. Seeking to reward his new allies, and to make use of them at the same time, he took a large contingent of Presbyterians into his service: Monck, Manchester, Annesley, Robartes, Holles, Ashley Cooper, Morice, Grimston and others. It was this 'Presbyterianised' Court which was to aid and abet King and Chancellor in their strivings for a pacificatory settlement of religion – much to the dissastisfaction of the Anglican Cavaliers.

There is no reason to suspect the ecclesiastical allegiance of Charles or Clarendon. They belonged by upbringing and interest to the Church of England. What is more they recognised in an episcopally-governed church an invaluable prop to monarchy. Their promptitude in filling the vacancies which had occurred in cathedral chapters – itself a preliminary to replenishing a much-depleted episcopate – argues more than an appreciation of the legal rights of Crown patronage; it declared a keenness to reassert royal control over the church, its personnel and organisation. Even so, they were prepared to modify the institutions of the church and lower the terms of conformity in order to retain moderate Presbyterians within the establishment. Given continuing puritan objection to 'the diocesan form' of episcopacy and the Prayer Book, this could best be done by reducing the traditional powers of the episcopate and revising the liturgy. Charles, temperamentally averse to persecution and personally indebted to Roman Catholics and Presbyterians, as well as Anglicans, for his preservation and restoration, had no desire to part with the services of any of his subjects. A tolerant settlement of religion would permit him to command the talents of all, as he saw fit. Clarendon's position was somewhat different. Though devoutly attached to the old church, he was a convinced erastian, holding that the function of a state-church was to unite, not divide, the nation. Consequently, he was strongly in favour of Protestant union, and seems genuinely to have mistrusted Cavalier militancy. He doubted the immediate practicality of restoring the church, and advised caution, hoping that 'the Church will be preserved in a tolerable condition, and by degrees recover what cannot be had at once'.[17]

The Court worked hard and long to implement the Breda Declaration. Besides encouraging the prospect of a general toleration Charles strove to unite the Presbyterians to the church. His repeated 'promises of peace' to their delegation in Holland; his appointment of nonconformist chaplains; his admission of their patrons to the Council and Household; his attempt to take religion out of the parliamentary arena; his sponsorship of talks between their representatives and the episcopal divines, culminating in the highly advantageous Worcester House Declaration of 25 October and the associated offer of bishoprics and deaneries to their chief spokesmen[18] – all point to the elaboration, however fitful, of a consistent policy: consistent in its ends and in the means chosen to realise them. Charles and Clarendon believed in their ability to achieve an accommodation between churchmen and Presbyterians by direct negotiation. That way they hoped to by-pass the Convention, with its menacing Cavalier votes, and to isolate the intransigent Anglican clergy from their intransigent lay allies. Having survived to charm its old enemies into obedience, the monarchy did not wish to fall victim to its old friends, the Cavaliers.

In backing Comprehension (church-union) and Indulgence (toleration) Charles's motive was unmistakably political. For all his easy-going ways, he was a prince who inwardly yearned for independence. Like the rest of the Stuart race he prized the prerogatives of the Crown, and none more so than those which belonged to him by virtue of the Royal Supremacy. To him the ecclesiastical sphere seemed not only the area of government where his authority was least likely to be questioned, but also the most promising quarter in which to try to advance towards the distant goal of monarchical emancipation. If he could but obtain a broader measure of Protestant union inside the church, and extend a degree of toleration to peaceable Dissenters, including loyal papists, he would improve his political options by enlarging the ranks of his potential supporters in government and, thereby, escape the worst restrictions which Cavalier orthodoxy, with its addiction to law and property, might impose on him. Charles II, like James II after him, was no disinterested advocate of religious toleration, but a monarch bent on making much of monarchy.[19] It was a tribute to his determination that he held out against the Cavalier backlash for so long. Not until November 1661 did he admit that the ecclesiastical settlement had proved 'too hard' for him, and surrender to the Cavaliers.[20]

IV

There can be no mistaking the mood of the country. It was violently Anglican. Preoccupation with the intricacies of national politics had produced the illusion that they decided what happened, when, in fact, it was on a local level that many decisions were made. There opinion ran counter to the Court right from the start. Roused by the fever of the hustings in two successive general elections, and driven on by a passion to regain their influence in county society, the Cavaliers took charge of the conservatism of the shires, shaping it in accordance with their own prevailing partisanship. They demanded the restoration of their church 'under the ancient apostolical government by bishops',[21] and repeatedly urged Charles to settle religion 'as it was in the time of his royal grandfather and father of ever blessed memory'.[22] From County Durham to Surrey, from Northamptonshire to North Wales,

the nobility and gentry clamoured for the restitution of diocesan episcopacy: 'sovereign bishops', whose spiritual authority, owned by the
inferior clergy, enjoined by the canons of the church, enforced by statute and sustained by landed revenues, would keep the people from
that 'endless dividing into sects and factions', which had destroyed
the unity of church and state. By implication they rejected any 'reduc-
tion' of episcopacy, along the lines conceded by the Court to its
Presbyterian allies. They had too high an appreciation of episcopacy
as an instrument of stability to concur in lessening its powers.

Yet, there was more to the episcopalianism of the counties than a dis-
guised response to social and political imperatives. It signified a real
love for the Church of England. The inhabitants of County Durham
(well over 1500 of them) declared that their 'temporal burdens and
sufferings' had been 'light and ease' to them, compared with the banishment of their Bishop and orthodox clergy:

> the consequence whereof hath deprived us not only of all divine and
> public worship of God by the constitutions of Holy Church and the
> laws of this land established, but even of the holy sacraments,
> decent marriages and burials, and caused us to be overrun
> with errors, heresies, schisms and atheism.

Having learnt 'the value which ought to be put upon these blessings
by the want . . . of them', they petitioned for the restoration of the
'ancient, legal and primitive government of the Church', together
with the 'ancient and (until now) never questioned County Palatine';
the one for 'the good' of their souls, the other for that of their estates.[23]
For them the re-enthronement of their accustomed prince-bishop
betokened first and foremost the recovery of their religion – a valid
ministry, regular sacraments and wholesome doctrine; and only
secondarily a return to constitutional and economic normalcy.

In 1660 events did not wait on King and Parliament. They anticipated them. In reviving the traditional Anglican order church and society responded to the persistence of vested interests: the interests of a
dispossessed, hereditary, Anglican oligarchy, which had not been laid
aside by legal agreement, but by brute force. The Interregnum simply
had not lasted long enough to efface the memory of better days, when
thousands of families, lay and clerical, had profited from a share in the
temporal revenues of the church. The sheer number of survivors from

the pre-war church, their wide distribution through all ranks of society, their unimpaired corporate consciousness, their unbroken
spirit and close co-operation in reclaiming their lost local inheritance,
was sufficient to carry religion back into its old channels. Deprived
dignitaries, redundant officials, discarded tenants, discharged servants and deserted clients – many of them goaded by the pinch of
poverty – lost little time in seeking reinstatement or redress. At times
the spontaneity of Anglican recovery was phenomenal. Within weeks
of returning from exile Dean Cosin, once one of Laud's most hated
disciples, hastened to Peterborough, 'invited thither by the pre-
bendaries and divers tenants of the church, who desired to renew
their leases'. In July he took possession of the cathedral, and, 'to
the great satisfaction of the whole city', revived daily choir services. On 1
August he held his first chapter meeting, at which livings were filled,
leases granted and orders made for resuming the collegiate life of the foundation. Although Cosin's eagerness brought an angry reprimand from
Clarendon, who as always was concerned not to offend the Presbyterians,
it is clear that his decanal office won local recognition. By October his
greatest potential opponent, Oliver St John, a Cromwellian notable
who had purchased 'the royalties of Peterborough', had submitted to
the jurisdiction of his courts.[24]

This irresistible Anglican reflex was apparent on all levels of church
life – parochial, archidiaconal, diocesan and provincial. The un-
controversial clerical procedures of subscription, institution and
induction began again.[25] Ordinations, never discontinued by the
old bishops, were again publicly celebrated.[26] Testamentary business flooded back into the probate courts of Canterbury and
York.[27] The colleges of Oxford and Cambridge, like the cathedrals
of the church, reverted to their ancient statutes.[28] The use of the
liturgy was widely restored, as 'many ministers began of themselves
to read the Common Prayer'.[29] Elsewhere nonconformity was des-
ignated a criminal offence. In September the Dorset Grand Jury
indicted five ministers for their 'irreverent neglect' of the liturgy,
and presented 'divers dangerous and illegal conventicles' in terms
that foreshadowed the 1664 Conventicle Act. Such assemblies constituted a double affront to the propriety of Anglican landowners,
being 'infinitely to the dishonour of God and religion' and a 'great
disturbance of the peace of the kingdom'.[30] After Venner's desper-
ate Fifth Monarchy insurrection, in January 1661, few disputed
the Cavaliers' axiom that religious dissent and political subversion

were indistinguishable; soon it was to be elevated to the status of a
legislative principle.[31]

The weakness of the Court's position was shown by its inability to
restrain, let alone overcome, Cavalier prejudice in the localities. For
example, in 1661, it failed to prevent Richard Baxter's eviction from
Kidderminster, though he was a royal chaplain and a major sup-
porter of the policy of reconciliation. He was turned out by a collusive
action on the part of three local Cavaliers: Sir Ralph Clare, patron of
the living; Sir John Pakington, his neighbour; and Bishop Morley, the
diocesan. They wished to restore the sequestered Vicar, whom Clare
had patronised during the Interregnum. So solicitous were these 'two
knights of the country' to be rid of Baxter that one of them offered 'his
troop' to the Bishop to stop him from preaching. On removing to
London, Baxter found it impossible to escape their allegations of sedi-
tious behaviour; so much so that Gilbert Sheldon, bishop of London,
refused to license him without an express undertaking 'not [to]
preach against the doctrine of the Church, or the ceremonies established by law'.[32] Later, when elected a proctor in Convocation, he
found himself excluded by Sheldon, who preferred a conformist in his
place.[33] It was now the turn of the once-prosperous puritans to be
ejected from the church. During 1660 some 290 sequestered incumbents
were restored, and 695 Commonwealth ministers displaced. It was the
first round in a lengthy shake-up of the parochial clergy, which did not
end before the enforced mass exodus on St Bartholomew's Day (24
August) 1662 had added a thousand more to the list of nonconformist
casualties.[34]

Outside Whitehall the King's much-publicised 'lenity' carried less
weight. Old-fashioned churchmen, such as Sir Justinian Isham in
Northamptonshire or Squire Whalley in Nottinghamshire, marvelled
at Charles's flattering nonconformist expectations; but decided that,
for them, it was wiser and safer to abide by the known laws of the land.
By taking the onus of enforcing the Elizabethan Act of Uniformity
upon themselves, magistrates could dodge toleration and take a tough
line against those 'peevish spirits', who would ever have 'a chapel
wherever God hath a church'. Isham even ventured the enterprising
view that, where 'roughness' was to be used, it was 'better expressed
by those who act under his authority than by [the King] himself'.[35]
The renewal of prosecutions for nonconformity, spasmodic and
scattered though they were, indicated that some JPs were already
accepting the duty of disciplining dissidents. One thing is plain. The

country was moving in a quite contrary ecclesiastical direction from that advocated by the Court. In doing so it responded very largely to its innate conservatism and to the stimulus of unofficial Cavalier leadership. Lay intolerance, the joint product of experience and indoctrination, was the decisive factor in restoring the Church of England to its old form and its old ascendancy.

Baxter admitted as much, when, turning aside from clerical wrangling, he stated that the episcopal clergy 'carried it' against the Presbyterians 'by their parts and interest in the nobility and gentry'.[36] Not for nothing had the sequestered priests pursued their dedicated witness in the country houses of Cromwellian England. They had raised up a church party, the like of which had never been seen before. They and their patrons had entirely succeeded − as Cromwell feared they might − in entailing their quarrels on posterity.[37] To their enemies, the Presbyterians, they gave no quarter; and to those that attempted to get in their way, such as Charles and Clarendon, they gave scant heed.

The general election of 1661 − the last for eighteen years − was a triumph for the church.[38] When the Cavalier Parliament met in May, the House of Commons proved implacably Anglican. It imposed the sacrament on its members and insisted on kneeling at communion; it restored the bishops to the Lords and advowsons to their rightful owners; it burnt the Covenant and attacked the Quakers and other schismatics; it introduced a Bill 'to provide for an effectual conformity to the liturgy of the Church', though the Savoy Conference − the last of Charles's unsuccessful attempts to wrest concessions from the Anglican divines − was currently in session.[39] When it reassembled in the autumn, it chose to regard the hastily summoned Convocation, elected under episcopal supervision, not the Savoy Conference, nominated by the King and including Presbyterians, as the authoritative voice of the Anglican clergy. At long last Charles was forced to face the fact, however unpalatable to him, that the country would suffer nothing less than the re-establishment of the traditional Church of England. In passing the Corporation Act of 1661, which swept Presbyterians from municipal office, he gave Cavalier Anglicanism its head. Changing his tactics, but not his policy, he strove to ameliorate the terms of the Bill of Uniformity. He did not succeed. The Commons would neither abate their high notions of conformity, nor sanction his exercise of the dispensing power. The result was an exclusive and intolerant church settlement: the exact opposite of what he and Clarendon wanted. As such it represented a severe defeat for the restored monarchy, and one which Charles deeply resented.

V

The Restoration saw not only the resurrection of the Church of England, but also the creation of the Anglican establishment as it was to endure into the nineteenth century. The ecclesiastical legislation of the Cavalier Parliament may be said to conclude the final chapter in the long and painfully idiosyncratic history of the English Reformation. It did so in two respects; the one religious, the other political. First, it defined the state church – the Church of England – as an exclusively episcopal institution, served by bishops, priests and deacons, who were required to conform to the doctrine and use of a revised Prayer Book. Secondly, it erected a church state – the Anglican establishment – that is, a system of government in which churchmen enjoyed a monopoly of public office under a monarch who was at once Supreme Governor of the church and head of the state. The momentous sequence of Cavalier statutes, running from the Corporation Act of 1661 to the Five Mile Act of 1665,[40] had the cumulative effect of making communicant membership of the established church the test of political acceptability, and, in time, of social respectability as well. It introduced into the life of society a lasting division: a division between privileged conformist and unprivileged nonconformist, between 'Church' and 'Chapel'. Even when, in 1689, the Toleration Act grudgingly gave freedom of worship to most Protestant Dissenters, it denied them access to the jealously guarded preserves of public office. The Anglican establishment remained intact.

After 1660 the church continued to be the intellectual and emotive source of royalism. The Royal Supremacy was owned by statute and affirmed by the clergy. As defenders of the Faith and the Lord's Anointed, the Stuart kings were rendered an unqualified allegiance by the church. In the pulpits and from the press the clergy taught the necessity of non-resistance and passive obedience. These dogmas, deriving from belief in the hereditary divine right of kings, were not fond superstitions. They were the natural conclusions of the precept that all government was an ordinance of God, and that the authority of the civil magistrate – whether of superior prince, or inferior JP – proceeded from God. 'The foundation of government and obedience', declared Seth Ward in 1661, 'is deeply and firmly rooted

in the foundation of our religion.' Anglican political thought offered 'a
Christian theory of government' which was authoritarian and provi-
dential.[41] On both counts it had an instinctive attraction for a generation of churchmen who had surmounted the horrors of rebellion and
fanaticism. Dr South proclaimed the measure of Anglican commitment to monarchy when he declared at the consecration of Bishop
Dolben in 1666:

> The Church of England glories in nothing more than that she is the
> truest friend to kings, and to kingly government, of any other
> church in the world; that they were the same hands and principles
> that took the crown from the King's head and the mitre from the
> bishops'.[42]

Even that most exotic of contemporary cults, devotion to the Royal
Martyr, served to underline the nation's dread of revolution and the
churchman's investment in monarchy. In alliance with the church, its
hierarchy and its lay politicians, there was little which Charles and
James II could not have accomplished. They had it in them to be
strong monarchs, on one condition only – that they accepted and upheld the Anglican establishment. Had they been content to work
within the prescribed limitations of orthodoxy all might have been
well. Unfortunately they were not.

Of dubious faith, or none, Charles quickly got himself into trouble.
Though he gave his assent to the Act of Uniformity on 19 May 1662, he
had no intention of accepting defeat. Clarendon's speech at the close
of the session sounded an ominous note of defiance. He reminded the
MPs that 'the execution of these sharp laws depends upon the wisdom
of the most discerning, generous and merciful prince.'[43] During the
summer Charles made several attempts to evade the Act. In June his
plan to suspend the statute for three months met with the united
opposition of the bishops and judges. In August his proposal to issue
individual indulgences was defeated by Sheldon and the Duke of
York. In December he tried a new initiative. In issuing his Declaration on Boxing Day, he called on Parliament to recognise the dispensing power, which he deemed to be 'inherent' in the Crown. An unwise
reference to obliging his Roman Catholic subjects, in addition to Protestant nonconformists, occasioned intense suspicion of his motives in
seeking to alter the church settlement. In the 1663 session he spon-
sored a bill in the Lords for obtaining parliamentary authorisation of
his power to dispense with the penal laws in matters of religion, only

to find the Commons immovably against him. The MPs condemned outright any scheme for 'establishing a schism by law', and reaffirmed their conviction that:

> the asserting of the laws and the religion established, according to the Act of Uniformity, is the most probable means to produce a settled peace and obedience through the Kingdom; because the variety of professions in religion, when openly indulged, doth directly distinguish men into parties, and, withal, gives them opportunity to count their numbers; which, considering the animosities that, out of a religious pride, will be kept on foot by the several factions, doth tend, directly and inevitably, to open disturbance.[44]

The indivisibility of church and state was for them an article of faith; they believed, as did the intransigent episcopal divines, that 'it was not Indulgence which the schismatics desired, but empire'; they would have none of it.

Charles's efforts at Indulgence having got nowhere, he exploited the opportunity afforded by Clarendon's impeachment to employ new men. Making the most of the Cabal's un-Anglican sympathies, he reverted to Comprehension. He banished Sheldon from the Court, and had resort to underhand methods of engineering religious accommodation. Under the auspices of the duke of Buckingham, son-in-law of the Presbyterian Lord Fairfax, and Lord Chamberlain Manchester, he renewed contact with the nonconformist clergy and those conformists who desired to comprehend them within a modified church settlement. In 1667, and again in 1668, he backed informal 'conversations' between moderate churchmen and moderate Dissenters, and countenanced the introduction of private bills in Parliament in the hope of uniting his Protestant subjects. Even these noticeably more modest projects encountered fierce opposition at Westminster. The Cavaliers' unrelenting hostility to change was demonstrated by a Commons' motion, 'that if any people had a mind to bring any new laws into the House about religion, they might come as a proposer of new laws did in Athens, *with ropes about their necks'*.[45] A move to avoid further contention by referring the religious question back to the King, in April 1668, was overwhelmingly defeated by a vote of 176 to 70![46] Evidently there was considerable and, as the years went by, mounting distrust of the Court and its nefarious purposes – and with reason.

On 15 March 1672 Charles threw caution to the wind by issuing his Declaration of Indulgence, as part of a grander strategy to win political independence at home and abroad.[47] Unlike the Declaration of 1662, it did not defer to Parliament, but was, in itself, an exercise of 'that supreme power in ecclesiastical matters' to which the King had persistently laid claim. It summarily suspended the penal laws, and required 'all judges, judges of assize and gaol-delivery, sheriffs, justices of the peace, mayors, bailiffs and other officers', civil and ecclesiastical, to obey. The only restrictions on religious freedom were that dissenting ministers and meeting-houses should be licensed, and papists should refrain from public worship. Compared with the practical extent of royal toleration, the promise to preserve the Church of England 'entire in its doctrine, discipline and government', was paltry compensation for outraged churchmen.[48] The Indulgence had disastrous effects in the dioceses, undoing what good a hard-working episcopate had managed to achieve since 1662. On 1 January 1673 Bishop Sparrow of Exeter wrote to Sheldon:

I see daily to my heart's grief the poor sheep committed to my trust snatched out of the fold by cunning wolves, and I know not how to bring them back. The justices are almost all resolved to sit still; many of them love to have it so; the rest are apt to think, by what they see abroad, that it is no acceptable service to disturb our disturbers. Your Grace knows how short our arms are, and how weak our hands.

All Sparrow could hope for was relief from 'two or three of our greatest gentry'.[49] The Declaration of Indulgence was certainly Charles's most assertive and controversial act since ascending the throne. As such it was not to go unchallenged by the entrenched forces of Cavalier Anglicanism. Parliament was not reassembled until February 1673. When it met the Commons were ready for a show-down. They instantly attacked the suspending power, bluntly telling the King that he had been 'very much misinformed' on the subject of his prerogative, 'since no such power was ever claimed or exercised by any of your Majesty's predecessors'. On the contrary, statutes could only be repealed by statute, that is by the consent of King, lords and commons, and not by the King alone.[50] Humiliated beyond endurance, Charles bowed before the storm of protest. On 7 March he cancelled his Declaration. This was the last occasion on which he tried to overthrow the

Restoration church settlement. Parliament took its revenge on the King's mischievous ministers by passing the Test Act: an act which drove papists from office and wrecked the Cabal.[51]

VI

In the thirteen years between 1660 and 1673 the restored monarchy had done its best – sometimes directly, sometimes indirectly – to undermine the effectiveness of the Cavaliers' hold on church and state. During these troubled years a political tug-of-war had developed between Court and country, between the *politique* King and the zealous upholders of the Anglican establishment, led by Gilbert Sheldon, successively bishop of London (1660–63) and archbishop of Canterbury (1663–77). Intent upon advancing his prerogative at the expense of that establishment, Charles looked for support to a motley band of compliant churchmen, aggrieved Dissenters and ambitious papists; while Sheldon, pushed on to the defensive, insisted on the letter of the law and banked on the support of loyal churchmen. Truth to tell, Sheldon was in the better long-term position, for he knew the strength of his supporters. Having spent the entirety of the Cromwellian Interregnum ensconced in the bosom of the midland squirearchy, he appreciated the Cavaliers' solid social worth and their hatred of 'trouble-church' fanaticism. After 1661 he could depend on their representatives at Westminster. These 'prudent and religious patriots', as Bishop Hacket styled them,[52] proved more reliable friends to the church than either the King or his ministers, Clarendon included. In the recurrent crises of church and state – in 1662, 1663, 1667–8 and 1672–3 – Sheldon repeatedly invoked their assistance in resisting the harmful eccentricities of royal policy. They never failed him.

One consequence of the general election of 1661, which has been unaccountably overlooked, was the liberating effect that it had on Cavalier leadership inside the hierarchy of the church. It freed Sheldon and his episcopal allies from the uncongenial influence of a tolerationist Court, which had forced them, in turn, to engage in unwanted negotiations with the Presbyterian clergy, and to falter in the Lords' debates on Uniformity. The passage of the Act of Uniformity, 'a law so solemnly made', changed all that; for it allowed them to assert the rule of law against even the King. Henceforth Archbishop Sheldon ruled the Church with a rod of iron declaring, regardless of the vagaries of royal policy, that 'His Majesty's sense is no otherwise known than by his public laws, and by them, therefore, we are only to be guided in our duties'.[53] Fortunately for him his primacy coincided with the life of the Cavalier Parliament. He had the highest regard for its members and their devotion to church and state, but lamented the mischief wrought by Court faction and Charles's waywardness. In 1667 he wrote to his confidant, the Cavalier duke of Ormonde:

I really believe that the King never had, nor never is like to have, persons more willing to comply with his desires than this House of Commons . . . *were they treated as they might be*, for all the disorders have risen from the King's family and servants.[54]

During the eighteen years of its existence the loyalty and churchmanship of the Cavalier Parliament were never in doubt, and Sheldon did his best to maintain both. Yet it was not until the advent of Lord Treasurer Danby's administration that Charles was brought to 'reckon more particularly on his old friends' at Westminster and in the provinces.

Danby's policy was nicely calculated to the meridian of the Anglican establishment. Briefly stated, it was 'to keep up Parliament, to raise the old Cavaliers and the church party, and to sacrifice papists and Presbyterians'.[55] By the new year of 1675 he had effected a *rapprochement* between Whitehall and Lambeth – a crucial step towards making the Anglican system work to best advantage. Sheldon's return to Court favour inaugurated an era of close and beneficial co-operation between the twin authorities of church and state, which was to last into James II's reign.[56] A series of consultations, attended by ministers of state and bishops, resulted in Charles's belated espousal of the church interest.[57] Ever since 1660 royal inconstancy had been the Cavalier episcopate's worst headache, for it had played havoc with law enforcement in the dioceses and severely hindered their drive for uniformity. Instructively, in 1675, the bishops did not request new legislation, only the proper execution of the existing laws against nonconformity: in airing their grievance against past obstructions of the law they did not scruple 'to lay . . . something to His Majesty's door'.[58] The next four years saw the steady prosecution of Dissenters, in which the government lent its aid to the bishops and JPs, along with the active discouragement of Roman Catholicism, especially about the Court.

Alas for the peace of king and church, Danby's endeavours came too late to check the rising aspirations of Dissent, or to correct the 'popish' image of the Court. Years of royal patronage, reaching their climax in the Indulgence of 1672, had done more than assure the local survival of Protestant Dissent in the face of Cavalier Anglican intolerance: they had succeeded in revitalising its broken political spirit, as nothing else could have done, as was evidenced throughout the 1670s by the growth of the sectarian vote in the constituencies and the menacing vociferousness of the puritan 'rump' in Parliament. As for popery, a spent force if ever there was one in the life of the nation, Charles's contempt for the spiritual authority of the English Church, coupled with his dismissal of the 'Sheldonian' prelates from Court in 1667–8, had exposed his impressionable brother, James, duke of York, to the snares of Rome. Almost overnight the conversion of the heir presumptive to the Protestant throne of England gave popery an influence in politics out of all proportion to either its numbers or capabilities. More importantly, it lent a specious respectability to those malcontents who saw in Pan-protestantism a means of downing Danby and his exclusive Cavalier Anglican programme.

VII

Thus, by doggedly pursuing his mistaken quest for monarchical independence, by constantly undervaluing his 'old friends', the Church of England men, and by wilfully impeding their well-intentioned efforts to keep Dissenting minorities within the bounds set by statute, the King had seriously weakened the fabric of law and order: the very basis of the restored *régime*. In comforting the enemies of the Anglican establishment by his policies at home and abroad he unconsciously paved the way for a renewed bout of religious and political unrest, in which those watchwords of pre-war faction – 'popish affectation' and 'reformation' – were again given a new lease of life. That Charles was ultimately clever enough to get out of the trouble into which he had uncleverly got himself does not argue any superior political ability, still less perception, on his part. Moreover, in the last years of his reign he was exceptionally well served by his ministers in church and state – in the front rank of whom stood William Sancroft, Sheldon's successor in the primatial See of Canterbury (1677–91)[59]

The King's nomination of his trusted chaplain, over the heads of the entire episcopate, signified his resolution to demand from the clergy a higher standard of personal loyalty to himself and his family. Characteristically, he expected to extract the maximum advantage from his newfound alliance with the established church. In this he was not to be disappointed. As the first servant of the Crown, the new archbishop openly acknowledged that he ruled the church on behalf of the Stuart dynasty. A veteran loyalist, who had suffered sequestration and exile in the 1650s, and an energetic administrator who had tended the rebuilding of St Paul's Cathedral since 1666, Sancroft's principles and capacities were of a kind to put the Church into a forward gear, both politically and pastorally. His conduct revealed him to be heir general to the policies of Danby in the state and of Sheldon in the church. He was a stickler for the law, and a fervent believer in the high political role of his church. However, unlike Sheldon, he had to do without the backing of the Cavalier Parliament, which Charles rashly dissolved in 1679. As the Whig Exclusionists and their Dissenting allies in the boroughs came to dominate the House of Commons in the critical elections of 1679–81, he joined with the King in a concerted bid to resist the demand for the duke of York's exclusion from the throne. At Court he found willing partners among the Anglican nobility and ministers of state, while in the country he commanded the services of the Anglican episcopate and the ministers of religion. Under his direction the church was firmly committed to the defence of the legal establishment – this time not against the King, but against the declared enemies of divine rightist monarchy and episcopacy. Once again the harassed cry of 'the Church in danger' sounded from the press and pulpit, alerting the introverted conservatism of the shires and helping to create a Royalist party. Cavalier prelacy, fortified by Cavalier ideology, was a powerful driving force behind the rise of Toryism.

Through his friendship with the Hydes – Henry, second earl of Clarendon, and Laurence, earl of Rochester, the Anglican brothers-in-law of the duke of York – Archbishop Sancroft became a pivot of the 'Yorkist' reversionary interest, pledged to maintaining James's lawful inheritance as part of the Anglican scheme of things.[60] In the struggle with Whiggery he was unsparing in the duke's cause. He upheld his claims against Monmouth, the King's illegitimate son; he promoted propaganda on his behalf; he advanced James's adherents within the Anglican hierarchy; he prosecuted his opponents; he encouraged the integration of the Scottish episcopalians into James's

Edinburgh administration, and took care to relay to Tory England the grateful news that the Duke had inherited 'his blessed and royal father's concern for the poor broken Church' north of the Border. Such dedicated service to the dynasty redoubled the Stuart princes' appreciation of the Established Church as a prop to monarchy. On hearing, in November 1680, of the episcopate's unanimous denial of Exclusion in the House of Lords, James wrote from Edinburgh to Clarendon:

> Pray let the Archbishop of Canterbury and all the bishops know I never expected other from them than that they would be firm to the Crown, and put them in mind I have ever stuck to them, whatsoever my own opinion is [in religion], and shall continue to do so.[61]

In Scotland James's actions spoke even louder encouragement to the church. His suppression of field conventicles and his patronage of the down-trodden bishops gave the lie to Whig allegations that 'a popish successor' was incompatible with Protestant government.

As for Charles, he too supported the church to the hilt. In Parliament he refused to countenance any tampering with the Restoration Church settlement. When besought by a factious Commons to unite his Protestant subjects and to free Dissenters from the penal code – previously two of the most coveted goals of his personal policy – he stood by the Act of Uniformity and the laws of the land. After dissolving the third Exclusion Parliament in 1681 he threw the whole weight of the Court behind the episcopal campaign to discipline nonconformity in the dioceses. Convinced that schism in the church bred dissension in the state, the King systematically revised the commissions of the peace and set about regulating municipal corporations. His activities not only heralded the arrival in the localities of a magistracy that was dependably loyal; they also prepared the ground for unleashing the last great religious persecution seen in England: a persecution which brought the realm nearer to total outward conformity than at any time since the collapse of Laudian 'Thorough'. Church discipline, too long subject to the infirm procedure of the ecclesiastical courts, benefited as never before from the support of the intolerant Anglican laity, working through the parallel secular courts of petty and quarter sessions. In licensing the draconian prosecution of papists and dissenters Charles admitted that he had become the close prisoner of his 'old friends' and their Cavalier Anglican outlook. In short, he had succumbed to the fate which, at the outset of his reign, he had most wished to avoid. He had become the leader of a party – the leader of the intolerant, exclusive, high church Tories. For the present, at least, the restored Church of England, and the political interests which it represented, had succeeded in taming the restored monarchy.

8. The Debate over Science

MICHAEL HUNTER

RESTORATION science was controversial in its time and has remained so since. Indeed, scholarly debate over its different aspects has become a veritable minor industry in recent years, and the sheer bulk of often rather technical work on the subject might seem dismaying to the historical reader. This essay will try to give a few guidelines for approaching some of the more major controversies, but it will concentrate on the context of science as much as its content, for this too has been the subject of extensive discussion and its implications for the history of the period are wide. First, with science itself, what was its true character at this time and, in particular, how Baconian was it? How far was the period associated with the triumph of a mechanical world view at the expense of occult ones, and how close were the links between science and technology? More generally, how far were scientists concerned with the wider effects and potential benefits of their studies for society, as they had been in the Interregnum? How common was an interest in science, and how closely can it be linked with particular social classes or political or religious groups? Why was it that, though there is considerable evidence for science's popularity, it also encountered widespread hostility? What concerns underlay such opposition, and does its existence give warning against the danger of assuming that science was as dominant in the culture of the time as it was later to become?

I

One thing is not in doubt and that is the critical contribution to the Scientific Revolution made in England in these years, even if it is now clear that the role of the previous decades in the formation of ideas that were published only after 1660 has often been relatively neglected. Restoration England saw crucial advances in the classification

For Notes to Chapter 8, see pp. 224–8; for Bibliographical Notes, see pp. 203–4.

and study of plant and animal life, in the understanding of human physiology, of pneumatics, optics and other physical problems. At the same time, crucial steps were taken in the vindication of the corpuscular theory of matter, in the realignment of chemistry along mechanistic lines, in astronomical observation and in the articulation of a geometrical theory of the movement of the heavens. Attention has traditionally focused on the physical sciences, in which Isaac Newton's *Philosophiae Naturalis Principia Mathematica* (1687) is usually seen as crowning the age. But there is a danger of Newton's achievement overshadowing that of his contemporaries, whose contribution to more varied fields was in many ways more typical of the science of the time. In particular Robert Boyle, best known for his *Sceptical Chemist* (1661), made extensive and important experiments on a wide range of topics, while Robert Hooke, most famous for his *Micrographia* (1665), could claim sophisticated achievements in subjects from astronomy to geology. In the medical and biological sciences a different galaxy of names deserves attention, particularly those of John Ray and Nehemiah Grew in the analysis of plant life and Richard Lower and John Mayow in the elucidation of the mechanics of human physiology, and the achievement of each of these has been justly celebrated in the history of science.

When one turns from chronicling the achievement of such men to assessing the philosophy underlying them, however, one enters a more problematic area. Restoration science was self-consciously Baconian, its protagonists passionately devoted to the programme of inductive enquiry that Francis Bacon had articulated in the early 17th century as a means of superseding the sterile scholastic science of his day. The Royal Society, founded in 1660, was explicitly intended to forward by co-operative experiment and record the new 'system of natural philosophy' that Bacon had aspired to, as its publicists ceaselessly repeated. It is increasingly obvious, however, that those who have taken such views at their face value have been misled. Symptomatically the precise role of the Royal Society itself has now been questioned, for though it originally aspired to be a high-powered research institution along the lines of 'Solomon's House' in Bacon's *New Atlantis*, its performance in these terms was in fact disappointing. It had much more success in organising, co-ordinating and publicising research by scientists who tended to work on their own as they had before any such institution existed, an important but rather different function.[1] Similarly it now seems that Baconianism was at least to some extent a unifying slogan which (partly intentionally) gave an appearance of homogeneity to scientific activities and interests that were in fact extremely heterogeneous, and an over-emphasis on the influence of Bacon has led to a neglect of the more varied stimuli to scientific innovation in the period.[2]

Thus even in its technology science was acquiring in the Restoration period a sophistication which Bacon only dreamed of. The introduction and improvement of such instruments and devices as the microscope, the telescope and the micrometer gave a new scale of exactitude in observation and measurement which itself did much to transform scientists' terms of reference. More important was the fact that research in different subjects tended to be articulated along lines pioneered earlier in the seventeenth or even in the sixteenth century by continental and English scientists who owed little to Bacon, such as Johann Kepler, Galileo Galilei, William Harvey and René Descartes. Such men had isolated critical problems which gave a precise focus to research which a generalised programme of induction like Bacon's failed to provide.

This introduces perhaps the most important point of all. Traditionally the Scientific Revolution has often been considered significant primarily for turning away from the sterility of scholasticism towards precise observation and experiment, so that the advance of science at the time was principally associated with the accumulation of correct data from which improved theories were almost inevitably derived. But this is now seen as far too simple a mode of explanation of what actually went on. In fact it is clear – thanks not least to the work of such writers as Alexander Koyré, Herbert Butterfield and Thomas S. Kuhn – that in many ways the most critical advances in science at the time depended on changes in modes of explanation of natural and mechanical effects (often for insufficient reasons) rather than on more precise observation.[3] The corollary of this in the Restoration period has been to illustrate the importance of hypotheses based on already-deduced theory in the work of most of the more important scientists at the time.[4] Though it is possible to make Bacon seem more naïve than he really was in this respect, the fact remains that in his scientific theories as against his advocacy of inductive method he had relatively little of importance to offer. Recent research has vindicated the role of other thinkers, especially Descartes, as the men who – far more than Bacon – established the issues on which the science of the time focused.[5]

Yet some ambivalence on this point remains. For one thing it is clear that untrammelled induction was more important in some sciences than others. Thus in some of the areas in which Boyle worked, such as the study of heat, the chief advances of the period lay in the discovery of previously unknown experimental effects while theory was very underdeveloped in comparison with such 'classical' sciences as astronomy, statics and optics, where the opposite was the case.[6] But even in the latter there was a conscious appeal to Baconianism among English scientists, which inspired some hostility towards the *a priori* methods of some continental natural philosophers who were thought to devote insufficient attention to experiment and observation. Even Descartes himself (despite his major theoretical influence) was sometimes associated with the 'Modern Dogmatists' who betrayed the revolt against scholasticism by premature system-building.[7]

Moreover Restoration science could offer varieties of Baconianism, some of them more naïve than others. Though scientists like Hooke and Boyle clearly saw the need for a judicious mixture of theory and observation, realising the danger otherwise of natural philosophy being reduced to a mere heap of particulars, others were less sophisticated, as is shown by differing attitudes towards the great 'natural history' that Bacon had seen as the essential basis of science. Even figures like Hooke were enthusiastic about this, though seeing its limitations. But it is clear that for many lesser men it provided a charter for collecting a mass of miscellaneous data about the natural world in the belief, however misplaced, that they were thereby making an important contribution to the advancement of learning, a belief in which the Royal Society encouraged them.[8]

As a result one would misunderstand Restoration science if one did not take its natural history into account. A demonstrably popular and influential book like the *Natural History of Oxfordshire* (1677) compiled by Robert Plot, later curator of the Ashmolean Museum at Oxford and one-time Secretary of the Royal Society, is as characteristic of the science of the time as many more specialised treatises which proved critical in solving specific problems. Men like Plot were prominent in the scientific circles of the time, and this makes it less surprising that those who attacked the new science showed a constant tendency to conflate what we retrospectively evaluate as crucial with what we tend to write off as trivial.[9]

II

A corollary of this high valuation of inductive observation was the wide range of theory that was considered acceptable, for dogmatism was seen as having been one of the chief impediments to the advancement of learning. Boyle, for instance, presented his empirical findings so that they could be interpreted 'according to the differing hypotheses and inquisitions to which men are inclined', and this explains the wide range of alternative world-views that were able to coexist within scientific circles at the time, the discovery of which has sometimes surprised modern scholars.[10] Clearly the Royal Society included in its ranks not only men committed to the new mechanical philosophy but also others who preferred a wide range of more occult explanations of natural effects, often derived from sixteenth-century thinkers like the Swiss iatrochemist Paracelsus or seventeenth-century ones like J. B. van Helmont. Such confusion is hardly surprising in this intermediate period when Aristotelian science had been dethroned, but no satisfactory, all-embracing alternative had yet emerged, and we now know that several Fellows were even committed to the more arcane aspects of alchemy and astrology. There can be no doubt, however, that it would have been at variance with the Society's explicitly Baconian programme to ostracise them until induction had proved or disproved the validity of such concerns.

Indeed it was not just a case of such studies coexisting with science but of their actually contributing to the development of scientific ideas at the time, as recent studies of Newton have shown. For Newton was deeply committed to clearly arcane pursuits – it is even claimed that the *Principia* represents only a brief interlude in his working career whereas alchemy was a life-long interest – and there can now be no doubt that he was deeply influenced by mystical notions in formulating his world-view.[11]

But, in spite of this, there is clear evidence of tension on this point, which itself illustrates the direction in which things were moving at the time. Leading Fellows of the Royal Society such as Boyle, Hooke and William Petty were all outspoken in their championship of the mechanical philosophy at the expense of its more occult rivals, and in Boyle's case there was a positive attempt to establish a new orthodoxy on this point.[12] A number of scientists were outspoken in their attack on 'superstition', particularly judicial astrology, while Thomas Sprat in his *History of the Royal Society* (1667) was scathing about the aspirations of alchemical theorists: 'their writers involve them in such darkness, that I scarce know which was the greatest task, to understand their meaning or to effect it'.[13]

The surviving minutes suggest that occult theories were not often discussed at meetings of the Royal Society and there is evidence that on the rare occasions when they were this caused some friction, which might be taken to suggest growing antipathy towards them.[14] Similarly whatever the influence of mystical ideas on Newton, what was important about his system of the universe was that it was mathematically defined, and it was worlds apart from the old, vague, occult cosmologies which contributed to it. There can be little doubt that the traditional view of the Restoration period as marking the emerging triumph of mechanisation contains an element of truth, even if the occult interests of scientists at the time show that the process was a gradual and highly complex one.

The equivocal state of affairs in scientific circles, however, helps to explain the evident slowness with which occult beliefs were expunged from more popular mentalities, a slowness on which Keith Thomas has remarked in *Religion and the Decline of Magic* (1971). The championship of mechanisation did extend to this sphere, for scientists complained of the low quality of the standard astrological almanacs that sold so well in this period and would have liked to replace them with others more scientifically acceptable.[15] But this proved difficult to achieve, and it seems likely that the impact of the new science on the lower strata of society took longer than is sometimes supposed: indeed, there is evidence that scientists generally encountered problems in their attempts to extend their influence beyond the narrow circle of the intelligentsia.

The confused situation concerning the occult can be paralleled on the question of the relations between science and technology at this time. A violent controversy has raged over the closeness of the connection between the two in the Restoration period as in the 17th century generally, which again defies easy evaluation.[16] One thing is clear, and that is that scientists stressed the utility of what they were engaged in, in true Baconian style, and they contrasted it with the uselessness of the intellectual pursuits which they hoped that theirs would supersede. As Sprat put it, 'while the old [philosophy] could only bestow on us some barren terms and notions, the new shall impart to us the uses of all the creatures, and shall enrich us with all the benefits of fruitfulness and plenty'.[17]

The argument stems from the question of precisely what they meant by 'useful', and how closely really practical, everyday needs shaped the priorities of intellectual life. One should never forget that only a section of Boyle's book, *The Usefulness of Experimental Natural Philosophy* (1663, 1671) concerned utility of this sort: the others dealt with the value of natural knowledge in its own right and in terms of religious enlightenment. It is grotesque to credit much of the intellectual effort of Restoration scientists to a narrowly utilitarian viewpoint, as controversy over the stimuli to Newton's *Principia* has revealed. Clearly an intellectual momentum which was not of any direct practical significance supported most of the crucial conceptual advances of the period.[18]

But, true to their Baconian principles, most scientists genuinely believed that it was possible not only to pursue intellectual goals but to assist the needs of life as well. The Royal Society devoted considerable time and effort in its early years to technology, perhaps most strikingly in its project for a 'history of trades', which was in effect the technological counterpart of the great planned natural history. Its achievements included some valuable factual accounts of industrial processes, such as the 'History of Dyeing' by Petty which Sprat incorporated in his *History of the Royal Society*.[19] Interest was also expressed in agricultural improvement, and a 'georgical' questionnaire that was sent out produced numerous replies, while it was on the related topic of silviculture that the Society commissioned its most popular book, John Evelyn's *Sylva* (1664), which (it was claimed) was 'the occasion of propagating many millions of useful timber trees throughout this nation'.[20]

Despite such hopeful beginnings, however, on the whole the contribution of scientists to technology in this period was disappointing in comparison with the interest in the subject that they expressed. The programme for a co-operative history of trades lapsed after a few years, and though some scientists continued individually to pursue an interest in topics of immediate contemporary concern, such as naval technology, far less was achieved by the learned than Bacon and his enthusiastic followers had hoped.[21] Intellectuals were increasingly preoccupied by pure knowledge while the study of technology went its own way in other hands – those, for example, of the book- and map-seller Joseph Moxon, author of the classic *Mechanic Exercises, or the Doctrine of Handiworks* (1678, 1683) and other similar works. For Moxon was only peripherally connected with the circle of the Royal

Society although elected a Fellow in recognition of his achievement, while other similar writers had still less to do with the science of their day.[22]

Traditionally this has been associated with a growing élitism in Restoration science, and there is undoubtedly an element of truth in this, illustrating a significant characteristic of the intellectual life of the time.[23] Yet there is a tendency to draw overhasty conclusions from this, particularly in making invidious comparisons between the practitioners of Restoration science and their Interregnum precursors, many of whom, it is generally accepted, placed a high value on strictly utilitarian considerations. For there had been élitism in the Interregnum and it was not universal in the Restoration; in general insufficient stress has been laid on the difficulties that a technological programme encountered – not just the obvious problems of conceptualising ship design that evidently held up nautical theory, but, more important, the difficulty of getting suggestions for technical improvement through to those for whom they were intended, who had a tendency to write off the suggestions of the educated as 'the whimsies of contemplative persons'.[24] These were problems which the Interregnum had also had to face, not always with much success in comparison with the grandiose schemes of the time which have attracted perhaps disproportionate attention in such works as Charles Webster's *The Great Instauration* (1955). There was a constant tendency for intellectuals to withdraw to intellectual affairs where achievement and acclaim came more easily.

III

The question of the effect of the events of 1660 on the scientific movement also emerges in considering the link between science and reform at the time. For though most of such schemes as had been implemented by the revolutionary regime were now suppressed, plans for major reform of the kind that had been common in the Interregnum did not die out. In fact it is only the prejudice of modern scholars that has made it appear that such aspirations were the prerogative of religious and political radicals, and it is symptomatic that whereas attention has been drawn to the almost millenarian aspirations for science in Sprat's *History of the Royal Society* as evidence of the residual influence of 'Puritanism',it is now clear that the association of such ideas exclusively with the Puritans is quite mistaken; in fact they were part of the general intellectual equipment of the age and could equally easily be used to justify any programme, whether revolutionary or royalist.[25]

Perhaps most striking in showing the belief of the Restoration period in the potential of intellectual effort radically to reshape human affairs are the schemes of the time for a new and rational 'universal' language, plans which had originated in the Interregnum but which only now came to fruition.[26] No less significant were the projects of these years for educational reform, for these presented a major challenge to the techniques and content of orthodox education, though it should be pointed out that the notions of social engineering that had been present in at least some of the schemes emanating from Samuel Hartlib and his circle in the earlier period were now dropped.[27] Equally far-sighted were hopes that the application of accurate mensuration to the problems of government would make possible a more efficient use of national resources: this was the rationale of the 'political arithmetic' that William Petty championed in these years.[28]

The fruit of such schemes in the Restoration period, however, was on the whole disappointing. In the case of the language schemes this was due to technical difficulties, but educational reform (with a few exceptions) was blocked by conservatives who defended the utility of the traditional curriculum. Although there is some evidence of sympathy for the ideas of Petty and other scientists in government circles, in general they encountered apathy and hostility: Petty was said to be 'notional and fanciful near up to madness'.[29] Even when the government was convinced in the 1670s of the value of the relatively limited project of establishing an observatory at Greenwich to provide a more precise set of observations of the movements of the celestial bodies for navigational use, the early history of that institution shows a halfheartedness in its patronage that is almost as striking as its original foundation and which certainly hampered the efforts of the first astronomer royal, John Flamsteed.[30]

In general, after the Restoration as before, plans for scientifically inspired improvement were constantly blocked by more or less articulate defenders of the *status quo*, and it is significant that the reaction of disappointed protagonists of reform, as of technological change, was to resort to the advocacy of highhanded treatment in dealing with such obstruction.[31] In fact this gives a clue to a possible generalisation about the political implications of science in this period, and that is that scientists tended to aspire to strong and efficient government –

monarchist in this period, republican in the Interregnum – giving short shrift to the obfuscatory influence of vested interests. Thus, though the opponents of such schemes were quick to allude to the Interregnum by tarring their opponents with the brush of 'fanaticism', the unconcealed envy of scientists at the time for the use of science in the service of the state in contemporary France suggests a different perspective. The absolutist potential even of the Royal Society's agricultural enquiries was illustrated by a Huntingdonshire yeoman who refused to answer them, claiming 'there is more reason of state in this Royal Society than at first I was aware of'.[32]

Such suggestions must be hesitant, however, and in general it has proved difficult to find specific ideological connections for the new science. This is, in fact, a subject that has attracted an inordinate amount of attention, due largely to those who have polemically sought to establish a connection between science and 'Puritanism' in the seventeenth century in general. It is now clear, however, that at least as far as the Restoration is concerned, such a correlation will not do unless 'Puritanism' is so broadly defined (as it was, for example, by the American sociologist R. K. Merton) that it includes almost all English churchmen of the period.[33] Detailed analysis (for instance of the affiliations of the nucleus of the Royal Society in its early years) tends to illustrate the heterogeneity of the political and religious commitments of those devoted to science, and there can be little doubt that scientific pursuits both could be and were combined with a wide range of ideological viewpoints. Though it seems likely that the varying preconceptions of scientists helped to differentiate their concerns to some extent (as they clearly did in the Interregnum) this has yet to be demonstrated.[34]

The most convincing claims that have been made for a significant (though not necessarily exclusive) link between science and a particular religious group have concerned its association with the Latitudinarians, in other words with the party in the Restoration Church who aspired to a middle way between dogmatism and scepticism, advocating rationalism and simplicity in theology and tolerance and good works in the Church. There is certainly good evidence of an overlap between the advocates of Latitudinarianism and the leading scientists and patrons of science at the time.[35]

Some have seen this link between science and the men of latitude as a symptom of the withdrawal of science from religious and political commitment. Others, however, have seen it as a more positive ideology, writ large in the books of those associated with science who also wrote on religious topics such as Boyle, Sprat and John Wilkins, bishop of Chester. Such authors argued for religious moderation and the pursuit of science not merely in their own right but as part of a philosophy which justified both the social order of Restoration England and its mercantile potential.[36] Though the vagueness of 'Latitudinarianism' as an ecclesiastical group means that this attempt to give science a more precise religious and political linkage can easily merge back into a generalised view of its potential appeal to people of many vaguely similar opinions, the arguments concerning this link have on the whole been convincing.

With this philosophy went the hope, expressed in Sprat's *History of the Royal Society*, that the new science would gain widespread support from people of all classes, including those, such as the merchants, who were achieving that mercantile prosperity with which science and moderate religion were thought so naturally to concur.[37] The question of the extent to which science succeeded in obtaining the audience to which it aspired is one on which recent research has some findings to offer. Attention has focused primarily on the Royal Society, partly because its printed membership lists offer a fixed sample for statistical analysis which is otherwise not easily available among the scientific enthusiasts of the period, and partly because the membership of that body had a real significance in providing the financial and moral support without which it could not have performed such functions as it did in the world of science at the time. Although this creates some difficulties, since it is clear that as a sample of contemporary scientific interest the Society's membership was distorted in certain ways, other evidence does not suggest that conclusions based on it are particularly misleading in indicating where science found support at the time.[38]

Thus if one can separate the activities associated with the Society from the technological concerns that it increasingly abdicated, it seems clear that, though there was a large market for technical handbooks, primers in elementary mathematics and suchlike which went well down the social scale, a concern for more varied scientific activities on the whole did not, being predominantly associated with the professional and leisured classes. What is particularly interesting is that, despite the hopes of Sprat and others that science would advance hand in hand with commerce, few practising merchants were Fellows of the Royal Society. Those who were were often rather exceptional in their class, and indeed the mercantile community seems to have shown some scepticism about the grandiose claims of scientists at the time.[39]

In so far as one can find a significant social connection for science it is not directly with commerce but more with a nexus between landed wealth, trade and government. This has been ably sketched in connection with the financier Sir John Banks and it is represented, for instance, by such active Fellows of the Royal Society as Sir John Lowther of Whitehaven, landed gentleman and entrepreneur, or Thomas Povey, government official and merchant.[40] It is doubtless this kind of environment which helps to explain the indolently utilitarian character of science at the time – its ambivalence between the grandiose ambitions of Sprat and others that it should be of direct assistance to human life (which scholars have too often uncritically echoed), and its actual tendency to fail to realise these hopes and instead to settle down as a primarily intellectual activity to which men of affairs devoted their leisure in common with scholars and dilettantes.

But there is a danger of overemphasising specific social links for science as there is of making too much of its connection with Latitudinarianism. For what is significant about Restoration science is that it clearly became general in its appeal, and in the course of this process it tended to shed such specific connections, spreading widely among the educated classes. Clearly it was primarily a metropolitan activity: it was in London that science was fashionably pursued in coffee-house clubs and elsewhere and London was also the seat of the Royal Society, which was invigorated (and often trivialised) by similar enthusiasm. But interest spread further afield, to Dublin, where a comparable society was set up in 1683, and, more generally, to the English provinces where correspondence illustrates the activity of numerous more or less scattered enthusiasts.[41]

Even the universities were more receptive to the new ideas than has sometimes been thought, although science was not made integral to the undergraduate curriculum for nearly two centuries. Facilities for scientific study were widely available, as defenders of the *status quo* were quick to point out to their antagonists, after the Restoration as in the Interregnum. Oxford even acquired a philosophical society and a natural history museum, in the form of the Ashmolean, in the 1680s.[42] There can be no doubt that an interest in science, pursued by a vigorous dedication to experiment, correspondence and discussion on a wide range of topics, spread throughout Restoration England: the 'virtuoso', as a man devoted to such studies was called by contemporaries, became a familiar figure.

IV

In view of this it may seem surprising that science encountered hostility at the time, a hostility that clearly worried its supporters although it has sometimes been written off as insignificant by modern scholars. To some extent this may be associated with the reaction of vested interests like the universities and the medical profession to the threat which they felt that the aspirations of science presented, although they were not actually realised. The merest rumour that the Royal Society was espousing educational ambitions was enough to provoke outspoken enmity at Oxford, while the College of Physicians was also deeply jealous of its professional monopoly and at least some of its Fellows showed considerable rancour towards the newer institution.[43]

To some extent, too, the hostility reflects the ambivalence towards science of the London 'wits', who partook of a general sport of poking fun at the virtuosi enjoyed even by Charles II himself, despite his patronage of the Royal Society. The most significant outcome of this was perhaps Thomas Shadwell's comedy, *The Virtuoso* (1676), which shows a delicate eye for the laughable, and numbered both greater and lesser men among its victims.[44] Such satire caused the scientists some embarrassment – 'people almost pointed', Hooke noted in his diary when he went to see Shadwell's play – and attempts were made to reply to similar squibs in the early Restoration period, though the fact that these were not followed later suggests that the sting of satire soon wore off.[45]

Far more serious, however, was the suspicion that science encountered at the time due to its association with movements that were widely held to be destructive of the religious and moral values on which contemporary society was based. For one thing a problem was presented by the espousal of science by the religious radicals of the Interregnum, due to the general revulsion against fanaticism after the Restoration epitomised by the vast popularity of Samuel Butler's *Hudibras*. But the more intellectual heresies that had become popular during the Interregnum were also suspect, particularly the materialism that had been associated with ancient and modern philosophical ideas common in the revolutionary decades. Thus the atomist ideas that had come to England through Lucretius, and through the writings of the French scientist Pierre Gassendi, seemed pernicious because of their relationship with the well-known moral views of Epicurus, and modern materialists were also suspect. Indeed part of the ambivalence of scientists towards Descartes was due to a desire to dissociate themselves from implications of his philosophy that some saw as pernicious, and difficulties were presented above all by the views of Thomas Hobbes, himself also a scientist. For Hobbes's influence was widely held responsible for the atheism and libertinism which were seen as dangerously prevalent among the rising generation, and orthodox theologians therefore attacked him assiduously.[46]

The alarm that scientists felt at the possibility of being tarred with the brush either of illuminism or atheism is shown by the eagerness with which they sought to dissociate themselves from both. Thus Sprat in his *History of the Royal Society* was outspoken in his opposition to the 'enthusiasm' of the preceding period, and Robert Boyle also attacked what he saw as the dangerous implications of the radical occult ideas that had flourished in the Interregnum and which saw something of a revival in the 1660s, deliberately devoting himself to the articulation of a rival corpuscular system to reply to them. He also encouraged the collection of accounts of cases of witchcraft in an attempt to counter the materialism of Epicurus and Hobbes.[47]

In fact the Royal Society's ambivalent relations with Hobbes are particularly interesting in this connection, for though Hobbes was on quite good terms with a number of leading Fellows and the two parties enjoyed considerable mutual respect, he was never a Fellow himself. To some extent it is clear that older opinions that Hobbes was deliberately 'excluded' from the Society entailed views of the inclusiveness of its membership in relation to the scientific community at the time which have now been exploded. Hobbes was not the only person with known scientific interests who failed to join the Society, and at least part of the reason for this in his case was that he was known to be dogmatic and argumentative and that the Society did not want to be saddled with a club bore.[48] But this is only half the answer, since the point is not just that Hobbes was never a Fellow but that he was actually attacked by leading Fellows such as Boyle and John Wallis. They did this to dissociate the scientific programme to which they were devoted not only from Hobbes's dogmatic and non-experimental method but also from his philosophical ideas and their pernicious implications.[49]

Indeed the protagonists of the new science moved from the defence to the attack. Against those contemporaries who perceptively saw the danger that too much study of secondary causes might lead to a neglect of primary ones, they argued that, on the contrary, the study of the natural world contributed to God's glory, an argument from natural theology that can be traced at least back to Bacon and which now became increasingly prominent.[50] Sprat went on from his advocacy of inductive reasoning in reaction against the fanaticism of the Interregnum to argue for a natural alliance between the revived Anglican church and the scientific spirit, and scientists made much of natural theology, arguing that scientific investigation could cool religious controversy, ending empty verbal disputes, quite apart from manifesting the power and wisdom of God in his creation. The argument is epitomised by the title of one of the works of Joseph Glanvill, another assiduous protagonist of the new science, *Philosophia Pia, a discourse of the religious temper and tendencies of the experimental philosophy which is professed by the Royal Society, to which is annexed a recommendation and defence of reason in the affairs of religion* (1671).

Such arguments are particularly associated with the Latitudinarian party in the church, the links between which and science have already been mentioned. But what should be remembered is that, in so far as such parties were differentiated in the Anglican church in the Restoration period, the Latitudinarians were not the dominant group. A clue to the intellectual attitudes of other parties who took a different view of the new philosophy is provided by the most serious attacks on science that were made at this time: those of Meric Casaubon and Henry Stubbe. For though Stubbe was a ready controversialist whose pen had earlier been employed in a number of disputes and who easily moved to exaggeration and rather facile polemic, both he and Casaubon employed a number of more serious arguments with wider appeal. Indeed one suspects that it often took a polemicist to articulate views that were really commonplace, and there can be little doubt that many would have echoed the view of the Warwickshire lawyer Thomas Mariet on Stubbe's death in 1676: 'he is by many lamented, and by some as holding a rod over the Royal Society, who for him durst not trouble the world with their impertinances'. Even the warmest advocates of scientific investigation stood in awe of 'the huge clatter' made by Casaubon, 'so great a name amongst the critics and antiquaries'.[51]

What evidently worried such men most about the new science, apart from its unrealised aspirations and its potential atheistic connotations, was its genuine and self-conscious iconoclasm. Scientists prided themselves on the small number of the books that they had read; they attacked pedantry; they valued highly the observations of 'plain, diligent and laborious observers: such, who, though they bring not much knowledge, yet bring their hands and their eyes uncorrupted'.[52] So paradoxically to Stubbe and Casaubon as guardians of a learned culture, scientists seemed similar to the fashionable 'wits' whose satire they themselves feared. Stubbe explicitly placed them in this category, as implicitly did the divine, Robert South, and scientists like Petty were at pains to dissociate themselves from it, distinguishing his and the Royal Society's aims '(both as to difficulty and dignity) from what is commonly called wit'.[53]

What is more there was evidently an element of truth in the views of their antagonists, for it is clear that science's iconoclasm did have the effect of encouraging a disrespect for learning. Scholars complained of how young 'gallants' took up ideas that they had heard at the Royal Society or in talk at coffee-houses and proceeded to attack Aristotle and the universities, and even those who approved of science criticised its noisy and ignorant hangers-on.[54] Stubbe was not so far from the truth when he complained how fashion had turned against 'antiquated studies' in favour of poetry, plays and 'toyish experiments', which were claimed to be 'cares of such high concernment, that all philology is but pedantry and polemical divinity controversies with which we are satiated'.[55] The anti-intellectualism that can be discerned in Sprat is taken to an even further stage in a book like the *Treatise of the Bulk and Selvedge of the World* (1674) by the Suffolk virtuoso Nathaniel Fairfax, in which he professed to prefer a bricklayer to an Aristotelian philosopher, and the writings of Grew on the sprouting of a bean to shelves full of books on church government and the like.[56]

Fairfax's view may sound almost rhetorical, and by the middle of the eighteenth century it might have been dismissed as such. But in the Restoration period it was not, for many felt strongly about the need for learned activity of just the kind he attacked, espousing a traditional, learned, theologically and historically oriented view of the proper functions of intellectual life that was at odds with the priorities of science. Perhaps the clearest statement of this position is to be found in the attack on the new science made by Meric Casaubon, son of the celebrated classical scholar Isaac Casaubon and himself a distinguished scholar and divine, who assailed its pretensions as philistine and pernicious, rather as Stubbe poured scorn on those who preferred aphorisms of cider and suchlike to real wisdom.[57] Casaubon's scholarly criteria were quite different, and they were articulated by a clear view of the essential role of scholarship in the exposition and elucidation of Protestant Christianity and its defence against the ever-present threat from Rome.

Casaubon criticised as naïve or dangerous those who, like Sprat and Glanvill, appealed to pure reason as the basis of religion and claimed that the scriptures alone, interpreted in this light, were a sufficient basis for doctrine.[58] In his view Christianity had always inevitably had a controversial element and hence considerable value attached to the views of the Fathers and the councils of the early church on such topics: it was thus vital for the protagonists of Protestantism to be armed with a knowledge of these. More important still, however, was the 'general learning' in erudite languages and the history of rites and customs that was essential to the vindication of the authority of the scriptures themselves and to their proper understanding. Casaubon argued that intellectual activity devoted to this end had an importance that science could never aspire to.[59]

That others agreed on the need for erudition of this kind is illustrated, for instance, by the alarm that greeted the *Critical History of the Old Testament* by the heterodox French divine, Richard Simon, which sought to demonstrate the uncertainties of the literal text of the Bible. So it is not surprising that scholarship of the kind advocated by Casaubon did, in fact, flourish in Restoration England, where it was associated primarily (though not exclusively) with the high churchmen who dominated the ecclesiastical hierarchy at the time.[60] Its most spectacular centre was at Oxford, where John Fell, Dean of Christ Church, presided over the setting up of a printing house devoted to scholarly aims like Casaubon's. But similar attitudes and activities can also be found in others elsewhere – in John Pearson at Cambridge, for example, or Dudley Loftus in Dublin, who attacked the philosophical society there in terms similar to Casaubon's onslaught on the new science in England. All these men shared Casaubon's enthusiasm for the study of biblical texts and respect for patristic authority.[61]

Related to this concern for ecclesiastical scholarship was a more general interest in learned enquiry into historical precedent.

Nourished by similar polemical concerns, this was equally characteristic of the age, for these years saw infinite energy expended over
the collation and exposition of erudite historical sources by a whole
generation of scholars. And though the affiliations of such activity
were wider (particularly in connection with the constitutional issues
of the age, on the antiquarian arguments concerning which there was
lively debate), the evidence suggests that this dense erudition was, to a
disproportionate extent, the work of high churchmen.[62] What is more,
even when its protagonists did not make their views on the subject
explicit, their implicit sympathies were with the priorities articulated
by Casaubon, for one can certainly find evidence of their hostility to
the common disrespect of the age for the values they stood by.[63]

v

Science and learning were not totally polarised. The Latitudinarians
who made so much of science were less hostile to the learned argument from antiquity than is sometimes thought. There was also an
overlap between the patrons of the two traditions and their participants in such men as Sir Joseph Williamson, statesman and diplomat,
or Edward Bernard, Savilian Professor of Astronomy at Oxford, who
played an important role in encouraging both science and biblical
scholarship there, while his name is associated with a major catalogue
of antiquarian manuscripts that was compiled under his supervision
and published in 1697.[64] Fell encouraged science as well as learning,
too, and it is perhaps surprising to discover that even Stubbe and
Casaubon, though taking issue with the less restrained protagonists
of science, could both boast modest scientific interests themselves.[65]

But what is significant is that the science that interested them
and others like them tended to be innocuous natural history rather
than the critical conceptual advances of the new philosophy.
Though they were prepared to give science a minor place in their
scheme of knowledge, they failed (or refused) to acknowledge its
potential. Such men generally showed a sympathy for the 'ancients'
as against the 'moderns' in natural knowledge which has often been
seen as the central point of the dispute between them and their
scientific antagonists, while Casaubon was just unable to see what
all the fuss was about Descartes' 'cogito' principle. Most crushing of
all was Stubbe's indictment:[66]

All that is said about the erecting of mechanical or sensible philosophy of nature is but empty talk: human nature is not capable of such achievements. 'Tis evidently impossible to attain any exact knowledge of the surface of our whole terrestrial globe, and the depths of the earth and water are no less unsearchable. And as to the component particles, their nature, figure, motions and combinations are known only to the Deity: so that no prudent person is to be amused with these Rosicrucian promises.

This dismissive attitude clearly found its echo in others less articulate, and this makes it easier to understand why, despite the evidence for science's wide popularity – epitomised by Sprat's view that experimenting represented 'the present prevailing genius of the English nation' – this was balanced by scepticism concerning its potential as anything but an amusing way of spending time. This underlies John Evelyn's complaint concerning the Royal Society in 1679 that ' 'tis impossible to conceive how so honest and worthy a design should have found so few promoters and so cold a welcome in a nation whose eyes are so wide open'.[67] It is, indeed, symptomatic that Sprat's *History of the Royal Society* was not reprinted in the Restoration period, although it soon became scarce, since its large ambitions and strident iconoclasm clearly aroused hostility in a way that a more restrained devotion to scientific enterprise did not.[68]

But, equally significantly, the *History* was reprinted three times between 1702 and 1734, and it may not be fanciful to see this new acceptability as an index of the change that was by then coming over intellectual life. The transition had begun by 1688 and it accelerated thereafter, and though it was associated to some extent with the triumph of the Latitudinarians in the Church, it can also be linked to a more general shift in English and European culture in the late seventeenth and early eighteenth centuries.[69] For this is a period that is marked by a steady decline in respect for the Fathers in theological circles and by the eclipse of the tradition in theology and ecclesiastical scholarship that Fell and others had championed. Meanwhile, in historical research, the controversial ardour that had fuelled the concerns of the so-called 'Laudian' school subsided, and though scholarly historical achievement in this tradition continued at least up to the 1720s, it was disproportionately associated with the High Church party and shared in that party's gradual eclipse.[70]

At the same time, under the presiding genius of Newton, science became increasingly orthodox, systematic and influential, and the religious and philosophical values with which it was associated came to dominance in the aftermath of the publication of Locke's major works. More and more, men saw the pointlessness of basing the defence of religious orthodoxy on authorities for which its antagonists had little respect, and hence natural theology became all the more important.[71] There is also evidence of a growing concern for science in such areas of national life as government and education, with more attention to statistics in the former and to scientifically-oriented curricula in the latter, and though science continued to meet with satire, even its slighters increasingly respected its aspirations and achievements.[72]

So the Restoration period may be able to boast major scientific discoveries and a considerable amount of fashionable concern for science. But it is dangerous to read backwards from the high prestige that science enjoyed subsequently to assume that it was equally dominant in the Restoration. In fact learned traditions held a respect that science was later to usurp, while the general failure to implement scientifically-inspired reform indicates the indifference that persisted concerning science's potential. It is important not to lose sight of this ambivalence, in spite of all the period's positive achievement: for arguably this, more than anything else, is the key to the intellectual character of the age.

List of Abbreviations

(for Bibliographical Notes, and Notes and References)

Add. MSS	Additional Manuscripts, British Library
AHR	*American Historical Review*
BIHR	*Bulletin of the Institute of Historical Research*
BL	British Library
Bodl.	Bodleian Library, Oxford
CSPD	*Calendar of State Papers, Domestic*
CJ	*(House of) Commons' Journals*
EcHR	*Economic History Review*
EHR	*English Historical Review*
HJ	*Historical Journal*
HMC	Historical Manuscripts Commission
JBS	*Journal of British Studies*
PLMA	*Publications of the Modern Language Association of America*
PRO	Public Record Office, London
SP	*State Papers*
TRHS	*Transactions of the Royal Historical Society*
XVIIe siècle	*Le Dix-septième siècle*

Bibliographical Notes

Note: Place of publication is London unless otherwise stated.

I. THE LATER STUART MONARCHY

There has been no study of the later Stuart monarchy as such. Perhaps the nearest to such a study was J. R. Western, *Monarchy and Revolution: The English State in the 1680s* (1972) which contained some interesting ideas, but was marred by conceptual rigidity and confusion and by a lack of detailed archival research. The best general study of the Stuart constitution is that by Kenyon. On later Stuart constitutional theory, see the later chapters of J. G. A. Pocock, *The Ancient Constitution and the Feudal Law* (Cambridge, 1957), P. Laslett's introduction to his edition of Sir Robert Filmer, *Patriarcha and other Political Writings* (1949) and B. Behrens, 'The Whig Theory of the Constitution in the Reign of Charles II', *Cambridge Historical Journal*, VII (1941). There is no satisfactory biography of Charles II, but K. H. D. Haley's Historical Association pamphlet, *Charles II* (1966) is judicious and perceptive. For James II see J. Miller, *James II: A Study in Kingship* (Hove, 1978). The two kings' decision making can also be approached through three excellent biographies of Restoration politicians: A. Browning, *Thomas Earl of Danby*, 3 vols (Glasgow, 1951) (vols 2 and 3 consist of a valuable collection of documents); K. H. D. Haley, *The First Earl of Shaftesbury* (Oxford, 1968) and, above all, J. P. Kenyon, *Robert Spencer, Earl of Sunderland* (1959) which gives a superb account of the workings of court politics. The court itself has received little systematic attention, but for an indication of the sort of research that is needed, see D. Allen, 'The Political Function of Charles II's Chiffinch', in *Huntington Library Quarterly*, XXXIX (1976).

Turning to constraints of the monarchy, there is little sign as yet in the Restoration period of that reassessment of the relationship of Crown and Parliament which Conrad Russell and others have undertaken for the early part of the century. However, D. T. Witcombe, *Charles II and the Cavalier House of Commons, 1663–74* (Manchester, 1966) contains much useful material, though for a rather limited period. Charles's finances have been very well covered by C. D. Chandaman, *The English Public Revenue, 1660–88* (Oxford, 1975) and H. Roseveare, *The Treasury, 1660–1870: The Foundations of Control* (1973). Almost nothing has been published on county government in this period and only a little on urban history, notably in J. R. Jones, *The Revolution of 1688 in England* (1972) and J. H. Sacret, 'The Restoration Government and Municipal Corporations', *EHR*, XLV (1930). There is no satisfactory study either of the Crown's means of coercion: J. Childs, *The Army of Charles II* (1976) is rather narrowly military and stops in 1685, while J. R. Western, *The English Militia in the Eighteenth Century* (1965) leans too heavily on printed sources and central government records.

Finally, this period is rich in primary sources which offer insights into the working of monarchy, notably Clarendon's *Life*, Reresby's *Memoirs*, Burnet's *History* and, of course, Pepys's *Diary*.

2. PARTIES AND PARLIAMENT

There is no single systematic examination of the structures and workings of politics throughout the Restoration period. Particular phases are analysed in detail in J. R. Jones, *The First Whigs* (1961) and *The Revolution of 1688 in England* (1972); D. T. Witcombe, *Charles II and the Cavalier House of Commons* (Manchester, 1966); M. Lee, *The Cabal* (Urbana, 1965); R. S. Bosher, *The Making of the Restoration Settlement* (1951). For some more general perspectives see J. H. Plumb, *The Growth of Political Stability in England, 1675–1725* (1967) and his article 'The Growth of the Electorate in England from 1600 to 1715' in *Past and Present* 45 (1969). Sir Keith Feiling, *History of the Tory Party, 1640–1714* (Oxford, 1924) is still useful. A. Browning first reconnoitred the subject of parties in 'Parties and Party Organization in the Reign of Charles II' *TRHS* 4th ser. xxx (1948), and then proceeded to write the definitive biography of the pioneer of the techniques of parliamentary management, *Thomas Osborne, Earl of Danby* 3 vols (Glasgow, 1944–51). He was also the editor of the fullest collection of documentary and primary printed material, *English Historical Documents* VIII (1966) which covers the years 1660–1714. The other modern collection is also excellent; J. P. Kenyon, *The Stuart Constitution* (Cambridge, 1966) deals with the period 1603–88. The latter's biographical study, *Robert Spencer, Earl of Sunderland* (1958) gives a clear insight into the politics of the Court. K. H. D. Haley, *The First Earl of Shaftesbury* (Oxford, 1968) not only deals with his organisation of opposition but with his earlier career as a minister. Maurice Ashley has written many biographies of leading figures: *Charles II* (1971); *General Monck* (1977) and *James II* (1977); the latter should be compared with John Miller, *James II: A Study in Kingship* (Hove, 1978).

For general surveys of the period see D. Ogg, *England in the Reign of Charles II* (Oxford, 1955) and *England in the Reigns of James II and William III* (Oxford, 1957). See also J. R. Jones, *Country and Court; England 1658–1714* (1978).

3. LAW, COURTS AND CONSTITUTION

An admirable introduction to the Restoration and its historiography is J. Thirsk (ed.), *The Restoration* (1976). The fullest modern account of the period is D. Ogg, *England in the Reign of Charles II* (Oxford, 1934, 2nd edn 1955), and *England in the Reigns of James II and William III* (Oxford, rev. edn, 1963).

Books on constitutional history abound: one of the most helpful, despite its age, remains M. A. Thomson, *A Constitutional History of England, 1642 to 1801* (1938); while two newer books dealing with political and constitutional history in this period are G. E. Aylmer, *The Struggle for the Constitution,*

1603–1689 (1963) and B. Kemp, *King and Commons, 1660–1832* (1957). The most stimulating modern work is the extended essay by J. R. Western, *Monarchy and Revolution: the English State in the 1680s* (1972). J. P. Kenyon, *The Stuarts: A Study in English Kingship* (1958), is biographical in approach and small in scale, but lively and interesting. Two good sets of documents, each with excellent accompanying commentary, are A. Browning (ed.), *English Historical Documents, 1660–1714*, VIII (1966) and J. P. Kenyon (ed.), *The Stuart Constitution, 1603–1688* (Cambridge, 1966); H. Roseveare, *The Treasury, 1660–1870* (1973), in the series called 'Historical Problems: Studies and Documents', is also first class. Among numerous articles and monographs some of the most useful are: R. E. Boyer, *English Declarations of Indulgence, 1687 and 1688* (The Hague, 1968); C. D. Chandaman, *The English Public Revenue, 1660–1688* (Oxford, 1975); J. Childs, *The Army of Charles II* (1976); J. R. Jones, *The Revolution of 1688 in England* (1972); J. H. Plumb, *The Growth of Political Stability in England, 1675–1725* (1967); J. G. A. Pocock, *The Ancient Constitution and the Feudal Law* (Cambridge, 1957); C. Roberts, *The Growth of Responsible Government in Stuart England* (Cambridge, 1966); J. H. Sacret, 'The Restoration Government and Municipal Corporations', in *EHR*, XLV (1930) 232–59; L. G. Schwoerer, *'No Standing Armies!' The Antiarmy Ideology in Seventeenth-Century England* (Baltimore, 1974); C. C. Weston, *English Constitutional Theory and the House of Lords, 1556–1832* (1965); D. T. Witcombe, *Charles II and the Cavalier House of Commons, 1663–74* (Manchester, 1966). Two inaugural lectures deserve notice; G. Holmes, *The Electorate and the National Will in the First Age of Party* (Lancaster, 1976); and J. P. Kenyon, *The Nobility in the Revolution of 1688* (Hull, 1963).

The law is less well served than the constitution, but the breadth of vision and mastery of detail in W. S. Holdsworth, *History of English Law* still impresses – for this period volume VI (1924) is the most relevant. A. Harding, *A Social History of English Law* (1966), is the best brief introduction. Specialised modern studies include B. L. Anderson, 'Law, Finance and Economic Growth in England: Some Long-term Influences', in B. M. Ratcliffe (ed.), *Great Britain and her World 1750–1914. Essays In Honour of W. O. Henderson* (Manchester, 1975) pp. 99–124; W. H. Bryson, *The Equity Side of the Exchequer: Its Jurisdiction, Administration, Procedures and Records* (Cambridge, 1975); J. S. Cockburn, *A History of English Assizes, 1558–1714* (Cambridge, 1972); A. F. Havighurst, 'The Judiciary and Politics in the Reign of Charles II', in *Law Quarterly Review*, LXVI (1950) 62–78, 229–52; 'James II and the Twelve Men in Scarlet', ibid., LXIX (1953) 522–46; E. G. Henderson, *Foundations of English Administrative Law* (Cambridge, Mass., 1963); J. R. Hertzler, 'The Abuse and Outlawing of Sanctuary for Debt in Seventeenth-Century England', in *HJ*, XIV (1971) 467–77; G. W. Keeton, 'The Judiciary and the Constitutional Struggle 1660–88', in *Journal of the Society of Public Teachers of Law*, new ser., VII (1963) 56–68; *Lord Chancellor Jeffreys and the Stuart Cause* (1965); M. Landon, *The Triumph of the Lawyers; Their Role in English Politics, 1678–1689* (Alabama, 1970); B. Osborne, *Justices of the Peace, 1361–1848* (Shaftesbury, 1960); R. J. Sharpe, *The Law of Habeas Corpus* (Oxford, 1976); D. E. C. Yale (ed.), *Lord Nottingham's Chancery Cases*, (Selden Soc., LXXIII (1957) and LXXIX (1961); *Sir Matthew Hale's The Prerogative of the King*, ibid.,

XCII (1975); 'A View of the Admiral Jurisdiction: Sir Matthew Hale and the Civilians', in D. Jenkins (ed.), *Legal History Studies, 1972* (Cardiff, 1975) pp. 87–109; L. A. Knafla, 'Crime and Criminal Justice: a Critical Bibliography' in J. S. Cockburn (ed.), *Crime in England, 1550–1800* (1977) pp. 270–98.

4. FINANCIAL AND ADMINISTRATIVE DEVELOPMENTS

As yet there is no complete modern synthesis of the financial and administrative developments of this period, although chapters of two modern general books may be recommended: J. R. Western, *Monarchy and Revolution: The English State in the 1680s* (1972) chs 4 and 5, and J. H. Plumb, *The Growth of Political Stability in England, 1675–1725* (1967) (ch. on the executive). D. Ogg's *England in the Reign of Charles II*, 2 vols (2nd edn, Oxford, 1955) has not been entirely superseded by these works.

There are a number of important monographs on this theme. The most monumental is C. D. Chandaman's *The English Public Revenue, 1660–88* (Oxford, 1975), which supersedes W. A. Shaw's introductions and tables in the *Calendar of Treasury Books*, although the volumes themselves remain (in Professor Chandaman's words) 'an indispensable tool for historians of public finance'. Edward Hughes's *Studies in Administration and Finance, 1558–1825* (Manchester, 1934) contains a valuable section on the customs and excise in this period. There are two important books on the Treasury by H. G. Roseveare: *The Treasury: The Evolution of a British Institution* (1969), a general survey, chapters 2 and 3 of which are relevant for this study; and *The Treasury, 1660–1870: The Foundations of Control* (1973), which is more detailed and contains a number of illuminating documents illustrating Treasury development. S. B. Baxter's *The Development of the Treasury, 1660–1702* (1957) is suspect for this period. Professor Baxter minimises the importance of 1667 and overemphasises the importance of 1676 in the Treasury development (largely through a misconception of the relationship between the Treasury and Privy Council) and under-estimates the work of Sir George Downing. E. R. Turner's works on the Privy Council (*The Privy Council of England in the Seventeenth and Eighteenth Centuries,1603–1784*, 2 vols (Baltimore, 1927–8) and *The Cabinet Council of England in the Seventeenth and Eighteenth Centuries, 1622–1784*, 2 vols (New York, 1970)) are massive but are also flawed. Professor Turner attached too much importance to Cabinet development, and neglected the administrative work of the Privy Council. Dr Jennifer Carter's unpublished thesis, 'The Administrative Work of the English Privy Council, 1679–1714' (University of London Ph.D. thesis, 1958) deals with this aspect and puts the decline of the Privy Council in perspective. There are two important monographs on the Secretaries of State, parts of which are relevant for this period: F. M. G. Evans, *The Principal Secretary of State, 1558–1680* (Manchester, 1923) and Mark A. Thomson, *The Secretaries of State, 1681–1782* (Oxford, 1932). For details of the expansion of naval, military and colonial administration, J. Ehrman, *The Navy in the War of William III* (Cambridge, 1953) has a number of relevant passages on naval administration in this period. J. Childs, *The Army of Charles*

II (1976) contains a chapter on the Army's staff and administration; the present author's *Guns and Government: The Ordnance Office Under the Later Stuarts* (1979) assesses the development of an important but hitherto neglected department of state in the context of late seventeenth-century government; and an older monograph, C. M. Andrews, *British Committees, Commissions and Councils of Trade and Planations, 1622–75* (Baltimore, 1908) is still useful. There is no equivalent for this period to G. E. Aylmer's works on civil services of Charles I and the English Republic, but J. C. Sainty's books in the Office-Holders in Modern Britain series (*Treasury Officials, 1660–1870* (1972); *Officials of the Secretaries of State, 1660–1782* (1974); *Officials of the Boards of Trade, 1660–1870* (1974) and *Admiralty Officials, 1669–1870* (1975) are relevant for Restoration England) contain lists of officials and valuable introductions. His two articles on tenures of office in *EHR*, LXV (1965) 448–75, and *BIHR*, XLI (1967) 150–71, are important. G. A. Jacobsen's *William Blathwayt: A Late Seventeenth-Century Administrator* (Yale, 1932) is still probably the best administrative biography of a Restoration civil servant, although for an insight into the conditions of government service the student cannot do better than dip into *The Diary of Samuel Pepys*, the new edition of which by R. C. Latham and W. Matthews is almost complete.

5. RESTORATION ENGLAND AND EUROPE

It would, of course, be pointless in this context to attempt to list the myriad works relevant to the history of Europe in this period, but useful introductions can be found in F. L. Carsten (ed.), *The Ascendancy of France, 1648–88* (The New Cambridge Modern History, vol. v) (Cambridge, 1961) and John Stoye, *Europe Unfolding, 1648–1688* (1969). Also there is much useful material, in a short space, in G. Zeller, *Les temps modernes: II, De Louis XIV á 1789* (Histoire des relations internationales, vol. III) (Paris, 1955).

The nature of French policy and its effects on Europe at this time are best approached through J. B. Wolf, *Louis XIV* (1968); Ragnhild Hatton (ed.), *Louis XIV and Europe* (1976); and Robert Mandrou, *Louis XIV en son temps* (Paris, 1973); together with the contributions to the special issue of the journal *XVIIe siècle* XLVI–XLVII (1960) concerned with French international relations in this period.

The situation of the Dutch Republic, especially in its relations with England, is important. M. A. M. Franken, 'The General Tendencies and Structural Aspects of the Foreign Policy and Diplomacy of the Dutch Republic in the Latter Half of the Seventeenth Century', *Acta Historiae Neerlandica*, III (1968) 1–43, is a helpful introduction, as are the first chapters of Alice C. Carter, *Neutrality or Commitment: The Evolution of Dutch Foreign Policy, 1667–1795* (1975). Although first published in Dutch in 1939, P. Geyl, *Orange and Stuart* (New York, 1969) is still essential reading; while by far the best treatment of its subject in English is Stephen B. Baxter, *William III* (1966). Dutch relations with the Austrian Habsburgs are considered in a fascinating study by Václav Cihák, *Les provinces-unies et la cour impériale 1667–1672* (Amsterdam, 1974); while some interesting new perspectives on Spanish policy are given by R. A. Stradling, 'A Spanish Statesman of Appeasement: Medina de las Torres and Spanish

Policy, 1639–1670', HJ, XIX (1976) 1–31, which concentrates on the 1660s.

J. R. Jones, *Britain and Europe in the Seventeenth Century* (1966) is a brief but stimulating introduction to its subject, while G. M. D. Howat, *Stuart and Cromwellian Foreign Policy* (1974) is a competent survey. In general, however, English foreign policy has been largely neglected by historians, and it is still necessary to rely on the treatment of foreign affairs in the standard works on English history in this period, such as David Ogg, *England in the Reign of Charles II* (Oxford, rev. edn 1955) and *England in the Reigns of James II and William III* (Oxford, rev. edn 1963); though Charles Wilson, *Profit and Power: A Study of England and the Dutch Wars* (1957) is an interesting, brief discussion, and K. Feiling, *British Foreign Policy, 1660–1672* (1930) deals in some detail with his chosen period. On one particular episode, K. H. D. Haley, *William of Orange and the English Opposition*, 1672–74 (Oxford, 1953) has uncovered enough interesting material to suggest that similar research for other years would be very enlightening. Until such work is undertaken we must make do with the, often incidental, treatment of foreign policy in such works as A. Browning, *Thomas Osborne, Earl of Danby and Duke of Leeds, 1632–1712*, 3 vols (Glasgow, 1951), and J. P. Kenyon, *Robert Spencer, Earl of Sunderland, 1641–1702* (1958).

6. TRADE AND SHIPPING

There are four excellent general studies covering the period before and after 1660: L. A. Clarkson, *The Pre-Industrial Economy in England, 1500–1750* (1971); D. C. Coleman, *The Economy of England, 1450–1750* (1977); B. A. Holderness, *Pre-Industrial England: Economy and Society, 1500–1750* (1976); C. Wilson, *England's Apprenticeship, 1603–1763* (1965).

On more specialised subjects see: R. Davis, *The Rise of the English Shipping Industry* (1962); K. G. Davies, *The Royal African Company* (1957); D. C. Coleman, *Sir John Banks, Baronet and Businessman* (Oxford, 1963); L. A. Harper, *The English Navigation Laws* (1939). Related topics covered by articles include R. Davis, 'English Foreign Trade, 1660–1700', *EcHR* 2nd ser. VII (1954); R. Grassby, 'English Merchant Capitalism in the Late Seventeenth Century', *Past and Present* 46 (1970); M. Priestley, 'Anglo-French Trade and the "Unfavourable Balance" Controversy, 1660–1685', *EcHR* 2nd ser. IV (1951); C. Wilson, 'The Other Face of Mercantilism', *TRHS* 5th ser. IX (1959).

7. THE RESTORATION CHURCH

The restored Church of England is currently the subject of active research, of which little has so far been published. Despite its lack of sympathy for Restoration churchmanship, N. Sykes, *From Sheldon to Secker* (Ford Lectures for 1958, Cambridge, 1959) is the most useful introduction.

R. S. Bosher, *The Making of the Restoration Settlement: the Influence of the Laudians* (1957) is an important study, which is strongest on the role of the Anglican clergy in reviving the old episcopal order in the Church, and weakest on the political context of Anglican restoration. For the political manoeuvres governing the struggle between Presbyterians and Anglicans, see G. R. Abernathy,

'The English Presbyterians and the Stuart Restoration, 1648–1663' in *Transactions of the American Philosophical Society* (new ser. 55 1965); D. R. Lacey, *Dissent and Parliamentary Politics in England, 1661–1689* (New Brunswick, 1969); Sir Keith Feiling, *History of the Tory Party 1640–1714* (Oxford, 1924) and D. T. Witcombe, *Charles II and the Cavalier House of Commons 1663–1674* (Manchester, 1966). F. Bate, *The Declaration of Indulgence, 1672* (1908) investigates the maturing crisis of Charles II's ecclesiastical policy.

Anne Whiteman, 'The Re-establishment of the Church of England, 1660–1663' in *TRHS* (5th ser. v 1955) highlights the conservatism of the institutional Church. R. A. Beddard, 'Sheldon and Anglican Recovery' in *HJ* xix (1976) indicates Sheldon's significance as an administrator. His article, 'The Commission for Ecclesiastical Promotions, 1681–84: an Instrument of Tory Reaction' in *HJ* x (1967) traces the politicisation of church preferment. R. Thomas, 'Comprehension and Indulgence' in *From Uniformity to Unity, 1662–1962* (1962) ed. G. F. Nuttall and O. Chadwick sketches the abortive irenical projects of the period.

P. E. More and F. L. Cross, *Anglicanism* (1935) is a convenient anthology of Anglican divinity. G. R. Cragg, *From Puritanism to the Age of Reason* (Cambridge, 1950) and H. R. McAdoo, *The Spirit of Anglicanism* (Hale Lectures, 1965) chart the shifting currents of theology and theological method. The best episcopal biography is C. E. Whiting, *Nathaniel, Lord Crewe, Bishop of Durham* (1940).

On Dissent, see G. R. Cragg, *Puritanism in the Period of the Great Persecution, 1660–88* (Cambridge, 1957); G. F. Nuttall, *Richard Baxter* (1965); R. A. Beddard, 'Vincent Alsop and the Emancipation of Restoration Dissent' in *JEH* xxiv (1973). On popery, see J. A. Williams, 'English Catholicism under Charles II' in *Recusant History* vii (1963) and J. Bossy, *The English Catholic Community 1570–1850* (1975).

8. THE DEBATE OVER SCIENCE

Some idea of the kind of work that is at present being done on the history of science in the Restoration period may be gained from a perusal of the articles in periodicals and volumes of essays referred to in the notes to the early part of this chapter. Few works of synthesis that have yet appeared adequately reflect this research, but mention may be made of R. H. Kargon, *Atomism in England from Hariot to Newton* (Oxford, 1966), chapters 9 to 11 of which deal with this period. For a general account of the achievements of these years from the point of view of 'classical' history of science, see A. R. Hall, *From Galileo to Newton, 1630–1720* (1962), while for a brief attempt to approach the variety of explanatory frameworks held by different scientists there is Hugh Kearney *Science and Change, 1500–1700* (1971). Recent work on the organisation of science at the time is similarly to be found more in the periodical literature than in book form, but there is a good account of the Dublin Philosophical Society in K. T. Hoppen *The Common Scientist in the Seventeenth Century* (1970). Information on individual major scientists of the time is best sought in the authoritative and up-to-date articles in C. C. Gillespie (ed.), *The Dictionary of Scientific Biography* (New York, 1970–6).

On the social and technological bearing of science at this time much has been written, not all of which is of great value: in fact, the best general introduction to the subject remains in many ways Sir George Clark's *Science and Social Welfare in the Age of Newton* (2nd edn, Oxford 1949; reprinted 1970). R. K. Merton's celebrated *Science, Technology and Society in Seventeenth-Century England* (New York, 1970; originally published in *Osiris*, IV (1934) should be treated with caution; a useful collection of articles indicating the range of opinions on this and related topics will be found in Charles Webster (ed.), *The Intellectual Revolution of the Seventeenth Century* (1974). On the Interregnum background, Dr Webster's *The Great Instauration: Science, Medicine and Reform, 1626–1660* (1975) is fundamental, though sometimes controversial.

On the relations between science and religious thought general accounts will be found in R. S. Westfall, *Science and Religion in Seventeenth-century England* (New Haven, Conn., 1958); H. R. McAdoo, *The Spirit of Anglicanism* (1965), and G. R. Cragg, *From Puritanism to the Age of Reason* (Cambridge, 1950). For an attempt to give the science of the time a more precise correlation in ecclesiastical politics, see M. C. Jacob, *The Newtonians and the English Revolution* (Hassocks, 1976), chapter 1 of which relates to the Restoration period. On the opposition to Hobbes and atheism the best work is S. I. Mintz, *The Hunting of Leviathan* (Cambridge, 1962).

Of the many accounts of opposition to science at this time perhaps the best is R. H. Syfret, 'Some Early Reactions to the Royal Society', in *Notes and Records of the Royal Society*, VII (1950) 207–58, and 'Some Early Critics of the Royal Society', in ibid., VIII (1950) 20–64, but in R. F. Jones, *Ancients and Moderns* (2nd edn, St Louis, 1961) chs 8 and 9 are also useful. The scholarly preoccupations underlying such attacks have been less fully studied, but on ecclesiastical learning in the period some relevant material will be found in Norman Sykes, *From Sheldon to Secker* (Cambridge, 1959) and H. R. McAdoo *The Spirit of Anglicanism*, while on historical scholarship D. C. Douglas *English Scholars, 1660–1730* (2nd edn, 1951) is a classic, though now seeming a little over-rhetorical and dated. The Restoration universities and their values are surveyed in Hugh Kearney *Scholars and Gentlemen* (1970) chs 9 and 10.

One source may be singled out: Thomas Sprat, *History of the Royal Society* (1667), perhaps the most frequently cited contemporary work on Restoration science and its context, though not as straightforward as some who have used it have imagined. There is a modern edition by J. I. Cope and H. W. Jones which includes useful critical apparatus (1959).

Notes and References

For abbreviations used here, see page 196 above.

INTRODUCTION   *J. R. Jones*

1. The whiggish interpretation of James Mackintosh, *History of the Revolution in England in 1688* (1834), Henry Hallam, *The Constitutional History of England* (1855) and T. B. Macaulay, *The History of England from the Accession of James II*, ed. C. H. Firth (1913–15), influenced the last generation of historians. See G. M. Trevelyan, *England under the Stuarts* (1966) and *The English Revolution, 1688–1689* (1938), and also D. Ogg, *England in the Reign of Charles II* (2nd edn 1955) and *England in the Reigns of James II and William III* (rev. edn 1963).

2. See especially A. Bryant, *King Charles II* (1955) and C. H. Hartmann, *Clifford of the Cabal* (1937) and *The King my Brother* (1954).

3. The most notable victim, Oliver Plunket, has recently been canonised, and many others beatified. As well as the Vatican, contemporary French Jansenists (notably Antoine Arnauld) joined in denouncing the persecution of English Catholics.

4. See G. Ascoli, *La Grande Bretagne devant l'opinion française* (Paris, 1930).

5. Edward Hyde, earl of Clarendon, *The Life . . . being a Continuation of the History* (1827) vol. I, pp. 358–62, 368–9; vol. II, pp. 154, 211, 222.

6. Nine volumes of Pepys's *Diary* have appeared (1970–6) edited by R. C. Latham and W. Matthews. The edition is completed by a companion and an index volume.

7. Only Blathwayt has received a satisfactory biography: G. A. Jacobsen, *William Blathwayt: A Late Seventeenth-Century English Administrator* (New Haven, Conn., 1932) which also gives a great deal of information on the detailed workings of government.

8. See R. Colie, *Light and Enlightenment* (Cambridge, 1957) and M. Purver, *The Royal Society: Concept and Creation* (1967) especially pp. 206–35.

9. For a general description of the debates over toleration see A. A. Seaton, *The Theory of Toleration under the Later Stuarts* (Cambridge, 1911).

10. The texts of the Declarations are well worth comparative examination: J. P. Kenyon, *The Stuart Constitution* (Cambridge, 1966) pp. 403–6 (1662), 407–8 (1672), 410–13 (1687).

11. Clarendon's own account in the *Life* was hopelessly embittered; for his outlook in 1660 see his speech to the Convention, *CJ*, VIII, 172–4.

12. A. Browning, *Thomas Osborne, Earl of Danby* (1951) vol. I, p. 117, vol. II, p. 63.

13. The text of *Absalom and Achitophel*, with notes, has been edited by J. and H. Kinsley (1961).

14. K. Feiling, *British Foreign Policy, 1660–1672* (1930) pp. 267–307; C. H. Hartman, *Charles II and Madame* (1934) pp. 243–312. The text is most accessible in A. Browning (ed.), *English Historical Documents*, vol. x (1966) pp. 863–7.

15. S. Pepys, *Diary*, 2 September 1666.

16. See below (pp. 87–8)

17. J. R. Western, *The English Militia in the Eighteenth Century* (1965) chs 1 and 2.

18. L. G. Schwoerer, *'No Standing Armies!' the Antiarmy Ideology in Seventeenth-century England* (Baltimore, 1974).

19. R. S. Bosher, *The Making of the Restoration Settlement* (1957) pp. 143–277; A. Whiteman, 'The Re-establishment of the Church of England, 1660–1663', in *TRHS*, 5th ser., v. V. D. Sutch, *Gilbert Sheldon* (The Hague, 1973); I. M. Green, *The Re-establishment of the Church of England, 1660–63* (Oxford, 1978).

20. George Morley, *A Sermon preached at the . . . Coronation of . . . Charles II* (1661).

21. Browning, *Danby*, vol. i, pp. 282–3.

22. I. B. Cowan, *The Scottish Covenanters 1660–1688* (1976) pp. 82–93.

23. A. Grey, *Debates of the House of Commons* (1763) vol. iii, pp. 24–34, 107–12, 211–18; vol. v, pp. 358–84.

24. Western, *English Militia*, pp. 12–13, 15, 44–6.

25. Grey, *Debates*, vol. ii, pp. 74–8, 79–82, 200–14, 215–22. J. Childs, *The Army of Charles II* (1976) pp. 221–3.

26. Grey, *Debates*, vol. vi, pp. 15–26, 39–48, 214–15, 268–70, 278–84, 386. Childs, *Army*, pp. 224–8.

27. A new study by Dr Childs, *The Army, James II and the Glorious Revolution*, is to be published by the Manchester University Press.

28. J. R. Jones, *The Revolution of 1688 in England* (1972) pp. 128–75.

29. See *The History of the Ecclesiastical Commission* (1711).

30. M. Priestley, 'Anglo-French Trade and the "Unfavourable Balance" Controversy', in *EcHR*, 2nd ser., iv (1951–2).

31. T. H. Lister, *Life and Administration . . . of Clarendon* (1837) vol. iii, pp. 346–8.

32. PRO Baschet transcripts, Barrillon's despatches of 24 and 27 March 1681. Sir John Dalrymple, *Memoirs of Great Britain and Ireland* (1771–3) vol. ii, pp. 292–5, 298–301.

33. C. D. Chandaman, *The English Public Revenue 1660–1688* (1975) pp. 249–61.

34. John Eachard stated the case of poverty in *The Grounds and Occasions of the Contempt of the Clergy* (1670). See also A. T. Hart, *The Country Priest in English History* (1959) pp. 111–27.

35. Milton's publication of *The Ready and Easy Way to Establish a Free Commonwealth*; the text can be found in any edition of his prose works, or see S. E. Prall, *The Puritan Revolution* (1969) pp. 286–305.

36. A. Olson, *The Radical Duke* (Oxford, 1961) p 1.

37. J. P. Kenyon, *The Popish Plot* (1972) pp. 107, 191, 212–13.

38. D. R. Lacey, *Dissent and Parliamentary Politics in England, 1661–1689* (New Brunswick, 1969) pp. 150–2, 157–8. On the general effects see G. R. Cragg, *Puritanism in the Period of the Great Persecution* (Cambridge, 1957).

39. See G. S. Thomson, *The Russells in Bloomsbury, 1669–1771* (1940).

40. R. North, *Lives of the Norths* (1890 edn; repr. Farnborough 1972) vol. I, pp. 185–6.

41. E. M. G. Routh, *Tangier: England's Lost Atlantic Outpost* (1912) pp. 349–53, 361–3.

42. See M. Foss, *The Age of Patronage: the Arts in Society, 1660–1750* (1971) especially chs 2, 3 and 4.

43. His final conversion was achieved by Gilbert Burnet who, with his usual flair for self-advertisement, published *Some Passages in the Life and Death of John Wilmot, Earl of Rochester* (1680).

44. M. Cranston, *John Locke* (1959) pp. 202–3, 220–1, 228–30.

45. George Bull, a country parson, received recognition from Oxford at the instigation of Dr Fell and Archbishop Sancroft, after publishing his *Defensio Fidei Nicaenae* (1685).

46. J. G. A. Pocock, 'Robert Brady . . . a Cambridge Historian of the Restoration' in *Cambridge Historical Journal*, X, 2 (1951).

1. THE LATER STUART MONARCHY *John Miller*

(The writer would like to thank John Morrill for reading and commenting on the first draft of this essay.)

1. J. R. Western, *The English Militia in the Eighteenth Century* (1965) pp. 11–16.

2. C. H. Hull (ed.), *Economic Writings of Sir William Petty* 2 vols (Cambridge, 1899 edn, repr. 1971–5) vol. II pp. 630–2.

3. R. North, *Examen* (1742) pp. 427–8.

4. This was made especially clear in the Act declaring the King's sole right to direct the militia: J. P. Kenyon, *The Stuart Constitution* (Cambridge, 1966) p. 374.

5. For the reinterpretation of Elizabethan and early Stuart parliamentary history, see J. S. Roskell, 'Perspectives in English Parliamentary History'; in E. B. Fryde and E. Miller (eds), *Historical Studies of the English Parliament* 2 vols (Cambridge, 1970) vol. II, pp. 296–323; G. R. Elton, 'Tudor Government, the Points of Contact: I. Parliament', *TRHS*, 5th series, XXIV (1974) 185–200; C. Russell, 'Parliamentary History in Perspective, 1604–29, in *History*, LXI (1976) 1–27.

6. C. D. Chandaman, *The English Public Revenue* (1975) pp. 190–3, 85–8. With reference to the Hearth tax, it should perhaps be added that the Commons' hostility followed the passing of an Act whereby royal officials were to assess and collect the tax, instead of local constables acting under the supervision of the JPs: ibid., pp. 81–5.

7. A. Browning, *Thomas, Earl of Danby*, 3 vols (Glasgow, 1951) vol. II, p. 70; Sir W. Temple, *Memoirs, 1672–9* (1692) pp. 153–4.

8. M. Hawkins, 'The Government: Its Role and Its Aims', in C. Russell (ed.), *Origins of the English Civil War* (1973) p. 37.

9. A. Browning (ed.), *Memoirs of Sir John Reresby* (Glasgow, 1936) pp. 112–13; L. von Ranke, *History of England*, 6 vols (Oxford, 1875) vol VI p. 78.

10. See for example, Bodl., Carte MS 32, fos 390, 597; *CSPD 1667*, p. 428;

1675–6, p. 315; E. Berwick (ed.), *Rawdon Papers* (1831) pp. 220–1.

11. B. L. Egerton MS 2539, fos 180–2.

12. G. Burnet, *History of My Own Time*, 6 vols (1833) vol. II, p. 173; J. Miller, *James II: A Study in Kingship* (Hove, 1978) pp. 80, 90, 97–8.

13. C. H. Hartmann, *The King my Brother* (1954) p. 314; J. Dalrymple, *Memoirs of Great Britain and Ireland*, 3 vols. (1773) vol. II; Appendix p. 94. (For doubts about Charles's sincerity in the Secret Treaty of Dover see Miller, *James II*, pp. 59–62.)

14. See for example I. M. Green, *The Re-establishment of the Church of England, 1660–63* (Oxford, 1978) pp. 26–9. It seems to me that to show that Bellings enjoyed Charles's favour and that Bellings thought that these were Charles's views is far from conclusive proof that these were in fact Charles's views. There was no hint of toleration for Catholics in 1668–9 and Charles showed no qualms about authorising the persecution of Catholics in the 1670s.

15. T. H. Lister, *Life of Clarendon* 3 vols (1837–8) vol. III, pp. 198–201; Bodl., Carte MS 47, fos 343, 359; Pepys, *Diary*, vol III, pp. 229, 237, 252; Miller, *James II*, pp. 54–5; T. Brown (ed.), *Miscellanea Aulica* (1702) p. 66.

16. Chandaman, *Public Revenue* pp. 256–61 and *passim*.

17. J. Sheffield, duke of Buckingham (earlier earl of Mulgrave), *Works* 2 vols (1753) vol. II, pp. 58–9; Clarendon, *Life* 3 vols (Oxford, 1827) vol. II, p. 144; Pepys *Diary* vol. IX, p. 387; see also G. Savile, marquis of Halifax, *Complete Works*, ed. J. P. Kenyon (Harmondsworth, 1969) pp. 247–67; Miller, *James II*, pp. 37–41; K. H. D. Haley, *Charles II* (1966).

18. Temple, *Memoirs, 1672–9*, p. 274.

19. C. Roberts, 'The Impeachment of the Earl of Clarendon', *Cambridge Historical Journal* XIII (1957) 1–18; D. T. Witcombe, *Charles II and the Cavalier House of Commons* (Manchester, 1966) ch. 6.

20. Clarendon, *Life*, vol III, p. 64.

21. Archives Nationales, Paris, K1351, no. 4, fo. 58 (report of Usson de Bon-repaus, September 1688).

22. See J. P. Kenyon, *Robert Spencer, Earl of Sunderland* (1958) chs 4–6; Miller, *James II*, chs 9–14.

23. B. Behrens, 'The Whig Theory of the Constitution in the Reign of Charles II', in *Cambridge Historical Journal* VII (1941) 42–71, especially 59–60; *CSPD 1677–8*, p. 145.

24. R. North, *Lives of the Norths*, ed. A. Jessopp 3 vols (1890) vol. III, pp. 181, 186; Pepys, *Diary* vol. VIII, p. 512; HMC Portland MSS vol VIII, p. 15; E. W. Thibaudeau (ed.), *Autograph Letters in the Collection of Alfred Morrison: Bulstrode Papers* (1897) p. 315; E. Newton, *The House of Lyme* (1917) pp. 242–3; Witcombe, *Charles II* pp. 76, 102.

25. A. Grey, *Debates in the House of Commons, 1667–94* 10 vols (1763) vol. VI p. 190; vol. VIII, pp. 260–1.

26. See, for example, Ruvigny to Louis XIV, 6–16 April 1674 and 29 March–8 April 1675; PRO Baschet transcripts, bundles 131, 132.

27. Elizabeth's most serious defeat came in the 1559 religious settlement; for defeats of Henry VIII see G. R. Elton, *Reform and Renewal* (Cambridge, 1973) pp. 103–6, 123–8. There were also considerable disputes about taxation in 1523 and the Proclamations Bill in 1539, not to mention the Statute of Uses.

28. A. F. Havighurst, 'The Judiciary and Politics in the Reign of Charles II' and 'James II and the Twelve Men in Scarlet', in *Law Quarterly Review*, LXVI (1950) 240–52; LXIX (1953) 522–46; Kenyon, *Stuart Constitution*, pp. 401–3, 420–6, 438–47; Barrillon to Louis XIV, 6–16 October 1687, Baschet transcripts, bundle 173.

29. Chandaman, *Public Revenue* pp. 11, 42, 51–2, 81–2, 100–7; J. Miller, *Popery and Politics in England, 1660–88* (Cambridge, 1973) pp. 56–63, 132–3, 142, 162–9, 191–4, 256–8; J. Miller, 'The Militia and the Army in the Reign of James II', in *HJ*, XVI (1973) 667–73.

30. C. Brooks, 'Public Finance and Political Stability: The Administration of the Land Tax, 1688–1720', in *HJ*,XVII (1974) 281–300.

31. J. R. Jones, *The Revolution of 1688 in England* (1972) pp. 43–50; *CSPD 1682*, pp. 238–40, 274–5, 472; *Jan–June 1683*, pp. 95–6; *July–Sept 1683*, pp. 104, 150.

32. See R. J. Frankle, 'The Formulation of the Declaration of Rights' in *HJ*, XVII (1974) 265–79; C. Roberts, 'The Constitutional Significance of the Financial Settlement of 1690', in *HJ*, XX (1977) 59–76.

33. Both Charles II and William III offered, of their own volition, to allow the Commons to inspect their accounts: Witcombe, *Charles II* pp. 5n., 17; H. Horwitz, *Parliament, Policy and Politics in the Reign of William III* (Manchester, 1977) pp. 32, 58–9, 64.

34. After 1714 the Commons lost interest in the detailed scrutiny of the Crown's accounts: see H. Roseveare, *The Treasury: The Evolution of a British Institution* (1969) pp. 88–93.

2. PARTIES AND PARLIAMENT *J. R. Jones*

1. R. Walcott, *English Politics in the Early Eighteenth Century* (Oxford, 1956) particularly pp. 71–5, 77–80.

2. The subject of the study by Sir L. Namier, *The Structure of Politics at the Accession of George III*(1965).

3. A. Browning, *Thomas Osborne, Earl of Danby* 3 vols (Glasgow, 1944–51) gives the fullest account, with copious lists in vol. III.

4. W. C. Abbot, 'The Long Parliament of Charles II', in *EHR*, XXI (1906).

5. *CJ*, VIII, 254, 276, 291.

6. Ibid., 440 (25 February 1663).

7. Edward Hyde, earl of Clarendon, *Life* (Oxford, 1827) vol. I, pp. 361–2; vol. II, pp. 206–10.

8. Ibid., vol. II, pp. 206–11. D. T. Witcombe, *Charles II and the Cavalier House of Commons* (Manchester, 1966) pp. 11–12, 38–9, 44–6, 50–2, 56–7.

9. The most accessible example of a libel attacking Danby is *A Seasonable Argument*; this contains a list of alleged pensioners and it is printed in A. Browning (ed), *English Historical Documents*, vol. VIII, pp. 237–49.

10. H. M. Margoliouth (ed.) *The Poems and Letters of Andrew Marvell*, revised by L. Legouis, (1971) vol. II, pp. 1–236 contains 294 of his letters to the corporation and civic officers of Hull during the years 1661–78.

11. D. Hirst, *The Representatives of the People? Voters and Voting in England under the Early Stuarts* (Cambridge, 1975); see also J. H. Plumb, *The Growth of Political Stablility in England, 1675–1725* (1967), and his article 'The Growth of the

Electorate in England from 1600 to 1715', in *Past and Present*, 45 (1969).

12. J. R. Jones, 'Restoration Election Petitions', in *Durham University Journal*, XLIII (1961) 49–57.

13. H. N. Muckerjee, 'Elections for the Convention and Cavalier Parliaments', in *Notes and Queries*, XCVI (1934); R. H. George, 'Parliamentary Elections and Electioneering in 1685' *TRHS*, 4th ser., XIX (1936).

14. J. R. Jones, 'Political Groups and Tactics in the Convention of 1660', in *HJ*, VI (1963) 159–63.

15. For this see R. G. Pickavance, 'The English Boroughs and the King's Government: A Study of the Tory Reaction of 1681–5'(Oxford D. Phil. thesis 1976).

16. *CSPD 1685* pp. 21–2, 24–6, 30, 32–3, 36, 54, 63, 75; HMC 14th report, IX, 484; N. Luttrell, *A Brief Historical Relation of State Affairs* (1857) vol. 1 p. 341.

17. J. R. Jones, *The First Whigs* (1961) pp. 92–106, 159–73.

18. For an impression of the effects of this split compare J. R. Jones, 'Shaftesbury's "Worthy Men": a Whig View of the Parliament of 1679', in *BIHR*, XXX (1957) 232–41, and A. Browning and D. Milne, 'An Exclusion Bill Division List', in ibid., XXIII (1950) 205–25.

19. Jones, *First Whigs* pp. 167–74; PRO Shaftesbury Papers viB, 399; A. Grey, *Debates of the House of Commons* (1763) vol. VIII, pp. 309–10, 325, 326–7.

20. Jones, *Whigs* pp. 172–3.

21. J. R. Jones, 'The Green Ribbon Club', in *Durham University Journal*, XLIX (1956) 17–20. 17 November was the anniversary of Elizabeth's accession in 1558.

22. On the original Tories nothing has been published to supersede K. Feiling, *History of the Tory Party, 1640–1714* (1924).

23. For this background see J. P. Kenyon, *The Popish Plot* (1972); J. Miller, *Popery and Politics in England, 1660–1688* (Cambridge, 1973); F. S. Ronalds, *The Attempted Whig Revolution of 1678–81* (Urbana, 1937).

24. K. H. D. Haley's biography, *The First Earl of Shaftesbury* (1968), is immensely impressive in its scholarly account of every facet of his career, but the attempt at characterisation (pp. 740–6) is disproportionately brief and not altogether convincing.

25. John Dryden's *Absalom and Achitophel* is best studied in the edition by J. and H. Kinsley (1961).

26. There are many contemporary manuscript copies of the letter to Carlisle in which he announced his turn to opposition in archival collections; it is printed in the unsatisfactory biography by L. F. Brown, *The First Earl of Shaftesbury* (New York, 1933) pp. 226–7. See also Haley *First Earl* pp. 369–71.

27. Jones, *First Whigs* pp. 55–7, 65–71; Haley, *First Earl* pp. 463–6, 516–26, 597–602. The text of the 1680 bill is in *English Historical Documents*, vol. VIII, pp. 113–14, and J. P. Kenyon, *The Stuart Constitution* (Cambridge, 1966) pp. 469–71.

28. Whig strategy and its assumptions, and the scale of Exclusionist propaganda and canvassing, are comparable with those of such nineteenth-century causes as the Chartists and the Anti-Corn Law League.

29. Furthermore limitations were explained in full detail only at a late stage, in a Commons debate at Oxford in 1681; Grey, *Debates* vol. VIII, pp. 317–20.

30. Jones, *First Whigs* pp. 9–16.

31. Grey, *Debates* vol. VII, pp. 418–20; vol. VIII, p. 328.

32. J. H. Sacret, 'The Restoration Government and Municipal Corporations', in *EHR*, XLV (1930) 232–59.

33. D. R. Lacey, *Dissent and Parliamentary Politics in England, 1661–1689* (New Brunswick, 1969) reduced the value of an excellent and informative study by assuming that opposition MPs were 'dissenters' or 'presbyterians' and 'congregationalists'; see particularly chs 5 and 6.

34. D. Allen, 'The Role of the London Trained Bands in the Exclusion Crisis', in *EHR*, LXXXVII (1972) 287–303; J. Levin, *The Charter Controversy in the City of London, 1660–1688* (1969).

35. Haley, *First Earl* pp. 707–13; D. J. Milne, 'The Results of the Rye House Plot, and their Influence upon the Revolution of 1688', in *TRHS*, 5th ser., I (1951) 91–108.

36. Haley, *First Earl* pp. 512–15; Jones, *First Whigs* pp. 61–3.

37. Jones, *First Whigs* pp. 96–102.

38. *True Protestant Mercury*, nos XXI and XXII; *Loyal Protestant*, nos III and IV.

39. Jones, *First Whigs* p. 63; Grey, *Debates* vol. VII, 265–78.

40. Jones. *First Whigs* pp. 198–206.

41. J. R. Jones, *The Revolution of 1688 in England* (1972) pp. 61–5.

42. Ibid., pp. 128–75.

3. LAW, COURTS AND CONSTITUTION *Jennifer Carter*

1. These issues are well explored in C. Roberts, *The Growth of Responsible Government in Stuart England* (Cambridge, 1966) chs 5 and 6; M. Ashley, 'King James II and the Revolution of 1688; Some Reflections on the Historiography', in H. E. Bell and R. L. Ollard (eds), *Historical Essays 1600–1750 Presented to David Ogg* (1963) pp. 185–202, gives a helpful summary of how views on the Revolution had changed up to 1963. D. H. Hosford, *Nottingham, Nobles and the North: Aspects of the Revolution of 1688* (Hamden, Connecticut, 1976) especially pp. 1–8 and 120–5, provides a revisionist view of the events leading up to the Revolution and a stimulating local study.

2. C. Robbins, *The Eighteenth-Century Commonwealthman* (Cambridge, Massachusetts, 1959) p. 24.

3. Since the publication of D. Ogg, *England in the Reign of Charles II* (Oxford, 1934; 2nd edn 1955) and *England in the Reigns of James II and William III* (Oxford, 1955), the most important reinterpreters of the Stuart monarchy have been: J. P. Kenyon, *The Stuarts: a Study in English Kingship* (1958); *Robert Spencer, Earl of Sunderland* (1958); *The Stuart Constitution* (Cambridge, 1966); J. R. Western, *Monarchy and Revolution: The English State in the 1680s* (1972); J. R. Jones, *The Revolution of 1688 in England* (1972).

4. C. Hill, *Reformation to Industrial Revolution* (1967) p. 110.

5. O. Airy (ed.), *Burnet's History of My Own Time* (1897) vol. I, p. 151.

6. C. D. Chandaman, *The English Public Revenue, 1660–1688* (Oxford, 1975). C. Roberts, 'The Constitutional Significance of the Financial Settlement of 1690', in *HJ*, XX (1977) 59–76.

7. Chandaman, *Public Revenue* p. 277.

8. The dates of parliamentary sessions may be found most conveniently in F. M. Powicke and E. B. Fryde, *Handbook of British Chronology* (2nd edn 1961) pp. 538–9. There is a diagram conveying the same information less exactly in A. Browning (ed.), *English Historical Documents, 1660–1714*, vol. VIII, (1953) pp. 162–3.

9. Chandaman, *Public Revenue* p. 278.

10. Kenyon, *The Stuarts*, pp. 146–7.

11. M. A. Thomson, *A Constitutional History of England, 1642–1801* (1938) p. 54. See also Browning, *Documents* p. 145 and W. S. Holdsworth, *History of English Law*, vol. VI (1924) p. 162.

12. Thomson, *History* pp. 61 n. 1, 86.

13. Browning, *Documents* pp. 50–1; Kenyon, *Stuart Constitution*, pp. 401–3; Thomson, *History* pp. 87–93.

14. Quoted in Kenyon, *Stuart Constitution*, p. 402.

15. G. R. Abernathy, 'Clarendon and the Declaration of Indulgence' in *Journal of Ecclesiastical History*, XI (1960) 62.

16. Kenyon, *Stuart Constitution*, p. 3.

17. *CJ* IX, 581. See also J. Childs, *The Army of Charles II* (1976) p. 232 and *passim*; L. G. Schwoerer, *'No Standing Armies!' The Antiarmy Ideology in Seventeenth-Century England* (Baltimore, 1974) chs 5, 6 and 7.

18. J. R. Western, *The English Militia in the Eighteenth Century: The Story of a Political Issue, 1660–1802*(1965); J. Miller, 'The Militia and the Army in the reign of James II', in *HJ*, XVI (1973) 659–79; Browning, *Documents*. pp. 787–8.

19. D. Allen, 'The Role of the London Trained Bands in the Exclusion Crisis, 1678–81' in *EHR*, LXXXVII (1972) 287–303; W. M. Sachse, 'The Mob and the Revolution of 1688', in *JBS*, IV (1964) 37–8.

20. Chandaman, *Public Revenue* p. 261; Western, *Monarchy and Revolution*, p. 125.

21. Miller, *Militia* p. 662; Hosford, *Aspects of the Revolution* pp. 75–6.

22. Western, *English Militia* p. 154; Miller, *Militia* p. 664.

23. J. Miller, 'Catholic Officers in the Later Stuart Army', in *EHR*, LXXX VIII (1973) 35–53; C. D. Ellestad, 'The Mutinies of 1689', in *Journal of the Society for Army Historical Research*, LIII (1975) 4.

24. Quoted by Western, *English Militia* p. 135.

25. Kenyon, *Stuart Constitution*, pp. 423–4; Holdsworth, *English Law* vol. VI, p. 509.

26. G. Holmes (ed.), *Britain after the Glorious Revolution* (1969) p. 44.

27. Holdsworth, *English Law* vol. VI, p. 424; D. Veall, *The Popular Movement for Law Reform, 1640–1660* (Oxford, 1970) pp. 226–7; A. Harding, *A Social History of English Law* (1966) pp. 226–7; M. Landon, *The Triumph of the Lawyers: Their Role in English Politics, 1678–1689* (Alabama, 1970); A. F. Havighurst, 'The Judiciary and Politics in the Reign of Charles II', in *Law Quarterly Review*, LXVI (1950) 251–2.

28. T. Siderfin, *Les Reports des Divers Special Cases* (1683) p. 85.

29. *State Trials*, vol. II, pp. 434, 446, 450; J. Keble, *Reports*, vol. I (1685) pp. 304, 324.

30. *State Trials*, vol. IV, p. 312.

31. Holdsworth, *English Law* vol. VI, p. 527; Kenyon, *Stuart Constitution*,

pp. 426, 433.

32. Kenyon, *Stuart Constitution*, p. 362; J. Thirsk (ed.), *The Restoration* (1976) p. xiii.

33. A. Hast, 'State Treason Trials During the Puritan Revolution, 1640–1660', in *HJ*, xv (1972) 52–3; Thomson, *History* pp. 145–6.

34. G. E. Aylmer, *The Struggle for the Constitution, 1603–1689* (1963) p. 201.

35. Western, *English Militia* p. 61.

36. L. Radzinowicz, *A History of English Criminal Law and its Administration from 1750*, vol. I (1948) pp. 3–4, 7ff.; Holdsworth, *English Law* vol. VI, pp. 402–3; J. H. Plumb, *The Growth of Political Stability in England, 1675–1725* (1967) pp. 21–2, on the gentry as a law to themselves. On the gap between law and enforcement see E. W. Ives, *The English Revolution, 1600–1660* (1968) chs 2 and 8; J. R. Hertzler, 'The Abuse and Outlawing of Sanctuary for Debt in Seventeenth-Century England', in *HJ*, XIV (1971) 467–77.

37. W. H. Bryson, *The Equity Side of Exchequer* (Cambridge, 1975) p. 168.

38. Harding, *Social History* p. 282; D. E. C. Yale (ed.), *Lord Nottingham's Chancery Cases*, vol. I (Selden Soc., 1957) vol. LXXIII, pp. CXXIII–CXXIV.

39. H. J. Habbakuk, 'The English Land Market in the Eighteenth Century', in J. S. Bromley and E. H. Kossmann (eds), *Britain and the Netherlands* (1960) pp. 154–73; B. L. Anderson, 'Law, Finance and Economic Growth in England: Some Long-Term Influences'; in B. M. Ratcliffe (ed.), *Great Britain and her World, 1750–1914: Essays in honour of W. O. Henderson* (Manchester, 1975) pp. 99–124.

40. Holdsworth, *English Law* vol. VI, pp. 379–97, 407; Harding, *Social History* pp. 278–81; C. H. Fifoot, *English Law and its Background* (1932) pp. 123–5.

41. Holdsworth, *English Law* vol. IX, pp. 217–18, 230–1; Western, *English Militia* p. 68.

42. E. G. Henderson, *Foundations of English Administrative Law* (Cambridge, Mass., 1963) p. 5.

43. R. J. Sharpe, *The Law of Habeas Corpus* (Oxford, 1976) pp. 16–19, 125.

44. D. Ogg, *England in the Reigns of James II and William III*, pp. 175–9, argues that the Ecclesiastical Commission was not illegal, but this is not the only possible interpretation of the evidence. On ecclesiastical jurisdiction see also R. E. Head, *Royal Supremacy and the Trials of Bishops 1558–1725* (1962).

45. D. E. C. Yale, 'A View of the Admiral Jurisdiction: Sir Matthew Hale and the Civilians', in D. Jenkins (ed.), *Legal History Studies 1972*, (Cardiff, 1975) pp. 91, 108.

46. B. P. Levack, *The Civil Lawyers in England, 1603–1641* (Oxford, 1973) pp. 3, 201.

47. J. G. A. Pocock, *The Ancient Constitution and the Feudal Law* (Cambridge, 1957) p. 55.

48. Holdsworth, *English Law* vol. V, p. 355; vol. VI, pp. 508–11, quoting Halifax's *Character of a Trimmer*; W. R. Prest, *The Inns of Court under Elizabeth I and the Early Stuarts, 1590–1640* (1972) pp. 44–6, 170–3, 237; M. Landon, *Triumph of the Lawyers* pp. 40–1.

49. Kenyon, *Stuart Constitution*, p. 424.

50. W. J. Jones, *Politics and the Bench: the Judges and the Origins of the English Civil War* (1971) p. 148.

51. Havighurst, *Judiciary and Politics* p. 229.

52. Ibid., p. 247; and 'James II and the Twelve Men in Scarlet', in *Law Quarterly Review*, LXIX (1953) 522.

53. G. W. Keeton, *Lord Chancellor Jeffreys and the Stuart Cause* (1965) p. 96; J. P. Kenyon, 'The Acquittal of Sir George Wakeman', in *HJ*, XIV (1971) 707; J. S. Cockburn, *A History of English Assizes, 1558–1714* (Cambridge, 1972) p. 251.

54. G. Burnet, *The Life and Death of Sir Matthew Hale* (1682) pp. 76–108. For modern views: C. M. Gray (ed.), *Sir Matthew Hale: The History of the Common Law of England* (Chicago, 1971) p. 13; D. E. C. Yale (ed.), *Sir Matthew Hale's 'The Prerogatives of the King'* (1975) Selden Soc. vol. XCII, pp. LVI–LVII.

55. Kenyon, *Stuart Constitution* p. 707; *The Popish Plot* (1972) pp. 117–18.

56. J. R. Jones, *The Revolution of 1688 in England*, p. XVI; Keeton, *Lord Chancellor Jeffreys*; P. J. Helm, *Jeffreys* (1966).

57. Havighurst, *Law Quarterly Review*, LXVI (1950) 65–6; Cockburn, *English Assizes* pp. 59, 252; Western, *English Militia* pp. 60–1.

58. Kenyon, *Stuart Constitution*, p. 420; W. S. Holdsworth, *Some Lessons from our Legal History* (1928) p. 75; Kenyon, *Popish Plot*, p. 117.

59. Cockburn, *English Assizes* p. 249; Kenyon, *Stuart Constitution*, pp. 427–8.

60. Thomson, *History* p. 143; Kenyon, *Stuart Constitution*, pp. 420–1; Holdsworth, *English Law* vol. VI, p. 388; Cockburn, *English Assizes* p. 124.

61. Keeton, *Lord Chancellor Jeffreys* p. 97; Ogg, *England in the Reign of Charles II*, vol. II, p. 519.

62. Ogg, *England* p. 520; Kenyon, *Popish Plot*, p. 177; Western, *English Militia* p. 68.

63. Details are given in Appendix 3 of J. Miller, *Popery and Politics in England: 1660–1688* (Cambridge, 1973) pp. 269–72.

64. e.g. ibid., p. 60; S. A. Peyton (ed.), *Minutes of Proceedings in Quarter Sessions held for the Parts of Kesteven in the County of Lincolnshire, 1674–1695*, vol. I (Lincoln, 1931) Lincoln Record Soc. vol. XXV, pp. CXV-CXVI, CXXII-CXXIV.

65. B. Osborne, *Justices of the Peace*, 1361–1848 (Shaftesbury, 1960) p. 152, J. R. S. Phillips, *The Justices of the Peace in Wales and Monmouthshire, 1541–1689* (Cardiff, 1975) p. 13.

66. J. Carswell, *The Descent on England* (1969) Appendix A, p. 240.

67. J. Levin, *The Charter Controversy in the City of London, 1660–1688 and its Consequences* (1969), prints an amended list of new charters granted between 1680 and 1688 (Appendix A) and a list of English parliamentary boroughs whose charters were not remodelled (Appendix B) pp. 109–13.

68. Jones, *Revolution of 1688 in England*, ch. 6.

69. Ibid., p. 175; Hosford, *Aspects of the Revolution* p. 58.

70. J. S. Morrill, *The Revolt of the Provinces: Conservatives and Radicals in the English Civil War, 1630–1650* (1976) pp. 26–9, 34–5.

4. FINANCIAL AND ADMINISTRATIVE DEVELOPMENTS *Howard Tomlinson*

1. Quoted in P. Zagorin, *The Court and the Country: The Beginning of the English Revolution* (1969) p. 14.

2. For an outline of these developments, see two works by G. E. Aylmer, *The King's Servants: The Civil Service of Charles I, 1625–42*, 2nd edn (1974) pp. 433–7; *The State's Servants: The Civil Service of the English Republic, 1649–60* (1973) ch. 2.

3. C. D. Chandaman, *The English Public Revenue, 1660–88* (Oxford, 1975) pp. 254, 260.

4. Ibid., pp. 21–2, 51–3.

5. J. Beresford, *The Godfather of Downing Street: Sir George Downing, 1623–84* (1925) p. 205.

6. See Chandaman, *Revenue* pp. 285–95, for a discussion of these credit instruments (especially the payment tallies and their influence on Exchequer accounting procedures).

7. PRO SP For. 84/174, fo. 20: Downing to Sir H. Bennet, 17 Jan 1665. Quoted in Henry Roseveare, *The Treasury, 1660–1870: The Foundations of Control* (1973) p. 23.

8. Henry Roseveare, *The Treasury: The Evolution of a British Institution* (1969) p. 58. Roseveare, *Treasury: Foundations of Control*, p. 20. For Clarendon's outbursts see *The Life of Edward, Earl of Clarendon . . . by Himself*, 3 vols (3rd edn, Oxford, 1761) vol. III, pp. 790ff.

9. *Calendar of Treasury Books, 1667–8, passim*; minutes cited in Roseveare, *Treasury: Foundations of Control*, pp. 111–12, 134–6.

10. For these orders see PRO PC 2/59, p. 233; PC 2/60, pp. 46, 157–8, 176–7. They are reproduced in Roseveare, *Treasury: Foundation of Control*, pp. 113–15, 118.

11. Ibid., pp. 120–4; an extract from BL Add. MSS 28078, fos 11–15.

12. Roseveare, *Treasury: Foundations of Control*, pp. 27–30.

13. *Seventh Report of the Deputy-Keeper of the Public Records* (1846) Appendix ii, p. 11.

14. See Roseveare, *Treasury: Foundations of Control*, pp. 129–30, for extracts of minutes concerning orders for the starting of 'register' books for each branch of the revenue, petitions, orders from the King and Privy Council etc.

15. Pepys, *Diary* (1970–76 edn) 2 Jan 1668. A remark made by Sir William Coventry, upon which the King turned on his heel.

16. For the work of Danby and the 1679 commission, see Roseveare, *Treasury: Foundations of Control*, pp. 40–4, and Chandaman (who attaches more importance to the Commissions of 1679–84), *Revenue* pp. 231–55. It will be apparent from the foregoing account that the present author has followed Dr Roseveare's work (to which he is greatly indebted) in emphasising the importance of the year 1667 as being the turning-point in the history of the modern Treasury, rather than 1676, the date at which Professor Baxter claims the department reached maturity. (S. B. Baxter, *The Development of the Treasury, 1660–1702* (1957) p. 262). It seems to the present author at least that Dr Roseveare has convincingly exposed the weaknesses in Professor Baxter's argument, especially his misplaced emphasis on the 1676 retrenchment scheme.

17. For details see Chandaman, *Revenue* pp. 29, 73, 105.

18. This is certainly true of the customs (see E. E. Hoon, *The Organisation of the English Customs System, 1696–1786* (Newton Abbot, 1968) pp. 118–19) and

probably of the other revenues as well.

19. Edward Hughes, *Studies in Administration and Finance, 1558–1825* (Manchester, 1934) p. 138. The same case could not be made out for smaller branches of the revenue like the wine licences (directly administered, 1670–82, but farmed thereafter) and the law duty (farmed 1671–80 with the exception of the years 1672 and 1675–6), although after 1685 the farming of Post Office revenues was (permanently?) abandoned.

20. Ibid., pp. 139–40, 155–8.

21. Figures extrapolated from Chandaman, *Revenue* pp. 31–5, 75, 104, 106.

22. For the early history of the Office for Taxes see W. P. Ward, 'The Office for Taxes, 1665–1798', in *BIHR*, xxv (1952) 204–12; and Chandaman, *Revenue* pp. 181–3, 187. See ibid., p. 186, for the figures for the 1673 and 1677 Assessments.

23. For further details, see Roseveare: *Treasury: Foundations of Control*, pp. 24–5 and the letter from Southampton and Ashley to Auditor Long, 19 Dec 1665, quoted in W. A. Shaw, 'The Beginnings of the National Debt', in T. F. Tout and J. Tait (eds), *Owen College Historical Essays* (1903) pp. 419–20. Some of the repayment clauses of the 1665 Additional had already been foreshadowed in at least one spending department (The Ordnance Office). See PRO, SP 29/112, fos. 166–8, Orders 13 Feb 1665.

24. For a full description of both the unrestricted operation of the Order system prior to the Stop of the Exchequer and the working of the system itself, see Chandaman, *Revenue* pp. 224–6, 295–300.

25. For this period see P. G. M. Dickson, *The Financial Revolution in England: A Study in Development of Public Credit, 1688–1756* (1967).

26. E. I. Carlyle, 'Clarendon and the Privy Council, 1660–7', in *EHR*, xxvii (1912) 251–3, citing from *Continuation of the Life of Edward, Earl of Clarendon* (Oxford, 1857).

27. Aylmer, *King's Servants*, pp. 19–23.

28. For the increasing use of the term in this period see E. R. Turner, *The Cabinet Council of England in the Seventeenth and Eighteenth Centuries, 1622–1784*, 2 vols (New York, 1970) vol. i, pp. 233–6.

29. For Roger North's testimony see the Appendix to the article by Godfrey Davies, 'Council and Cabinet, 1679–88', in *EHR*, xxxvii (1922) 62–5.

30. See ibid., pp. 55ff. (especially Davies's marshalling of evidence against the objections of Turner *et al.*, that the 1679 Committee was a Cabinet). Also H. W. V. Temperley, 'Inner and Outer Cabinet and Privy Council, 1679–1783', in *EHR*, xxvii (1912) 688–9; E. R. Turner, 'Committees of Council and the Cabinet, 1660–88', in *AHR*, xix (1913–14) 781ff.; Sir W. R. Anson, 'The Cabinet in the Seventeenth and Eighteenth Centuries', in *EHR*, xxix (1914) 53. Both Turner and Anson believed that the informal Committee of Foreign Affairs was also a Cabinet in the early 1660s.

31. For these later developments see J. Carter, 'The Revolution and the Constitution', in Geoffrey Holmes (ed.), *Britain After the Glorious Revolution, 1689–1714* (1969) pp. 49–52; J. Carter, 'Cabinet Records for the Reign of William III', in *EHR*, lxxviii (1963) 95–114; and J. H. Plumb, 'The Organisation of the Cabinet in the Reign of Queen Anne', *TRHS*, 5th ser., vii (1957) 137–57.

32. For these committees see Davies, 'Council and Cabinet', pp. 53ff.,

Turner, 'Committees of Council', pp. 772 ff., and *The Cabinet Council*, vol. I, *passim*; J. Carter, 'The Administrative Work of the English Privy Council, 1679–1714' (unpublished London University Ph. D. thesis, 1958) ch. 3.

33. For much of the following see ibid., pp. 142 ff.

34. E. R. Turner, *The Privy Council of England in the Seventeenth and Eighteenth Centuries, 1603–1784*, 2 vols (Baltimore, 1927–8) vol. II, p. 74. The wealth of the assembly may be gauged from a remark of Temple, who claimed that the new council of 1679 was collectively worth £300,000 p.a. in land and offices, adding: 'authority is observed much to follow land'. See E. R. Turner, 'The Privy Council of 1679', in *EHR*, xxx (1915) p. 263 n. 78.

35. D. Ogg, *England in the Reigns of James II and William III* (Oxford, 1955) p. 333.

36. Charles II agreed to 'lay aside the use . . . . of any single ministry or private advices or foreign committees' in order to appease the opposition in parliament, but did not keep his promises. For this important event see Davies, 'Council and Cabinet', pp. 49 ff.; E. R. Turner, 'The Privy Council of 1679', in *EHR*, xxx (1915) 251–70; Clayton Roberts, 'Privy Council Schemes and Ministerial Responsibility in Later Stuart England', in *AHR*, LXIV (1959) 564–82.

37. Quoted in Carlyle, 'Clarendon and the Privy Council', p. 271.

38. BL Add. MSS 34349, fo. 21. Quoted in Davies, 'Council and Cabinet', p. 53, n.5.

39. The power of presiding may have been denied him earlier in the century (cf. BL Add. MSS 38061, 1628 orders with order of 20 Feb 1624, printed in H. W. V. Temperley, 'Documents Illustrative of the Powers of the Privy Council in the Seventeenth Century', in *EHR*, xxvii (1913) 129–30) but it is clear that by the 1690s he could preside. BL Add. MSS 38061, fo. 121, Southwell's 'mixt notes'.

40. Quoted in Temperley, 'Documents . . . ', p. 131.

41. For this see F. M. G. Evans, *The Principal Secretary of State, 1558–1680* (Manchester, 1923) pp. 235ff.; Mark A. Thomson, *The Secretaries of State, 1681–1782* (Oxford, 1932) pp. 42–3; W. T. Root, 'The Lords of Trade and Plantations, 1675–96', in *AHR*, xxiii (1917) 27–8.

42. The transaction of the 1678 peace proposals, for instance, was carried out 'with such secrecy that the Secretaries of State themselves know nothing of it', Danby to Montagu, Feb 1678, quoted in Evans, *Principal Secretary of State* pp. 139–40. Also see ibid., p. 131, for Trevor.

43. For the tentative advances made in this direction see J. C. Sainty, *Officials of the Secretaries of State, 1660–1782, passim*, and Evans, *Principal Secretary of State* pp. 192–3, 364–5, re. the staffing and organisation of the office, 1684 and 6 March 1689 (extracts from All Souls College MS 204, fos 119ff., and BL Add. MSS 38861, fo. 46).

44. For the Secretary at War and the other members of the Army's administrative staff – especially the Paymaster-General, appointed in 1662, to act as banker – see John Childs, *The Army of Charles II* (1976) pp. 94ff., and C. M. Clode, *The Military Forces of the Crown*, 2 vols (1869) vol. I, pp. 71, 73. Also Thomson, *Secretaries of State*, p. 67, for the military responsibilities of the Secretaries of State.

45. See G. F. James and J. J. Sutherland Shaw, 'Admiralty Administration and Personnel, 1619–1714', in *BIHR*, xiv (1936–7) 10–14, 166–83; J. Ehrman, *The Navy in the War of William III* (Cambridge, 1953) pp. 196ff.; J. C. Sainty, *Admiralty Officials, 1660–1870* (1975) pp. 1–2.

46. For the Navy Board see Ehrman, *Navy* 176ff., and for the Ordnance Office the author's *Guns and Government: The Ordnance Office Under the Later Stuarts* (1979).

47. For a clear outline of the rather confused colonial administrative arrangements in this period see J. C. Sainty, *Officials of the Boards of Trade, 1660–1870* (1974) pp. 1–3. For the work of these boards see C. M. Andrews, *British Committees, Commissions and Councils of Trade and Plantations, 1622–75* (Baltimore, 1908) pp. 61ff.; R. P. Bieber, 'The British Plantation Councils of 1670–4', in *EHR*, xl (1925) 93–106; E. E. Rich, 'The First Earl of Shaftesbury's Colonial Policy', in *TRHS*, 5th ser., vii (1957) 47–70; W. T. Root, 'The Lords of Trade and Plantations, 1675–96', *AHR*, xxiii (1917) 20–41.

48. J. H. Plumb, *The Growth of Political Stability, 1675–1725* (1967) p. 127; M. Lane, 'The Diplomatic Service Under William III', in *TRHS*, 4th ser., x (1927) 87–110; V. Barbour, 'Consular Service in the Reign of Charles II', in *AHR*, xxxiii (1927–8) 553–78.

49. For a fee table in a Secretary's Office in 1684 see Evans, *Principal Secretary of State* p. 192. The payment of £1 for every warrant bill or captain's commission in excess of £6. 5s. must have been a sizeable prerequisite.

50. E.g., see Ormonde's comment to Primate Boyle quoted in Hughes, *Administration and Finance* p. 162, and Pepys's remark that 'the expectation of profit will have its force and make a man the more earnest'; Pepys *Diary*, 19 Dec 1663.

51. J. R. Tanner, *Samuel Pepys and the Royal Navy* (Cambridge, 1920) p. 41.

52. See J. R. Western, *Monarchy and Revolution* (1972) p. 116, for some figures. In William's reign, the Lord Chancellor received £4000, the Secretaries of State £1950 each, the Lord Privy Seal £1825 and the Lord President £1500; PRO, SP 8/2, ii, fo. 154.

53. For the following see the two important articles by J. C. Sainty: 'The Tenure of Offices in the Exchequer', in *EHR*, lxv (1965) 448–75; and 'A Reform in the Tenure of Offices during the Reign of Charles II', in *BIHR*, xli (1967) 150–71.

54. He argued that he had an indubitable right to his Exchequer fee and to execute his office by deputy after he had been dismissed. See his begging letters to the Treasury, BL Sloane MSS 836, fos. 85–6; Sloane MSS 4067, fo. 148.

55. Nearly all the incidents of sale in the Ordnance occurred in the 1660s and the last example of the sale of the office of Clerk of the Council appears to have been in 1685. See the present author's 'Place and Profit: An Examination of the Ordnance Office, 1660–1714', in *TRHS*, 5th ser., xxv (1975) pp. 67–8; and J. Carter, 'The Administrative Work of the English Privy Council, 1679–1714' (London Ph.D. thesis 1958) f. 538.

56. For this see Plumb, *Growth of Political Stability*, pp. 24–6.

5. RESTORATION ENGLAND AND EUROPE *J. L. Price*

1. Quoted in Charles P. Korr, *Cromwell and the New Model Foreign Policy. England's Policy Toward France, 1649–1658* (Berkeley, 1975) p. 93.

2. Ragnhild Hatton, *Europe in the Age of Louis XIV* (1969) p. 93; Louis André, *Louis XIV et l'Europe* (Paris, 1950) p. 18.

3. A. F. Pribram, *Franz Paul Freiherr von Lisola, 1613–1674, und die Politik seiner Zeit* (Leipzig, 1894) p. 14.

4. Korr, *Cromwell*, p. 93.

5. Quoted in André, *Louis XIV*, p. 78 (present author's translation).

6. *The Works of Sir William Temple* (1770) vol. I, p. 305.

7. Václav Cihák, *Les provinces-unies et la cour imperiale, 1667–1672* (Amsterdam, 1974) p. 75.

8. See Charles Wilson, *Profit and Power* (Cambridge, 1957).

9. Temple, *Works*, vol. I. p. 333.

10. See the scathing remarks of G. C. Gibbs, 'The Revolution in Foreign Policy', in G. Holmes (ed.), *Britain after the Glorious Revolution, 1689–1714* (1969) p. 60.

11. A. Browning, *Thomas Osborne, Earl of Danby and Duke of Leeds* (Glasgow, 1951) vol. I, p. 20.

12. Browning, *Danby*, vol. I, p. 257.

13. M. A. M. Franken, *Coenraad van Beuningen's politieke en diplomatieke aktiviteiten in de jaren 1667–1684* (Groningen, 1966) p. 65; Andrew Lossky, '"Maxims of State" in Louis XIV's Foreign Policy', in Ragnhild Hatton and J. S. Bromley (eds), *William III and Louis XIV* (Liverpool, 1968) pp. 13–14.

14. Temple, *Works*, vol. I, p. 305.

15. Wilson, *Profit and Power*; J. B. Wolf, *Louis XIV* (1968).

16. N. Japikse, *Johan de Witt* (Amsterdam, 1915) p. 206.

17. K. Feiling, *British Foreign Policy, 1660–1672* (1930) p. 83.

18. David Ogg, *England in the Reign of Charles II* (Oxford, 1956) p. 283.

19. Feiling, *British Foreign Policy*, pp. 50–1.

20. Jean Berenger, 'An Attempted *Rapprochement* between France and the Emperor: the Secret Treaty for the Partition of the Spanish Succession of 19 January 1668', in Ragnhild Hatton (ed.), *Louis XIV and Europe* (1976).

21. André, *Louis XIV*, p. 78.

22. G. Pagès, *Le Grand Electeur et Louis XIV, 1660–1688* (Paris, 1905). 26.

23. Pagès, *Le Grand Electeur*, p. 250.

24. Ogg, *Charles II*, p. 349.

25. G. Zeller, *Les temps modernes, ii. De Louis XIV à 1789 Histoire des relations internationales*, ed. P. Renouvin, t. III, Paris, 1955) p. 50.

26. Franken, *Van Beuningen*, pp. 12–13; A. C. Carter, *Neutrality or Commitment* 1975.

27. J. R. Jones, *Britain and Europe in the Seventeenth Century* (1966) p. 65.

28. Ralph Davis, *The Rise of the English Shipping Industry in the Seventeenth and Eighteenth Centuries* (1962) pp. 18–19.

29. Jones, *Britain and Europe*, p. 72.

30. Browning, *Danby*, vol. I, p. 92.

31. K. H. D. Haley, *William of Orange and the English Opposition, 1672–74* (Oxford, 1953) p. 139.

32. Zeller, *De Louis XIV à 1789*, p. 49.

33. K. H. D. Haley, 'The Anglo-Dutch *Rapprochement* of 1677', in *EHR*, LXXIII (1958) 617.

34. A. J. Bourde, 'Louis XIV et l'Angleterre' in *XVIIe Siècle*, XLVI–XLVII (1960) 56–7.

35. Haley, 'The Anglo-Dutch *Rapprochement*', 619.

36. Browning, *Danby*, vol. I, p. 151.

37. Zeller, *De Louis XIV à 1789*, p. 46.

38. Franken, *Van Beuningen*, p 236.

39. Ogg, *Charles II*, pp. 622–3.

40. Wolf, *Louis XIV*, pp. 508–10.

41. G. Livet, 'Louis XIV et l'Allemagne', in *XVIIe Siècle*, XLVI–XLVII (1960) 38.

42. Pagès, *Le Grand Electeur*, 423.

6.   TRADE AND SHIPPING   *Gordon Jackson*

1. D. C. Coleman, 'An Innovation and its Diffusion: the "New Draperies"', *EcHR*, XXII, 417; P. J. Bowden, 'Wool Supply and the Woollen Industry' in *EcHR*, IX, 44; C. Wilson, 'Cloth Production and International Competition in the Seventeenth Century' in *EcHR*, XIII, 209.

2. F. J. Fisher, 'London's Export Trade in the Early Seventeenth Century' in *EcHR*, III, 151.

3. Quoted in J. H. Rose (ed.), *Cambridge History of the British Empire*, vol. I, p. 68. Chs. 2 and 3 are a useful account of early colonisation.

4. R. Davis, 'English Foreign Trade, 1660–1700' in *EcHR*, VII, 152.

5. E. A. Wrigley, 'A Simple Model of London's Importance in Changing English Society and Economy, 1650–1750' in *Past and Present* 37, 58.

6. J. A. Chartres, *Internal Trade in England, 1500–1700* (1977), *passim*.

7. J. Thirsk and J. P. Cooper (eds), *Seventeenth Century Economic Documents* (1972) p. 81.

8. Ibid., pp. 71, 76.

9. Ibid., p. 75.

10. R. Grassby, 'English Merchant Capitalism in the Late Seventeenth Century' in *Past and Present*, 46, 102.

11. Thirsk and Cooper, *Stuart Economic Documents* p. 686: 'The Origins of Banking'.

12. Ibid., p. 73.

13. Quoted in C. M. Andrews, *The Colonial Period of American History*, vol IV: *England's Commercial and Colonial Policy* (1964 edn) p. 56. This book is a most valuable guide to the Navigation Acts and their working. See also L. A. Harper, *The English Navigation Laws* (1939) *passim*.

14. A. P. Thornton, *West India Policy under the Restoration* (1956) p. 27.

15. For a detailed comparison of the Acts see Andrews, chs. 3 and 4.

16. The 1660 Act is printed partially in Thirsk and Cooper, pp. 520–4, and fully in C. Grant Robertson, *Select Statutes, Cases and Documents, 1600–1832* (5th edn, 1925) pp. 3–13.

17. Quoted in Andrews, p. 114.

18. Quoted in ibid., p. 121.

19. M. Lewis, *The History of the British Navy* (Harmondsworth, 1957) chs. 6–7. For Anglo-Dutch rivalry in general see C. Wilson. *Profit and Power. A Study of England and the Dutch Wars* (1957). The Dutch context is set admirably in C. R. Boxer's *The Dutch Seaborne Empire, 1600–1800* (1965) chs. 3–4.

20. Quoted in Andrews, pp. 60–1.

21. G. N. Clark, *The Later Stuarts, 1660–1714* (2nd edn, 1955) p. 63.

22. R. Davis, *The Rise of the English Shipping Industry* (1962) chs 2–3, and 'Merchant Shipping in the Economy of the Late Seventeenth Century', *EcHR*, IX, 59.

23. Andrews, pp. 77ff.

24. Davis, *Shipping Industry*, p. 51.

25. Ibid., p. 52.

26. Ibid., p. 17.

27. Davis, 'Merchant Shipping', p. 71.

28. Ibid.

29. Davis, *Shipping Industry*, p. 17. The available facts and full analysis are to be found in Davis, 'English Foreign Trade, 1660–1700' in *EcHR*, VII, 150. Excellent brief guides are his *A Commercial Revolution* (Historical Association Pamphlet LXIV 1967) and *English Overseas Trade, 1500–1700* (1973).

30. K. N. Chaudhuri, 'Treasure and Trade Balances: the East India Company's Exports Trade, 1600–1720' in *EcHR*, XXI, 482.

31. Ibid., 485.

32. A brief account of the slave trade and African settlements is in ch. 15 of the *Cambridge History of the British Empire*, vol. I. The standard work is K. G. Davies, *The Royal African Company* (1957).

33. For the role of the outports see, for example, R. Davis, *The Trade and Shipping of Hull, 1500–1700* (East Riding Local History Soc 1964), W. B. Stephens, *Seventeenth Century Exeter* (1958), P. McGrath, *Merchants and Merchandise in Seventeenth Century Bristol* (Bristol Record Soc. 1955), C. N. Parkinson, *The Rise of the Port of Liverpool* (1952) and T. S. Willan, *The English Coasting Trade, 1600–1750* (1938).

34. D. C. Coleman (ed.), *Revisions in Mercantilism* (1969) pp. 4–5.

7. THE RESTORATION CHURCH   *R. A. Beddard*

1. G. Isham (ed.), *The Correspondence of Bishop Brian Duppa and Sir Justinian Isham 1650–1660*, (Northamptonshire Record Soc., XVII 1951) 183 [8 May 1660].

2. A. Browning (ed.), *English Historical Documents* (1966) VIII, 58.

3. Bodl. Wood MSS A 21, fo. 76; F 39, fo. 327. A. G. Matthews, *Walker Revised* (Oxford 1948), pp. 24, 25.

4. J. Fell, *The Life of . . . H. Hammond* (1661), pp. 64–5. T. Fuller, *The Worthies of England*, ed. J. Freeman (1952) p. 670.

5. R. A. Beddard, 'Sheldon and Anglican Recovery' in *HJ* XIX (1976) 1008.

6. Bodl. MSJ. Walker c. 2, fos 204–5.

7. Ibid. fo., 345.

8. Dean and Chapter Library, Exeter MS 3559, pp. 65–8 (11 Dec 1660). *Mercurius Publicus*, no. 54 (27 Dec 1660–3 Jan 1661). Bodl. Clarendon MSS 75, fo. 337: 'The Loyal Society to Clarendon', 30 Nov. 1661.

9. R. S. Bosher, *The Making of the Restoration Settlement* (rev. edn. 1957) pp. 39–40.

10. G. Davies, 'The General Election of 1660' in *Huntington Library Quarterly* xv (1952) 211–35. G. R. Abernathy, 'The English Presbyterians and the Stuart Restoration, 1648–1663' in, *Transactions of the American Philosophical Society* new ser. IV (1965) 50–53.

11. L. F. Brown, 'The Religious Factors in the Convention Parliament' in *EHR* xxii (1907) 51–63.

12. T. W. Bramston (ed.), *The Autobiography of Sir John Bramston*, (Camden Soc., xxxii (1845) 116–17.

13. Quoted in B. H. G. Wormald, *Clarendon: Politics, History and Religion 1640–1660* (Cambridge 1951), p. 238.

14. *The Autobiography of Sir John Bramston*, p. 117.

15. O. Airy (ed.), *Burnet's History of My Own Time* (Oxford 1897) vol. I, p. 162.

16. *English Historical Documents* viii, 57.

17. Bodl. Clarendon MSS 71, fo. 221: Edward Hyde to John Cosin, 23 Apr. 1660.

18. M. Sylvester (ed.), *Reliquiae Baxterianae*, (1696), part ii pp. 218, 229, 231, 259 *et seq*.

19. For James II, see R. A. Beddard, 'Vincent Alsop and the Emancipation of Restoration Dissent' in *Journal of Ecclesiastical History* xxiv (1973) 173–84.

20. *Lords Journals* xi 333: 20 Nov. 1661.

21. *Petition of the Gentry of Northamptonshire* (1660).

22. *Mercurius Publicus*, no. 24 (7–14 June 1660): petition of the Somerset nobility and gentry. Cf. nos 27, 28, 38.

23. Dean and Chapter Library, Durham: Hunter MSS 7/38: 'The humble petition of the knights, gentlemen and inhabitants of the County Palatine of Durham'.

24. Dean and Chapter Library, Peterborough: Dean Cosin's Papers, folios 68; 77, 79v–81; 103: Cosin to Clarendon (undated copy); *Acta et decreta Decani et Capituli*; H. Austin to Cosin, Peterborough, 9 Oct. 1660. For capitular reconstruction elsewhere, see A. Whiteman, 'The Re-establishment of the Church of England, 1660–1663' in *TRHS* 5th ser. v (1955) 113–114.

25. E.g. York Minster Library Muniments S3/4/a, pp. 172 *et seq*; S3/4/e (subscriptions); Borthwick Institute of Historical Research Inst. AB 6, pp. 302 *et seq* (institutions). For Exeter diocese, see Devon RO Chanter 151a, 24.

26. Bodl. MS Oxf. Dioc. Papers d.106, fo. l (Skinner's register). Devon RO Chanter 50 (Gauden's entries in *Registrum de Ordinibus*, 1571–1667).

27. *Index of Wills proved in the Prerogative Court of Canterbury*, vol. vii (1925) p. xvi. Borthwick Institute of Historical Research (typescript), B. D. Till, 'The administrative system of the ecclesiastical courts in the Diocese and Province of York', part III (1660–1883).

28. F. J. Varley (ed.), 'The Restoration Visitation of the University of Oxford and its Colleges', in *Camden Miscellany* xviii (1948).

29. *The Auto-biography of Symon Patrick* (Oxford 1839) pp. 37–8. *Lords Journals* XI
50. Add. MSS 19526, fo. 41. Pepys *Diary* (ed. R. Latham) vol. I, p. 282.

30. Bodl. Clarendon MSS 73, folios 218v, 219: Dorchester, 10 Sep. 1660.

31. W. C. Abbott, 'English Conspiracy and Dissent, 1660–74' in *AHR* XIV (1908–9) 503–28.

32. *Reliquiae Baxterianae*, pt II 298–302. Matthews, *Walker Revised* pp. 383–4.

33. Bosher, *The Making of the Restoration Settlement* p. 215.

34. A. G. Matthews, *Calamy Revised* (Oxford 1934) pp. xii–xiv.

35. *The Correspondence of Bishop Brian Duppa and Sir Justinian Isham* pp. 185–6. For Whalley, see Bosher, op. cit.

36. *Reliquiae Baxterianae*, pt II 149.

37. Quoted in Bosher, op. cit., . 40.

38. Sir Keith Feiling, *A History of the Tory Party, 1640–1714* (Oxford 1924) p. 106; H. N. Mukerjee, 'Elections for the Convention and Cavalier Parliaments' in *Notes and Queries* CLXVI (1934) 417–21.

39. *CJ* VIII, 247, 254, 256, 259, 261, 270, 271, 273, 279, 296, 300.

40. *English Historical Documents* VIII, 375–84.

41. S. Ward, *Against Resistance of Lawful Powers* (1661) pp. 6, 7.

42. R. South, *A Sermon Preached . . . Upon the Consecration of . . . Dr John Dolben Lord Bishop of Rochester* (1666) pp. 25–6.

43. *Lords Journals* XI 475–6. For Clarendon's part in Charles's evasive acts, see G. R. Abernathy, 'Clarendon and the Declaration of Indulgence' in *Journal of Ecclesiastical History* XI (1960) 55–73.

44. *CJ* VIII, 442–3.

45. Pepys IX, 60. Author's italics.

46. *CJ* IX, 77.

47. F. Bate, *The Declaration of Indulgence 1672* (1908) pp. 56 *et seq.*

48. *English Historical Documents* VIII 387.

49. Bodl. Add. MSS c 305, fo. 267: [1 Jan 1672–3].

50. *CJ* IX, 257.

51. *English Historical Documents* VIII 389–91.

52. Bodl. Tanner MSS 45, fo. 295: Hacket to Sheldon, Lichfield, 16 Mar. 1667–8.

53. BL Harleian MSS 7377, fo. 55v: Lambeth House, 21 Sep. 1674.

54. Bodl. Carte MSS 45, fo. 212: Lambeth House, 25 Feb 1666–7. Author's italics.

55. C. Edwards Pike (ed.), *Selections from the Correspondence of Arthur Capel Earl of Essex 1675–1677*, in Camden Soc. 3rd ser. XXIV (1913) pp. 1, 62: Sir Robert Southwell, 4 Jul. 1676; Lord Conway, 27 Apr. 1675.

56. R. A. Beddard, 'The Church of Salisbury and the accession of James II' in *Wiltshire Archaeological Magazine* LXVII (1972) 132–48.

57. A. Browning, *Thomas Osborne Earl of Danby* (Glasgow 1944–51), vol. I pp. 147–9.

58. Bodl. Carte MSS 72, fo. 253: Sir Robert Southwell to Ormonde, 2 Jan. 1674–5. SP Domestic 29/367, no. 132.

59. For what follows, see R. A. Beddard, 'William Sancroft, as Archbishop of Canterbury, 1677–1691' (Oxford D. Phil. thesis 1965) chaps 1 and 2.

60. R. A. Beddard, 'The Commission for Ecclesiastical Promotions,

1681–84: an Instrument of Tory Reaction' in *HJ*, x (1967) 11–40.
  61. Bodl. Clarendon MSS 87, fo. 331: 23 Nov. 1680.

8. THE DEBATE OVER SCIENCE   *Michael Hunter*

  1. R. G. Frank, 'Institutional Structure and Scientific Activity in the Early Royal Society', in *Proceedings of the Fourteenth Congress for the History of Science (1974)* (Tokyo, 1975) vol. IV, 82–101.
  2. C. Webster, 'The Origins of the Royal Society', in *History of Science*, VI (1967) 106–28.
  3. Alexander Koyré, *Etudes Galiléennes* (Paris, 1939); Herbert Butterfield, *The Origins of Modern Science* (1949); T. S. Kuhn, *The Structure of Scientific Revolutions* (2nd edn, Chicago, 1970).
  4. See, for instance, R. S. Westfall, 'Unpublished Boyle Papers relating to Scientific Method', in *Annals of Science*, XII (1956) 63–73, 103–17; R. H. Kargon, *Atomism in England* (Oxford, 1966) ch. 10; D. J. Oldroyd, 'Robert Hooke's Methodology of Science as Exemplified by his "Discourse of Earthquakes"', in *British Journal for the History of Science*, VI (1972–3) 109–30.
  5. L. Laudan, 'The Clock Metaphor and English Probabilism', in *Annals of Science*, XXII (1966) 73–104; Kargon, *Atomism* chs 9–10.
  6. T. S. Kuhn, 'Mathematical versus Experimental Traditions in the Development of Physical Science', in *Journal of Interdisciplinary History*, VII (1976) 15.
  7. Thomas Sprat, *History of the Royal Society*, ed. J. I. Cope and H. W. Jones (1959) pp. 28–32.
  8. Cf. Michael Hunter, *John Aubrey and the Realm of Learning* (1975) ch. 2.
  9. See for instance, C. Lloyd, 'Shadwell and the Virtuosi', in *PMLA*, XLIV (1929) 472–94.
  10. *Philosophical Transactions*, II (1667) 592; P. M. Rattansi, 'The Intellectual Origins of the Royal Society', in *Notes and Records of the Royal Society*, XXIII (1968) 129–43; K. T. Hoppen, 'The Nature of the Early Royal Society', in *British Journal for the History of Science*, IX (1976) 1–24, 243–73.
  11. R. S. Westfall, 'The Role of Alchemy in Newton's Career', in M. L. Righini Bonelli and W. R. Shea (eds.), *Reason, Experiment and Mysticism in the Scientific Revolution* (1975) pp. 195–6; P. M. Rattansi, 'Some Evaluations of Reason in Sixteenth and Seventeenth Century Natural Philosophy', in M. Teich and R. Young (eds), *Changing Perspectives in the History of Science* (1973) pp. 148–66.
  12. R. Boyle, 'About the Excellency and Grounds of the Mechanical Hypothesis', in T. Birch (ed.), *Works*, (1772) vol. IV, pp. 67–78; R. Hooke, *Micrographia* (1665) preface; W. Petty, *A Discourse of Duplicate Proportion* (1674) sig. A5 and pp. 17–20. See also below, p. 189.
  13. M. Hunter, *John Aubrey*, p. 134; T. Sprat, *Royal Society*, p. 37.
  14. For example, of the case of Oliver Hill and his ideas: Thomas Birch, *History of the Royal Society of London* (1756–7) vol. III, pp. 363, 366–7, 371; Robert Hooke, *Diary, 1672–80*, ed. H. W. Robinson and W. Adams (1935) pp. 331, 335, 337–9.
  15. Cf. Christ Church, Oxford, Evelyn Collection Correspondence, nos 79,

93: John Beale to John Evelyn, 2 Jan, 18 Dec 1669 (this and all letters in the Evelyn Collection mentioned hereafter are cited by kind permission of the Trustees of the Will of the late J. H. C. Evelyn); Royal Society Early Letters F. 1. 81: John Flamsteed to John Collins, 1 Jan 1672.

16. For recent discussions see the essays by Hall and Mathias in P. Mathias (ed.), *Science and Society, 1600–1900* (Cambridge 1972); C. Webster, 'The Authorship and Significance of *Macaria*', in *Past and Present* 56 (1972) 34–48.

17. T. Sprat, *Royal Society* p. 438.

18. B. Hessen, 'The Social and Economic Roots of Newton's *Principia*' in N. Bukharin (ed.), *Science at the Crossroads* (1931) pp. 149–92; Sir G. Clark, *Science and Social Welfare in the Age of Newton* (2nd edn, Oxford, 1949), ch. 3; A. R. Hall, 'Merton Revisited', in *History of Science*, II (1963) 8.

19. T. Sprat, *Royal Society* pp. 284–306. Cf. T. Birch, *Royal Society* I, *passim*; W. E. Houghton, 'The History of Trades: its Relation to Seventeenth-century Thought', in *Journal of the History of Ideas*, II (1941) 33–60.

20. R. V. Lennard, 'English Agriculture under Charles II: the Evidence of the Royal Society's "Enquiries"', in *EcHR* IV (1929) 23–45; John Evelyn, *Diary and Correspondence* (1852) vol. III p. 317: Evelyn to the Countess of Sunderland, 4 Aug 1690; L. Sharp, 'Timber, Science and Economic Reform in the Seventeenth Century' in *Forestry*, XLVIII (1975) 51–86.

21. Sir G. Clark, *Science and Social Welfare* ch. 1; for two detailed recent accounts see J. A. Bennett, 'Studies in the Life and Work of Sir Christopher Wren' (Cambridge Ph.D. thesis, 1974) ch. 4; L. G. Sharp, 'Sir William Petty and Some Aspects of Seventeenth-Century Natural Philosophy' (Oxford D. Phil. thesis, 1976) fos 242–50.

22. On Moxon and the Royal Society cf. M. Hunter, 'The Social Basis and Changing Fortunes of an Early Scientific Institution: An Analysis of the Membership of the Royal Society, 1660–85', in *Notes and Records of the Royal Society*, XXXI (1976) 35 and n. 123, 108 (F348).

23. Cf. M. Espinasse, 'The Decline and Fall of Restoration Science', in *Past and Present*, 14 (1958) 71–89.

24. Royal Society Early Letters S.1.2: Peter Smith to John Beale, 18 Sep 1655 (transcript).

25. C. Webster, 'Introduction', in *The Intellectual Revolution of the Seventeenth Century* (1974) p. 22; M. McKeon, *Poetry and Politics in Restoration England* (Cambridge, Mass., 1975) esp. ch. 8.

26. V. Salmon, *The Work of Francis Lodwick* (1972); John Wilkins's *Essay*: 'Critics and Continuators', in *Historiographia Linguistica*, I (1974) 147–63; James Knowlson, *Universal Language Schemes in England and France, 1600–1800* (Toronto, 1975) ch. 3.

27. M. Hunter, *Early Scientific Institution*, pp. 50–5; W. A. L. Vincent, *The Grammar Schools . . . 1660–1714* (1969) ch. 5; R. Caudill, 'Some Literary Evidence of the Development of English Virtuoso Interests in the Seventeenth Century' (Oxford D. Phil. thesis, 1976) fos 329–65.

28. Cf. W. Letwin, *The Origins of Scientific Economics* (1963) ch 5; Sharp, *Economic Reform* ch. 4.

29. The Marquis of Lansdowne (ed.) *The Petty–Southwell Correspondence*,

(1928) pp. 103–4; cf. also pp. 105, 119–20, 129.

30. F. Baily, *An Account of the Revd. John Flamsteed* (1835)pp. xxvii–xxviii; E. G. Forbes, *Greenwich Observatory*, I (1975) 29, 38.

31. Sharp *Economic Reform* pp. 351–2; cf., for example, MS Sloane 1039, fo. 105: John Wilcox to Robert Hooke, 15 Sep 1681; Royal Society Classified Papers, xxv, fo. 132: Richard Greenwood to John Houghton, 14 Sep 1685.

32. *Petty–Southwell Correspondence*, p. 103; A. R. and M. B. Hall (eds) *The Correspondence of Henry Oldenburg*, 8 vols (Madison: Univ of Wisconsin Press, 1965–) e.g. IV, 498–9, 518; Oldenburg to Sir Joseph Williamson, 4 July, 8 July 1668; ibid., VIII, 348: T. Tenison to Oldenburg, 7 Nov 1671.

33. R. K. Merton, *Science, Technology and Society in Seventeenth-century England* (New York, 1970) ch. 4; cf. also ch. 6. For an introduction to this controversy, see C. Webster (ed.) *The Intellectual Revolution of the Seventeenth Century*.

34. C. Webster, *The Great Instauration* (1975) pp. 93–5, 497–8.

35. B. J. Shapiro, 'Latitudinarianism and Science in seventeenth-century England', in *Past and Present* 40 (1968) 16–41; *John Wilkins, 1614–72* (Berkeley, 1969).

36. J. R. Jacob, 'Restoration, Reformation and the Origins of the Royal Society', in *History of Science*, XIII (1975) 155–76; M. C. Jacob, *The Newtonians and the English Revolution* (Hassocks, 1976) ch. 1.

37. T. Sprat, *Royal Society* pp. 65, 76, 129–33, etc.

38. M. Hunter, *Early Scientific Institution*, 9–22.

39. Ibid., 35 and *passim*.

40. D. C. Coleman, *Sir John Banks* (Oxford, 1963) pp. 135–9.

41. K. T. Hoppen, *The Common Scientist in the Seventeenth Century* (1970); *The Correspondence of Henry Oldenburg, passim*.

42. J. Wallis, 'Letter against Mr Maidwell', T. W. Jackson (ed.), *Collectanea*, (Oxford Historical Soc., I, 1885), 315–7, 320–3; B. J. Shapiro, 'The Universities and Science in seventeenth-century England', in *Journal of British Studies*, X, 2 (1971) 47–82; R. G. Frank, 'Science, Medicine and the Universities in Early Modern England', in *History of Science*, XI (1973) 194–216, 239–69; R. T. Gunther (ed.), *Early Science in Oxford*, vols. iv, xii (Oxford 1925, 1939).

43. M. Purver, *The Royal Society: Concept and Creation* (1967) p. 72; J. Keevil, *The Stranger's Son* (1953) pp. 178–9.

44. S. Pepys, *Diary*, (ed.), R. Latham and W. Matthews, vol. v (1971) pp. 32–3; C. Lloyd, *Shadwell*.

45. R. Hooke, *Diary*, p. 235; D. Stimson, 'Ballad of Gresham College', in *Isis*, XVIII (1932) 103–17.

46. Cf. S. I. Mintz, *The Hunting of Leviathan* (Cambridge, 1962); Q. Skinner, 'The Ideological Context of Hobbes's Political Thought', in *Historical Journal*, IX (1966) 294–7.

47. J. R. Jacob, 'Robert Boyle and Subversive Religion in the Early Restoration', in *Albion*, VI (1974) 275–93; M. E. Prior, 'Joseph Glanvill, Witchcraft and Seventeenth-Century Science', in *Modern Philology*, XXX (1932–3) 167–93.

48. Q. Skinner, 'Thomas Hobbes and the Nature of the early Royal Society', in *Historical Journal* XII (1969) 217–39.

49. R. Boyle, 'An Examen of Mr. T. Hobbes, his Dialogue Physicus de Natura Aeris', in *Works* I (1772) 186–9; J. Wallis, *Elenchus Geometriae Hobbianae*

(Oxford, 1655) sig. A2–3; cf. R. F. Jones, 'The Background to the Attack on Science in the Age of Pope', in J. L. Clifford and L. A. Landa (eds.), *Pope and his Contemporaries* (Oxford, 1949) pp. 106–8.

50. Cf. R. S. Westfall, *Science and Religion in Seventeenth-Century England* (New Haven, 1958).

51. Bodleian MS Aubrey 12, fo. 327: Thomas Mariet to John Aubrey, 14 Nov 1676; Christ Church, Oxford, Evelyn Collection Correspondence, no. 82: John Beale to John Evelyn, 10 May 1669.

52. M. Hunter, *Early Scientific Institution* p. 40; T. Sprat, *Royal Society* p. 72.

53. H. Stubbe, *Plus Ultra Reduced to a Non Plus* (1670) p. 36; *A Censure Upon Certaine Passages Contained in the History of the Royal Society* (Oxford, 1670) pp. 56–8; R. South, *Sermons Preached upon Several Occasions* (Oxford, 1823) vol. 1, pp. 373–5; W. Petty, *Oldenburg*, sig. A6.

54. Christ Church Evelyn Collection Correspondence, no. 301: Ralph Bohun to John Evelyn, 1668; Richard Graham, Viscount Preston, *Angliae Speculum Morale* (1670) p. 45.

55. H. Stubbe, *Legends No Histories* (1670) p. 11.

56. N. Fairfax, *A Treatise . . .* (1674) sigs A5, A6v.

57. H. Stubbe, *Plus Ultra Reduced to a Non Plus* p. 13.

58. M. Casaubon, *A Letter . . . to Peter du Moulin D.D. concerning Natural Experimental Philosophie, and Some Books Lately Set Out about It* (Cambridge, 1669) p. 17.

59. Bodleian MS Rawlinson D. 36.1, fo. 3 and *passim*. This important unpublished exposition of Casaubon's views is edited and discussed in M. R. G. Spiller, 'Conservative Opinion and the New Science, 1630–80: With Special Reference to the Life and Works of Meric Casaubon' (Oxford B.Litt. thesis, 1968); cf. also his 'The Idol of the Stove: The Background to Swift's Criticism of Descartes', in *Review of English Studies* new ser. XXV (1974) 15–24.

60. Cf., for instance, John Evelyn, *Diary and Correspondence*, vol. III pp. 264–7: Evelyn to John Fell, 19 Mar 1682; H. R. McAdoo, *The Spirit of Anglicanism* (1965) chs 9–10.

61. M. Hunter, 'The Origins of the Oxford University Press', in *The Book Collector*, XXIV (1975) 511–34; McAdoo, *Anglicanism*, pp. 386–7, 397; K. T. Hoppen, *Early Royal Society*, 159–66.

62. D. C. Douglas, *English Scholars 1660–1730* (2nd edn, 1951) p. 248 and *passim*; J. G. A. Pocock, *The Ancient Constitution and the Feudal Law* (Cambridge, 1957) chs 7–8.

63. Douglas, *English Scholars* p. 245.

64. H. R. McAdoo, *Anglicanism* pp. 348, 387–94; on Williamson, Hunter, 'Social Basis . . . ', pp. 21, 87 (F101); Harry Carter, *A History of the Oxford Press* vol 1 (Oxford, 1975) pp. 50–3; Douglas, *English Scholars* p. 66; Sir G. Clark, *Science and Social Welfare* p. 25; on Bernard, *Correspondence of Scientific Men in the Seventeenth Century*, ed. S. J. Rigaud (Oxford 1841) *passim*; A. Fox, *John Mill and Richard Bentley* (Oxford, 1954) pp. 60–1; Douglas, *English Scholars* pp. 111–3.

65. M. Hunter, 'Oxford University Press', 516; H. Carter, *Oxford Press* pp. 237–9; M. Casaubon, *A Letter . . .* , p. 21; Bodleian MS Rawlinson D. 36.1, fos 33–4; Royal Society Early Letters S.1.89–91: Henry Stubbe to Sir Robert

Moray, 24 Mar, 27 May 1667; *Philosophical Transactions*, II (1667) 494–502, III (1668) 699–709; Stubbe's works, *passim*.

66. Bodleian MS Rawlinson D.36.1, fos 23–4; H. Stubbe, *Campanella Revived* (1670) p. 15.

67. T. Sprat, *Royal Society*, p. 78; J. Evelyn, *Sylva* (3rd edn, 1679) sig. A3v.

68. Cf. Christ Church Evelyn Collection Correspondence, no. 96: John Beale to John Evelyn, 11 June 1670.

69. M. C. Jacob, *Newtonians*, *passim*; P. Hazard, *La crise de la conscience Européenne* (Paris, 1934).

70. Norman Sykes, *From Sheldon to Secker* (Cambridge, 1959) p. 142; M. Hunter, 'Oxford University Press', 532–3; D. C. Douglas, *English Scholars* esp. ch. 13.

71. G. R. Cragg, *From Puritanism to the Age of Reason* (Cambridge, 1950).

72. Cf. C. Davenant, *Discourses on the Public Revenues* (1698) vol. i, pp. 1–35; N. Hans, *New Trends in English Education in the Eighteenth Century* (1951); M. Espinasse, *Restoration Science*.

Notes on Contributors

ROBERT BEDDARD is fellow and tutor of Oriel College, Oxford. Since completing his D.Phil thesis 'William Sancroft, as Archbishop of Canterbury, 1677–1691' (Oxford, 1965) he has published several articles including 'The Commission for Ecclesiastical Promotions, 1681–1684: an Instrument of Tory Reaction' in *HJ* x (1967); 'The Guildhall Declaration of 11 December 1688 and the Counter-revolution of the Loyalists', ibid xix (1968); 'Sheldon and Anglican Recovery', ibid xix (1976).

JENNIFER CARTER is lecturer in History at the University of Aberdeen, and was formerly at Makerere College in Uganda. Her publications include 'The Revolution and the Constitution' in *Britain after the Glorious Revolution* ed. G. Holmes (1969) and 'Cabinet Records for the Reign of William III' in *EHR* LXXVIII (1963). Her Ph.D thesis was on 'The Administrative Work of the English Privy Council, 1679–1714'.

M. W. HUNTER, who studied at both Cambridge and Oxford, is lecturer in History at Birkbeck College, London. He has published *John Aubrey and the Realm of Learning* (1975).

GORDON JACKSON is senior lecturer in History at the University of Strathclyde. He has published *Hull in the Eighteenth Century* (1972) and *The Trade and Shipping of Eighteenth-Century Hull* (1975).

J. R. JONES is professor of English History at the University of East Anglia, Norwich. He has published *The First Whigs* (1961); *Britain and Europe in the Seventeenth Century* (1966); *The Revolution of 1688 in England* (1972) and *Country and Court: England 1658–1714* (1978).

JOHN MILLER is lecturer in History at Queen Mary College, London. He was formerly a fellow of Gonville and Caius College, Cambridge. His first book, *Popery and Politics in England, 1660–1688*, appeared in 1973; it was followed in 1978 by *James II: a Study in Kingship*.

J. L. PRICE is lecturer in History at the University of Hull. He is a specialist in the study of the Netherlands, and in that area has published *Culture and Society in the Dutch Republic during the Seventeenth Century* (1974).

HOWARD TOMLINSON teaches at Wellington College. He has published *Guns and Government: the Ordnance Office under the Later Stuarts*, and is preparing an edition of Pepys's Admiralty Correspondence for the Navy Records Society.

Index